P9-DBR-435

Old-School COMFORT FOOD

Old-School COMFORT FOOD

The Way I Learned to Cook

Alex Guarnaschelli

Clarkson Potter/Publishers ❀ *New York*

for my wonderful parents and every dishwasher and prep cook working in a restaurant anywhere. You are the people who make the world go around and make sure it remains a happy, tasty place.

Published in the United States by Clarkson Potter/ Publishers, an imprint of the Crown Publishing Group, a division of Random House, Inc., New York.
www.crownpublishing.com
www.clarksonpotter.com

Library of Congress Cataloging-in-Publication Data has been applied for.

ISBN 978-0-307-95655-2
eISBN 978-0-307-95656-9

Printed in the United States of America

Book design by Marysarah Quinn
Cover design by Marysarah Quinn
Cover photography by Squire Fox

10 9 8 7 6 5 4 3 2 1

First Edition

BUTTER
415 Lafayette Street
New York, NY 10003
P: 212.253.2828
F: 212.477.0181
www.butterrestaurant.com

Thank you for dining at **Butter.** Ensuring that your dining experience was pleasurable is very important to us. We welcome your thoughts and ideas.

Alexandra Guarnaschelli

Each time I come here, I'm impressed with the tasty and imaginative combinations

We would also like to keep you informed of upcoming events and menu changes. Please take a moment to fill out the information below for our mailing list.

Date: you create. I wanted
Name: to say thank you to one
Address: of the few (still!)
City/State/Zip: women chefs!
Telephone: Gloria Steinem
Email: (GLORIA STEINEM)

contents

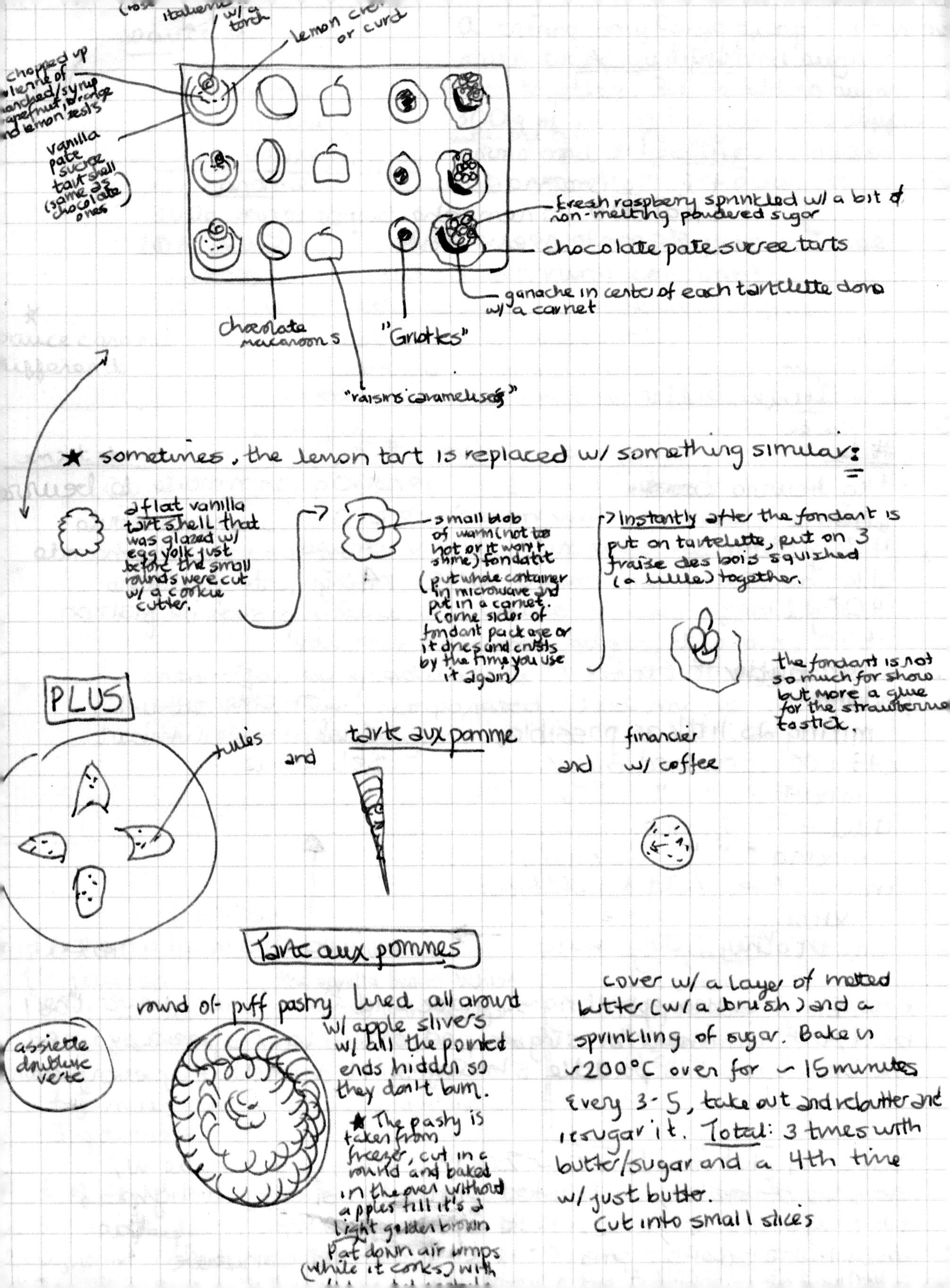

italienne w/ a torch
lemon cream or curd
chopped up julienne of blanched/syrup grapefruit, orange and lemon zests
vanilla pate sucree tart shell (same as chocolate ones)
fresh raspberry sprinkled w/ a bit of non-melting powdered sugar
chocolate pate sucree tarts
ganache in center of each tartlette done w/ a cornet
chocolate macaroons
"Griottes"
"raisins caramelisés"
★ sometimes, the lemon tart is replaced w/ something similar:
a flat vanilla tart shell that was glazed w/ egg yolk just before the small rounds were cut w/ a cookie cutter.
small blob of warm (not too hot or it won't shine) fondant (put whole container in microwave and put in a cornet. Cover sides of fondant package or it dries and crusts by the time you use it again)
Instantly after the fondant is put on tartelette, put on 3 fraise des bois squished (a little) together.
the fondant is not so much for show but more a glue for the strawberries to stick.
PLUS
tuiles
and
tarte aux pomme
and
financier w/ coffee
Tarte aux pommes
assiette doublure verte
round of puff pastry lined all around w/ apple slivers w/ all the pointed ends hidden so they don't burn.
★ The pastry is taken from freezer, cut in a round and baked in the oven without apples till it's a light golden brown
Pat down air lumps (while it cooks) with
cover w/ a layer of melted butter (w/ a brush) and a sprinkling of sugar. Bake in ~200°C oven for ~15 minutes
Every 3-5, take out and rebutter and resugar it. Total: 3 times with butter/sugar and a 4th time w/ just butter.
Cut into small slices

Introduction

My love affair with food began in the simplest of settings: my childhood kitchen on 55th Street and 7th Avenue in Manhattan. My mother was whipping up a cheese soufflé (a "casual" recipe, I should add, that included taking an entire wheel of Camembert and pushing the creamy insides through a strainer with a wooden spoon) and I was kneading bread dough from a *Beard on Bread* recipe. She folded in the fluffy egg whites, huffing and puffing over the bowl as she tried to retain all of the volume and still mix the ingredients. The batter made the tiniest, barely audible but intoxicating sound as it hit the bottom of the soufflé dish. She dashed from one end of the kitchen to the other and quickly (but gingerly) placed the dish in the center of the oven and closed the door. Her movements were more fluid than I had ever seen. I was mesmerized.

"Back that chair up against the oven door to keep it closed as the soufflé cooks, willya Al?" my mother instructed, wiping sweat from her forehead. The hinge on our oven door (a vintage 1940s GE model oven) was loose and would hang open slightly. That wouldn't work for a soufflé. I rinsed the bread dough off my hands and pushed the chair against the oven door. I stared through the small, grease-stained window as the soufflé doubled in volume. I sat in that chair, in fact, like a security guard would stand in front of the Hope Diamond. It was almost as if I could smell the various cheeses baking and browning as the soufflé cooked. Opera was blaring in the other room, the air conditioner blasting so hard it almost blew out the lit candles on the dining room table. The silverware was mismatched at each setting (I had even gotten a Mickey Mouse baby spoon into the mix). Various trivets and bowls littered the table. It was a hodgepodge haven of quality things. A stack of manuscripts (future cookbooks) and potential new projects ("Al, I just got in a great book proposal for a thousand-page book about garam masala. What do you think?") were in the mix as well.

ME, AROUND AGE 3

Once the soufflé was done cooking, my father, my mother, and I sat at the table, almost transfixed, as if watching a baby utter its first word. I swear the spoon made a sighing noise as it scooped out that first (boiling hot!) bit of cheese and eggs onto my plate. The steam coming off the soufflé snaked its way up my nostrils and my stomach growled. I think my ankles growled! "Eat it with a spoon," she instructed. There was some dry sherry and mustard that I remember tasting but not being able to identify. Just an alarm bell in my brain that something life-changing had occurred. And to tell you the truth, I had no idea what it was.

Now, don't get me wrong. I do not come from the type of Italian

American stock that one might quickly assign me to, given my last name. I did not have a grandmother who weighed 95 pounds but could carry an ox up a hill with a block of ice on her back. I didn't have an aunt who could make perfect gnocchi on the hearth with one potato and a small twig. The love of food simply emanated from my parents and their (still to this day) eternal push-pull collaboration-argument that surrounds the creation of a meal. The kitchen still has drawers filled with various utensils (I counted twenty-two paring knives), an astounding array of spices, and more china ("that's Ginori china," my mom whispered as if she were in church as I set the table with white plates with a simple orange rim) than one family of three could ever hope to use. The books, the shopping, the choices were the very thing that started it all for me and there is only one way to describe it: old school.

Old school: Any thing or things that refer to a previous generation of a subject/idea/object/etc. Typically, they are highly regarded and sometimes the very things that started it all.

What an exciting definition. And one that resonates deeply with my journey as a young eater all the way to the cook I am today.

So many books offer a dizzying array of "useful go-to tips" on how to get the same result in half the time with half the money or how to use half the ingredients or get a meal straight from your freezer to the table in 20 minutes.

I promise none of this.

This book is, instead, a result of my father's cooking, my mother's painstaking search for the ultimate pecan pie, mixed with the professional wisdom I have accumulated from sheer repetitive cooking in some pretty amazing restaurant kitchens. And these recipes, and my story, are old school because they are recipes that started something in me (a technique, a certain use of an ingredient) that became a common thread in my own cooking, because they consistently tip their hat to my culinary mentors (from my parents to Guy Savoy), and because they will make you feel like you are mixing a recipe with the spontaneity of the act of cooking itself.

It seems we chefs often describe the start of our culinary "education" and career path with the first cooking we did with our own hands. Makes sense. But in my case, it feels like it began long before that. I was my

MY MOM, IN THE 1970s, WITH HER DAILY COPY OF THE *NEW YORK TIMES*

parents' lone devoted spectator to the sport for many years before I became an amateur and then turned pro myself. Watching other, more experienced people make a meal is a critical part of learning how to cook.

Being watchful is also a critical part of cooking! The turning point with food often occurs when heat transforms it. Braised short ribs? Just mix the meat with salt, some vegetables, some wine, and some faith. At the end, peel back that foil and allow the tops of the ribs to poke out above the braising liquid and develop that beefy crust. There is no replacing heat and time with a recipe like that and the magic happens as we stand still and allow the ingredients to fulfill their delicious destiny.

Those years of watching and tasting shaped my idea of deliciousness—and the pursuit of that deliciousness in my adult life is my inspiration. It has gotten me through many a night when I looked up at a soup-spattered ceiling in a restaurant and asked myself: *Why does the dishwashing machine only break on Friday nights? Why did I just notice I served 8 sides of spinach that were washed but nonetheless still sandy and gritty? Why can't I just have an ergonomic chair and a desk with a mug on it that says* I love the Bahamas*?*

The tasting aspect of my culinary education began the minute my mother pulled a brick off the top of a pâté she had weighted down and cut me a slice. This wasn't that tube of liverwurst I had sampled (after desperately foraging in an empty fridge only to make a half sandwich on the end piece of Pepperidge Farm wheat bread). It was also not the bite of my friend's bologna sandwich at school the other day. This was a different level of complexity and one that I found riveting because my very own mother had whipped it up from scratch. Somehow all those other meats paled in comparison to the rough, almost handmade texture of the meat and the deep, rich flavor rolling over my tongue. It might have been the first time I encountered the power of animal fat as an ingredient.

Making these pâtés was just one of her seasonal food rituals. There was also the procession of Christmas cookies, each with its own tin encapsulating a singularly wonderful cookie experience. Linzer cookies, Greek *kourambiedes*, chocolate rum balls rolled in sprinkles (affectionately dubbed "shitballs"), and almond cookies were high points of my formative eating years. This was her repertoire, handed down from a mixture of family recipes and some good childhood eating.

But what really sealed the deal on my culinary education? The books. In 1979, my mother discovered and edited Julie Sahni's *Classic Indian Cooking* and, for almost a year, we ate a steady stream of dals, naan, lamb, and tandoori everything. Every year we moved from one specialty to another: from Rose Levy Beranbaum's sugary world of butter, flour, and eggs combined in showstopping cakes to the food of Emilia-Romagna with Lynne Rossetto Kasper—and thus a long stretch of balsamic, pasta, polenta cakes, and artichokes with Parmigiano-Reggiano.

What is it really like to grow up with a pretty famous cookbook editor? Fattening. Delicious. Embarrassing. Exhilarating beyond belief.

Most fattening moment to date? Christmas dinner circa 1978: digging into that now-mastered cheese soufflé followed by delicious sea scallops, gratinéed in their shells (page 170), and a huge piece of Dobos Torte (see Yellow Cake with Chocolate Frosting and Caramel Top, page 219).

Most embarrassing moment? Hands down, no contest: fourth grade school lunch. I open a somewhat stained but otherwise perfectly innocent looking brown bag to find the following:

- 2 beef meatballs (with a ton of sauce) somewhat smushed in tin foil
- a leaky, drippy, greasy plastic bag of enormous broccoli spears, doused with balsamic (before balsamic was ubiquitous) dressing
- 4 slices of bread

I looked to my left at my friend's juice box and thermos of soup and to my right at my other friend's peanut butter and jelly sandwich and two Oreos.

I gathered my lunch back into the grease-stained bag like one might shovel money during a bank heist and called my mother at work from the pay phone in the hall.

"Ma?" I said, cheeks burning. "What kind of lunch is that? Smushed broccoli and meatballs?"

“Al,” she began wearily, as if she were expecting my call, “you just put the meatballs, sauce, broccoli, and vinaigrette on top of the slices of bread to make a sandwich. If I had assembled it at home, it would have been all soggy by the time you went to eat it.”

ME, WITH MY CAT DENNIS, 1975

It was as if my mother were waiting patiently for me to reach an age where I would understand that flavor trumps appearances and normalcy. And that did eventually happen. I love the taste of my dad’s famous tomato sauce (page 95), the one that coated those meatballs, and the vibrant zing of his balsamic vinaigrette (page 283) on broccoli.

Exhilarating? Watching my mother tear through the pages of a manuscript, stirring a bubbling pot of pasta, checking a chicken with butter under the skin roasting in the oven, and tending a double boiler of dark chocolate and rum pudding. There is a kinetic energy that bubbles off the stove when you cook, whatever it is, however simple. As my mother enlisted my help with her cooking rituals and experiments, that energy traveled straight up my arms and into my brain and left me powerless when faced with the choice of profession. It was cook or die.

The professional cooking part of my education really began at Larry Forgione’s An American Place Restaurant on 32nd Street in Manhattan. It’s the early ’90s and I am clad in a black dress, and wearing three different shades of light blue eye shadow and “zinc pink” lipstick. (Wow.) I walk into the kitchen and am instantly met with a wave of coffee aromas mixed with some kind of tomato sauce and steamy (and slightly soapy?) air. The chef, Richard d’Orazi—a full head of jet-black hair, biggish eyebrows, and a loose form of goatee—is cutting an enormous piece of fresh tuna. He cuts carefully, methodically. In short: He looked terrifying.

I bop into the kitchen (I was even chewing gum that matched my lipstick) and explain I am there to work for free—to *stage*. He looks up and gives me the once-over. "I'll see you here tomorrow morning at 9 a.m. sharp."

"OK!" I smile enthusiastically and give him the thumbs-up.

"And, just for the record," he says as he pauses unnaturally, eyes spanning my manicured presence, "this is no glamour show in here, just so you know."

Flash to one month later. I am working in the pastry department. No makeup. Dark circles. Hair in a bun. Drab white coat and checked pants. I have never felt so good—like I was connecting my choice of profession with the life-affirming feelings from watching my parents cook all those years. Homemade biscuits and breads, apple and dried fruit crumbles, dark chocolate pudding—some of the true nuts and bolts of American food. The first time I went to make custard, I grabbed a "flat" of local eggs from the fridge and listened intently as my coworker Dino Rasi explained how much Larry Forgione values geography with ingredients: huckleberries from Oregon, blueberries from Maine, lamb from Colorado. "In Europe, we classify food by the seasons and by geography; we know about truffles from Piedmont, endive from Belgium. Why shouldn't we do the same in America?"

To tell you the truth, I wasn't yet ready for such a heady concept. I was driven by one motive only: avert disaster as frequently as possible. I cracked the first few eggs into the bowl, separating the yolks from the whites (and leaving in a few shell bits) and realized I needed to be farther away from the roaring hot oven to do this. I grabbed the flat and scooted to the other side of the pastry area. Midscoot, I looked up to see Larry Forgione trotting down the hallway to his office. I smiled and made some nervous attempt at a wave. A flat of eggs? A wave hello? Bad combo. I watched in slow motion as the flat of eggs slipped from my grip and landed (with a glorious splat!) at his feet. Or, really, *on* his feet: suede loafers with tassels ready to catch oozing yolk. To his credit, he just looked at me, smiled, shook his head, and walked around me to clean his shoes. I made a mental note of this and then forgot all about it. Every recipe I made, I wrote down avidly, with a voracious appetite for knowledge. But Larry Forgione's demeanor was something that never made it to the egg- and cream-stained pages of my first cooking notebook. He never lost his cool. Sure, he got impatient. He got frustrated. But he never lost it. And that was critical. He created an environment that nurtured me and gave me more confidence to learn, to enjoy the craft of cooking and take my innumerous mistakes in stride.

After working at Larry's for about a year and a half, I decided it was

IN LARRY FORGIONE'S KITCHEN, 1991

time to take this field seriously and get a degree. I certainly didn't have the money for the Culinary Institute of America or Johnson & Wales. So I bought a book, the *ShawGuide to World Culinary Schools*. Surely such a book could tell me where I could go and cut chicken for free somewhere. And it did: at La Varenne, headed by Anne Willan, in Burgundy, France. A work-study program. Some French culture. A change of scenery. A lot of dishwashing and one "La Varenne Grand Diplôme" later, I made my way up to Paris for what was supposed to be a three-day stint at the (then) two-Michelin star Guy Savoy before going home.

You ever meet someone and know that your life was about to change?

That was Guy Savoy.

"Welcome to my kitchen! My house is your house!" His hand swept the manicured kitchen filled with twenty-seven (most of them actually sneering) young French men. And me.

I got this, guys. I fit RIGHT in.

"You're a girl, but, worse than that, you're American," muttered one cook as he took the staircase with two boxes of baby arugula.

I spent the next few months in the basement peeling vegetables. I learned to "turn" an artichoke (how they start so big and end up so small), I opened fresh sea urchins (spiny little suckers), and I wiped what felt like every chanterelle in Paris with a damp cloth. Sure I felt sorry for myself. But self-pity can be a strange motivator. What I didn't realize until years later was how cooking with my parents in our kitchen at home was directly linked to this basement prep work. I was learning to appreciate ingredients. I can still close my eyes and conjure the aroma of a chanterelle, of a white truffle. I feel and turn an artichoke the same way today. Working repetitively with the same ingredient provided me with an understanding of how that taste will integrate into a dish. I took that, along with Larry Forgione's zen demeanor, and added it to my bag of tricks on the road to becoming a chef.

I wasn't allowed to cook anything (not even boil water for a cup of tea) for the first seven months at Guy Savoy. I came to regard the beautiful Bonnet stove and the elegant clatter of the heavy copper pans the way a hungry cat eyes a bowl of cream from across the room. One night, fed up with the seemingly invisible line drawn between me and the stove, I grabbed a copper pan and began to heat it up. I took some mushrooms—already seasoned, cooked, and cooled—to reheat them and put them on the plate of veal in front of me. Just as I was about to drop the mushrooms in the pan, the sous-chef, Laurent, swooped in and grabbed the pan from my hands.

"You are not ready," he sniffed and heated the mushrooms himself. He handed the pan to me with a spoon and watched as I carefully interspersed them with the veal on the plate.

I tasted the sauce. A hint of mustard, some lemon. Very unusual and bracingly acidic.

"You like the lemon?" Laurent asked me.

"I do," I replied. "It seems to really brighten the other flavors and it doesn't really taste like lemon!"

"Sometimes," he continued, "another ingredient, like lemon, can make veal taste more like itself without adding a distinctly lemon taste."

A revelation, and one that would reappear all the time while I was working there. Acidic ingredients, especially lemon, white wine, and various vinegars, suddenly piqued my interest because I realized how much they could illuminate the taste of things.

But there was an even more important, and, in a way, even simpler, revelation about French cooking that lodged its way into my brain. When I heated artichoke puree, I topped it with braised artichoke hearts and crispy artichoke leaves. Potato puree was topped with a layer of crisped potato rounds. Veal chops were completed with veal sweetbreads and a veal sauce. An ingredient

PART OF THE KITCHEN CREW AT GUY SAVOY, 1995

presented in many different forms of itself is a way to make something taste like the most intensely flavorful version of itself.

And let's talk about those ingredients. One day, a young guy appeared at the back door of the kitchen with two trays covered with cloth. The chef lifted it to reveal the most beautiful porcini mushrooms. The scent alone was intoxicating, a mixture of hazelnuts, barnyard, grass, and soil. I could wax poetic for pages about the parade of ingredients: tiny wild asparagus, white truffles from Alba, vibrant pink, almost pearl-colored sweetbreads. Instead I will only say that I began a love affair with great ingredients, one that had been started by Larry Forgione and continued by Guy Savoy.

A few years later I returned to New York and began working for Daniel Boulud. At that point in my career, I was thoroughly convinced that my years with Guy Savoy in France meant I had nothing left to learn about the craft of cooking.

Chef Alex Lee (who remains, to this day, one of the best chefs I have ever had the privilege of working with) greeted me affably.

"You hungry?" he asked.

Unusual. "Sure!" I smiled eagerly.

"Thomas!" he called to the back of the kitchen to one of the cooks. Thomas looked very busy prepping furiously for dinner service. "Make me and Alexandra a bunch of your dishes for her to taste." Thomas smiled (somewhat homicidally) and started heating up pans on the stove.

A few minutes later, Thomas appeared at the front of the kitchen with a couple of plates: grilled octopus on a bed of white beans and ravioli dotted with vibrant green peas and lemon zest. The food smelled delicious. I dug in. The ravioli was a pillow of peas and Parmesan cheese. The charred pieces of octopus were perfect: the kind that get stuck gloriously in your molars as you chew that mixture of the ocean and grill marks. And the

AT LA VARENNE COOKING SCHOOL IN BURGUNDY, FRANCE, 1992

beans, held together and made almost creamy by a white bean puree; they reminded me of Guy Savoy. Another bite. But the beans were a little salty. Were they too salty? Who was I to say? I wouldn't ever share that with the chef if he asked. The beans are too salty, the beans are too salty, the beans are too salty.

"What do you think?" asked Alex.

"The beans are too salty," I blurted.

"Thomas!" Alex shouted back at him. "She says your beans are too salty!"

My eyes scanned the kitchen. It felt as if every cook in the room were glaring at me. I had betrayed the "cooks' code" and tattled on a member of the very tribe I was trying to join. Alex smiled at me, somewhat satisfied, as if his experiment had worked. I had failed the first test.

"Thanks for the feedback," he said, putting the dishes aside. "You will be working with Thomas learning that station."

Welcome to the jungle, folks.

"Roll these croutons in melted duck fat and brown them in the salamander while you get some artichokes from the fridge downstairs," Thomas briskly gave me my first marching orders of the day.

I scurried to coat the croutons with the fat and arranged them in a single layer on a baking sheet. I whacked the tray in the salamander and ran downstairs to find the fridge. There were two full-size refrigerators: one for proteins and one for vegetables. All those years at Guy Savoy, prepping vegetables, making the same movements over and over, I was ready for this! I gathered a bunch of the most beautiful little chokes I have ever seen and turned to exit the fridge. As I rushed out, a tall, lanky cook named Vinnie came in and stopped when he found me.

"Uh, you may wanna go upstairs and check your croutons," he snickered a little.

I raced up the stairs, trailing artichokes, and saw that my tray was still in the salamander. The tray had actually caught fire, charring the bread beyond recognition, and duck fat flames were shooting out and licking the ceiling, which was actually starting to look charred, too! Thomas stood there, smirking a little. So much for oversalted beans. Welcome to Restaurant Daniel. (In fact, the entire time I worked there, they never completely fixed that ceiling; I used those marks as a reminder that I could always be having a worse day.)

My love of great ingredients eventually drove me out of Daniel and his perfect boxes of baby greens in search of the soil they came from. Whereas I had spent years in France learning various basic cooking techniques, I wanted to see how ingredients, produce in particular, came to make food taste so delicious. So I headed to California, naturally. I found a job working for Joachim Splichal at the original Patina restaurant in West Hollywood. Oh boy. The scent of nectarines from half a block away, artichokes and asparagus that looked as if they were still breathing. I went through my slice-a-tomato-with-some-sea-salt-and-smile-proudly-at-my-hard-work phase. It was refreshing to let the ingredients do most of the talking. I realized that a classic Béarnaise sauce, touched with Texas (as opposed to French) tarragon, could taste almost like licorice and illuminate lobster in a whole new way. I saw that Easter Egg radishes had a mustardy bite that made sour cream and caviar go together like cornflakes and milk. I tasted Santa Barbara spot prawns with slices of lemon and satsuma mandarin oranges that would make anyone rethink citrus as round and rich and not simply tangy, zesty, and acidic. California connected my palate with all of the cooking I had done so far through the oldest method in my personal playbook: eating! And I probably would have lived gloriously surrounded by mountains of Cherokee heirloom tomatoes and Tristar strawberries had the shores of my hometown not constantly beckoned my name.

You see, as cooks, we aren't always driven by the tides of the best tomato or working in the most demanding kitchen environment. Sometimes we are driven by the realization that, no matter where we are, we can always set up camp and earn our keep cooking. I had grown fond of having a car, a cute "new" VW Beetle, and puttering around, exploring the various farmers' markets and street-food carts that make Los Angeles amazing. But, as a person, I never felt I belonged there.

One day, I left my friend's condo, which we were sharing, and headed without thinking to the garage beneath it to get my car. I started the engine, drove around the corner, locked the car, put money in the meter, bought a cup of coffee, and drove right back without even realizing what I had done. It was time to get outta there.

Luckily, Joachim was opening a restaurant in Manhattan and I volunteered to work there in order to move back. Well. After all those palaces of fine cuisine and pretty little tomatoes, I wound up working at the base of Madison Square Garden in a steakhouse. It was a showdown between me, the start time of any Ranger or Knick game, and the deep-fryer. My senses became dulled by too many onion rings and crab cakes. But I learned the process of dry-aging meat, taking responsibility for aging a roomful (1,000 pounds or so at any given time) of beautiful prime beef. American beef.

I had spent so many years cooking fish at Guy Savoy and Daniel, and the rest just focusing on produce, that I never really learned enough about the beauty of meat. The basic food groups: fish, produce, grains, dairy, meat. They all need to have their proper day in the sun. And meat felt like the final frontier. The beef was beautiful, and if I close my eyes I can feel my arms twitch slightly as they remember the sweeping gestures of breaking down those beef shells the way dancers might remember a dance. The funky aroma of the aged meat as it parted from the bone, the smell of it as

PORTERHOUSE WITH MELTED MAÎTRE D' BUTTER (PAGE 114)

it spittled and charred under the 1,200-degree heat of the broiler. The steak melted ever so slightly the minute it hit that heat and developed a tasty crust as it browned, brushed with butter and sea salt.

But this gig felt final somehow. I came home stinking of blue cheese dressing and pecan pie and wondered what my next step was. I had lost my imaginary rope, the one that had, so far, pulled and tugged me through my journey in food. What I was cooking didn't feel like it came from distinctly anywhere. The ingredients were nice but they could have come from anywhere, been cooked anywhere, in the country.

I quit. I was going to find an office job with a desk, clipboard, and computer. And I got close. I took a job teaching at the Institute of Culinary Education and also as a private chef working for a family on Park Avenue: one quesadilla sliced in two, some macaroni and cheese, and a fruit bowl and I could be back at my apartment by 7 p.m. The teaching was also great. I learned so much about my own learning process by teaching people who were just starting out.

One morning, I was snoozing off a serious hangover in bed when I got an urgent call from the school. Come down and substitute teach. *Why not?* I threw on some electric green boots, sweats, and a chef's jacket. Hair in a bun. High fashion.

I arrived at the class and explained the cooking we would be doing for the day. The class was a fairly dry group except for one gentleman in the back who kept laughing at my jokes. That gentleman would become, a short year later, the father of my daughter, Ava. She is the light of my life and someone who opened my heart to a new joy, one I hadn't had the privilege of discovering working in all of these restaurants: cooking something out of love for another person (and not just out of love for the ingredients) and then having the joy of watching them eat it! Incidentally, those electric green boots remain one of my most sentimental possessions to this day. But I get a little ahead of myself by introducing Ava. Something else happened before that. And I really didn't expect it.

"My boyfriend's running a restaurant down on Lafayette Street and they need a chef," a fellow teacher whispered to me in the hallway one morning.

"No thanks." I smiled politely.

"Just go down there and see the place," she urged. "It's really beautiful and you just might change your mind."

So I did. The place was unique, covered in wood and built like a giant boat. I take that back—it looked like a giant wooden butter dish. The waiter sauntered up to the table moving as if there were a disco ball over his head. "What can I getcha guys?" He winked. Really? I had cooked a whole turbot for the president of the French Republic; I had sliced heirloom tomatoes for the likes of Brad Pitt. Was I really in a restaurant where food played second fiddle to ambiance? Is this how I was going to end up?

My friend and I ordered and ate. The food was really good and somehow suited the environs. And that was confusing. Was this really a "broken" restaurant in need of a chef? I went into the kitchen and found a group of young men all cooking furiously to keep up with the pace of the dining room. One cook in particular, Antonio, was cooking a pan full of scallops. He turned around to face me with a geisha-like smile. And I knew what that smile was. That smile was coming from the hum of the pan and those scallops as they developed a brown candylike crust. That hum was traveling up his arms and through his neck and up to his brain and making him smile. I had seen that look cross my mother's face from time to time when I was growing up.

"I'll take the gig. Just buy some mats for the floor," I murmured.

The menu was small and simple enough: 12 appetizers, 12 main courses. It had rice steamed in a banana leaf with some wasabi and pickled ginger mixed with a beurre blanc touched with lemongrass. A hodgepodge of well-executed dishes that somehow hung together. And I didn't see a reason to fix what wasn't broken. My first true menu, without any supervision or editing, would happen here and now at Butter. Even though I had twelve years' cooking experience to fall back on for ideas and inspiration. I made spinach mixed with hoisin sauce for a filet of beef. I made a mustard oil dressing to pool around grilled salmon. I made gnocchi with mushrooms doused with truffle oil. I felt like I had traded in a simple box with a few crayons for the motherlode box that has every hue, from Burnt Sienna to Vermilion, and the sharpener built into the side of the box to boot. I worked blindly but unbridled, galloping my way through various cuisines and flavors. This was fun!

One Saturday, I was running down the stairs to make sure we had enough of everything when one of my best cooks crossed me in the staircase. He was lugging two giant cans of hoisin sauce. "We're gonna need more of this for the weekend," he smiled at me. But as he said it I froze as if I had seen a ghost. I didn't sleep that whole night. How many gallons of hoisin sauce would it take? I had never used it before this gig and only eaten my father's occasional judicious and informed use of it on several of his Chinese dishes. Banana leaves? They were beautiful. I enjoyed the way they made perfect little packages for food, wrapping it neatly into a whole idea—and yet, for me, based on my experiences, they contained nothing of my spirit or training.

The next day, I woke up early, watched twelve episodes of *Star Trek* and headed out to the Greenmarket. I needed to go back to the well and drink the original Kool-Aid. I was going to buy 5 pounds of beets, pickle them, and somehow resolve my existential crisis.

Once at the Union Square Greenmarket, I went to the largest farmstand I could find. Paffenroth Gardens. Behind the sign ("from Warwick, New York") stood the quintessential farmer, overalls, flannel shirt, and a face like Santa Claus. I had come to the right place. I scanned the tables and saw so many things that pushed various buttons on my personal keyboard: baby carrots like I had seen littering the tables of the market in the 17th arrondissement in Paris, bunches of tarragon like those I had picked through in the markets in Los Angeles. The list went on.

I made my way over to "Santa" and introduced myself. Frosty stare.

"I am looking to buy a few pounds of beets." I smiled.

"What kind of beets?" he shot back. "I got candy stripes, slicing beets, golden beets, white beets . . ." His voice trailed off as he surveyed the table.

I looked at each kind of beet carefully, wondering which one would yield the lost taste I was searching for. Only one way to find out: I grabbed a bunch of bags and picked out about 15 pounds of each kind. Then baby carrots, in all colors, from vibrant red to almost pearly white. Radishes, mustard greens, kale, collards. The bags just piled up. I loaded everything into a taxi and took it to the restaurant.

Suffice it to say, my home pickling experiment never happened, but the menu at Butter changed forever. Gone were the sauces and flavors that were crowd-pleasing but not true to me, replaced with fresh vegetables cooked to coax out their best flavors—the way I had eaten them with my parents and cooked them with the likes of Daniel and Guy Savoy. With only fifteen years' experience in the field, I was happy with that achievement.

The Frugal Gourmet Cooks American
JEFF SMITH
COMPLETE BOOK OF
CHINESE NOODLES, DUMPLINGS AND BREADS
GOURMET COOKING SCHOOL COOKBOOK

キング

what kinds of stuff I like to use in the kitchen

First things first: I have always found it slightly arrogant to tell someone what to buy to have a well-stocked kitchen. Whatever equipment you gravitate to personally is what you should have. I am not a gadget person, but I grew up in a house that had more kitchen equipment than one could ever need. My mother has a pair of scissors designed to cut open the tops of fresh sea urchins. She has one drawer filled entirely with spatulas—at least thirty, at last count. And it makes her happy. My point is this: It doesn't matter how much or how little stuff you have to cook with. If a specific utensil makes you happy and that makes your food taste better, it belongs.

Knives

I feel as if knives are so personal. The best way to buy a knife? Test-drive it by holding it in your hands. Feel the grip. Figure out, firsthand, if it's relatively lightweight. Who wants to hold a heavy knife? It's only going to be, well, heavy, and weigh you down as you cut stuff. I like a sturdy slender knife that goes through food with ease, with a blade that I can keep sharp with minimal difficulty.

If I were transplanted to a kitchen on a desert island with my knife bag and asked to create a meal, what would I need? Here is a picture of an old-school knife roll as I see it:

A simple paring knife—I almost say the cheaper the better. My absolute favorite is a Sabatier knife (around 2½ inches) that retails for 6 or 7 dollars. The knife is lightweight and easy to hold, and the blade is pretty easy to keep sharp.

10-inch chef's knife—The first knife I ever had was two feet long, or so it seemed. And I loved the way it felt like I could cut through a whole watermelon with one swipe of the knife. With more experience, I favor something smaller and, though I generally like a lightweight knife, I like a chef's knife with a little heft to it and a little curve to the blade. This is the knife for splitting squash or slicing leeks and potatoes for soup. I don't use it much for butchering unless I'm dealing with a larger cut of meat.

5-inch boning knife—I like one with a thick, slightly flexible blade. This is the tool for some fish (like fluke, flounder) and some meat (like hanger steak or pork loins). I also use it for vegetables because it's longer than my paring knife but slender enough to allow for accuracy.

Serrated knife—I love this for slicing tomatoes and citrus. Sometimes I will just cut a few things with it to enjoy the feeling of cutting with a totally different kind of knife. Of course, it's also the go-to knife for cutting bread.

Diamond Steel knife sharpener—I know most knife buffs would tell me how wrong I am to recommend this steel because it "eats knives for lunch" and leaves you, eventually, with a paper-thin blade half the size you began with. But if that's true, it also means I have gotten a lot of use from the knife and made a lot of delicious food with it in the process! For home cooks, sharpening can be a daunting process. Don't worry about being perfect, just get in there and give it a try. This steel is a good place to start. There are certain foods, particularly citrus and more fragile fruits like grapes and tomatoes, where I always give the knife a little sharpening before I begin. Remember to wipe the blade clean of any metal after sharpening and before touching food with it.

A note about storing knives: Don't do a twenty-car pileup with all of your knives in a drawer. Every time you open and close it, they rattle around on top of each other and their blades become dull as a result. Keep them separate or upright somehow. If you do have to pile them for space reasons, cover each one with some type of guard to protect the blade. There are many kitchen clichés that hold true. One of the oldest in the book is that you are more likely to cut yourself with a dull knife. I have nearly lobbed a finger off with a knife so dull that it could have been mistaken for a spoon!

Other Tools You Might Need

A wooden spoon—What is it that feels so different about gripping a piece of wood and using it to stir whatever is cooking on the stove? There's something about the porous nature of wood that makes my hand feel more connected to whatever I stir with that spoon. I also love being able to leave it in most bubbling pots and pick it back up without burning myself.

A good rubber spatula—I like to spend money on a good heatproof spatula that can weather many temperatures and therefore uses. The first and simplest use for a rubber spatula is for delicately folding things (like whipped egg whites) into batters, but a heatproof rubber spatula is also great for hot food. I love tracing under the edge of an omelet or scraping up sticky edges of a potato cake. It's a diplomatic fixer in a lot of delicate situations.

Vegetable peeler—I like the square "Swiss" peelers. Plastic. Affordable. But they peel with even, clean strokes. Because this is a fairly cheap piece of equipment, keep it dry after using to avoid corrosion.

Microplane grater—I remember when the Microplane came on the scene. For the first few years, anytime anyone asked me for a favorite kitchen gadget, this was it. Grating ginger to get juice and pure pulp instead of woody, stringy bits? Getting garlic to a liquidy paste in seconds? Extracting just the top skin layer from citrus zest and leaving the pith behind? This tool remains a game changer.

Mandoline—I have one of those expensive metal French mandolines in my bottom kitchen cabinet. When I worked at Guy Savoy, I used to bring it out and use it to make the most beautiful potato garnishes. That mandoline and I were one. Whenever I go to grab it now, it feels like that sucker weighs fifty pounds! So I love a plastic Japanese mandoline for making thin slices of radishes, carrots, and potatoes. The trade-off? It has the capacity to cut you remorselessly. So be careful when using. Use the guard. Pay attention. Don't multitask.

A small fine-mesh "tea" strainer—I use this a lot for dusting things with an even layer of powdered spices and times when I want to strain a small quantity of something.

Outside the Knife Bag and on to the Kitchen Counter

Blender (Vitamix)—This is the one place where I believe that dropping a lot of money will change your life. This blender is expensive and worth it. It makes airy soups, amazing purees; it crushes ice and makes delicious blended drinks. I have enjoyed this piece of equipment from celery root soup in snowy December all the way to a tangy margarita in July.

Food processor—My mother often uses it for blending sauces, like her famous marinara, which yields a slightly rougher texture I love. To me, the food processor keeps things a little rougher, with more texture. It's also great for making doughs.

Mortar and pestle—I love using this to crush toasted spices. The aroma is so intense; it makes my stomach growl. I also love to grind garlic or onion to a paste and smear it on top of a roast just before cooking.

Pots and Pans

I almost never use lids. I honestly cannot remember the last time I covered anything I cooked. I think it's because smelling the aromas as things cook and watching them change and become tastier, more complex, is a big part of tasting for me. As far as pricing and buying pots and pans, I would rather have one expensive sauté pan and one pot than a whole array of cheaper things I don't love. You are going to look at your cookware for a long time so make sure it's love before you head to the cash register.

12-inch cast-iron skillet—My favorite. To me, this is like the wide-open country road. Great for getting red hot and searing a steak or hamburgers, fun for baking a pie or corn bread for a good crust and different presentation. I honestly would cook just about anything in one.

A good nonstick pan—I realize cast iron seems so old school and nonstick surprisingly synthetic in comparison, but there are times when only the nonstick will get you where you want to go. I love them for pancakes and omelets.

12-inch and 8-inch sauté pans/skillets—I favor the types of pans with walls that curve out because they allow more steam to escape as things cook. The result? Browner potato cakes, browner meat.

Ingredients and Shopping

It's wonderful to read about food and the shopping habits of chefs. But it's more important to buy what you love—I can't stress this enough. Good food is expensive and you should spend your hard-earned cash on what you want to eat. That said, I do hope that you can see the beauty in nature's seeming imperfections when it comes to fruits and vegetables. For example, the bits of black discoloration on the rind of grapefruit may look "ugly," but they are a sign that the sugar is emerging from the fruit and that it is ripe to eat. My motto: Buy imperfect, buy what you love.

While I love giving standard, across-the-board recommendations for kitchen essentials, I'm not one to consistently use the same ingredients. Here are a few instances where that holds true for the recipes in this book:

Parsley: curly or flat-leaf?—Some chefs feel adamant about one or the other. I believe each has its time and place. Because I grew up enjoying the deep grassy flavor of curly in meatballs, I believe that's where it best belongs. So when I want the "serious" parsley flavor to shine through, I turn to curly. Flat-leaf is a mellower cousin. I like a few leaves torn into a salad or to pair it with certain types of meat or fish for a hint of freshness.

Bread crumbs—I wish I used the same bread crumbs every time. Coarse, rough panko bread crumbs are great for breading things like squid and getting that substantial coating (and crust). Plain dried bread crumbs are just that: your standard can from the supermarket without any flavorings added in. They come pretoasted. I use these in my meatballs to add body. I also use plain dried bread crumbs whenever I am looking for a lighter coating or a sprinkle of a subtler ingredient.

Oil: olive vs. canola—I am a big fan of extra-virgin olive oil and used to use it with wild abandon on everything. But now I find I cook with it in a more specialized, careful way. For cooking at high temperatures on the stovetop, I usually reach for canola oil because it better tolerates high heats and olive oil becomes bitter if used at high temperatures. Canola is also less expensive. Olive oil shines through most in a salad dressing (often tempered with a bit of canola) or when drizzled over meat, fish, or vegetables as a last-minute touch to add richness.

Butter—I like unsalted butter and use it for almost everything. I season generously with salt when I cook and it actually confuses my seasoning when salt is built into unexpected places. I do keep a stick of lightly salted butter around in my freezer for occasional use.

Salt—I always use kosher salt for cooking. For boiling water for pasta, seasoning meat and fish before cooking, baking. . . . Also, I use Diamond Crystal brand. I find it categorically less salty than Morton's brand.

I fell in love with fleur de sel sea salt from the coast of Brittany, France, a long time ago and use it to season meat, fish, or vegetables that final time just before serving. My other favorite? Maldon salt from England. It looks like little snowflakes. A sprinkle of this salt leaves you crunching it between your teeth. It takes me back to biting into a piece of Chiclets gum as a kid, breaking through that hard (but ever-so-thin) sugary shell and chewing the gum hidden beneath.

Pepper—I love black pepper because it can bring out flavor in certain ingredients just like salt does. Black pepper also has somewhat of a heat-driven floral note (like fresh chiles) so I like it on red meats and other robust ingredients that can withstand (and almost need) the aggressive pepper. I grab white pepper whenever I want the flavor to be slightly subtler and not visible! At Guy Savoy, for example, I was trained (for years, so it's hard to erase this from my cook DNA) to put white pepper wherever black pepper would be unsightly, such as in mashed potatoes.

Soy sauces—Take one Italian-American father who loves French food and cooks Chinese food for a hobby and you end up confused about some ingredients—namely, soy sauce. My father had so many and it seemed like he never used the same one twice. I use dark soy for deep salt and reduced-sodium soy when I want a lighter note.

One final note: Cooking is a lifelong learning process. Whether cooking at home or becoming a chef, don't forget to be patient. Consider this:

In 1983, my parents took me on a trip to Paris. The second night, we ate at Chef Joël Robuchon's famous restaurant Jamin. At that time, Robuchon had been cooking for twenty-plus years and was considered the most important chef in Paris. As we ate our appetizers, we didn't utter a word. There were flavors so pure and so complex that speaking and eating at the same time was out of the question. My father turned to the waiter and exclaimed: "This is some of the best food I have ever eaten in my life!" The waiter tilted his head slightly in my father's direction and responded: "Yes, and in another ten years he will almost be a really great chef."

snacks
always bring a
family together

tomato slices on an english muffin
with cheddar

spicy cauliflower fritters

broccoli and onion dip

pickled grapes with prosciutto

white mushrooms on toast

roasted squash soup
with popcorn

chilled cucumber soup
with fiery yogurt sauce

overnight garlic bread

crispy squid with garlic,
red pepper flakes and basil

grilled clams with
charred zucchini and garlic

baked clams with bacon

chicken wings with marmalade

little spare ribs

I know when we say family meals, we mean dinners with our loved ones at home. My mother would often make soup to start a meal, one that could tell a story about the season: chilled tomato in summer and a velvety potato leek for winter. I have never made a menu without including a soup for that reason.

But I have also had a different family: one that forms in a restaurant. So, what would you expect the kitchen staff and waiter family at one of the finest restaurants in Paris to eat after hours? Caviar on brioche toast points? Fondue with truffle shavings? Not quite. Take a can of corn, a can of pickled beets, ice-cold slices of cucumber, wedges of tasty avocado, and mix together with some sherry vinaigrette and you have the perfect snack for a group of hungry cooks and waiters at 2 a.m. The textures, temperatures, and mixture of canned and fresh flavors comprise one of my most vivid taste memories as a young cook. Of course, I was so grateful to sit down and eat after a fifteen-hour workday and everything tastes better when you're so hungry.

When I make a snack, I chase the same feeling that salad gave me. I am not alone. My daughter, Ava, appeared in the doorway of the kitchen the other day and announced, "Ma, make me something delicious to eat."

"What would you like?" I asked, intrigued.

"Just something delicious, OK?"

Sounds about right to me . . .

tomato slices on an english muffin with cheddar

I don't make this for eight people or share it with anyone. Some things are to be enjoyed alone. **SERVES 1**

1 Thomas' English muffin, split open
3 (3/8-inch-thick) slices tomato
Kosher salt and cracked black pepper
Pinch of sugar
1½ ounces extra-sharp cheddar, cut into 4 or 5 slices

1. Toast the English muffin until those nooks and crannies are deeply browned.

2. Season the tomato slices with salt, pepper, and sugar.

3. Layer the tomatoes, one overlapping the other, on top of the bottom half of the muffin. Top with the cheddar. Put the muffin top over it and press down until some of the juice leaks out of the tomatoes. Close your eyes. Pretend you're eight years old. Enjoy.

tomatoes

Every summer while I was growing up, my parents would ship me off to my great-aunt Aggie's place in Newton, Massachusetts. Aggie lived in a house on a sloped street with a big backyard and a little tiny bit of land in front. There was an enormous rose of Sharon tree and a small patch of unruly yellow and orange flowers out front. Sitting out on the front steps one balmy Saturday afternoon, I was drawn to the aroma of the flowers. They were marigolds. It seemed to me, an eight-year-old, that this sea of flowers was just like the field of poppies in the *Wizard of Oz*. I crouched down and crawled in between the plants, elbows in the dirt. After all, there isn't much soil in your life when you grow up on 7th Avenue in Manhattan. It smelled good and was barely damp on my knees. Do you think it's possible that soil can make you hungry? It was only in the thick of these flowers that I realized they were interspersed with tomato plants.

The tomatoes were everywhere, hanging low and, in some cases, already on the ground. I grabbed a large red tomato defying gravity on a vine and bit into it like an apple. Warm from the earth, that tomato had an extra-special something. It wasn't even that sweet nor was it perfectly shaped. But it was so juicy and delicious. It became the tomato I have searched for from that day since.

My aunt came onto the porch calling my name. I grabbed a few more tomatoes and crawled out from my hiding place. My aunt looked relieved.

"The marigolds are so cool, Ags," I remarked, clutching the warm tomatoes.

"They keep the bugs away, Al. Come inside and I'll slice those up with some sharp cheddar and put it on a toasted English muffin."

ME WITH MY GREAT-AUNT AGGIE, 1976

spicy cauliflower fritters

I am a closet carnivore masquerading as a sometime somewhat vegetarian type. This recipe harnesses the best of both of those. Why? Cauliflower is already meaty in texture, and frying little pieces gives it more heft. I love it with a side of Harissa (page 285) or with some sour cream seasoned with lemon juice. **SERVES 4 TO 6**

BATTER

1½ cups all-purpose flour, plus more if needed
2 teaspoons coriander seeds, lightly crushed and toasted
2 teaspoons red pepper flakes
Kosher salt
2 teaspoons canola oil, plus 1 quart for frying
1½ (12-ounce) bottles beer, preferably Heineken

1 large head cauliflower, stem removed, broken into bite-size florets
1 tablespoon smoked hot paprika

1. Make the batter: In a medium bowl, combine the 1½ cups flour, the coriander seeds, red pepper flakes, and 1 teaspoon salt. Whisk in the 2 teaspoons oil and the beer. Set aside in a warm place. Like bread dough, it will puff up slightly.

2. Cook the cauliflower: In a large, deep, heavy-bottomed pot (or deep-fryer), heat the 1 quart oil to 375°F. Monitor the temperature of the oil with a thermometer. Line a baking sheet with a kitchen towel to drain the cooked florets.

3. Arrange the cauliflower pieces in a single layer on a separate baking sheet. Use a small fine-mesh strainer to dust the smoked paprika evenly over the cauliflower.

4. Stir the batter slightly and check its consistency by dunking a cauliflower floret into the batter, shaking off the excess. The batter should coat the piece lightly but completely. If the batter is too thick, whisk in a little water. If too thin, whisk in a little more flour.

5. Working in small batches, coat the cauliflower with batter, letting excess fall off, and lower into the oil. It should bubble slightly and the cauliflower should gradually rise to the top. Fry, turning once, until lightly browned, 2 to 3 minutes, and then transfer them to a kitchen towel to drain any excess oil. If the batter doesn't form a thin, crisp shell, don't be afraid to drop the cauliflower back in the oil and fry for an additional minute. Season with salt while the cauliflower is still hot. Serve immediately.

broccoli and onion dip

I never ate a single chipful of dip growing up in my house. For that reason, dip has fascinated me ever since. Chipping and dipping is an iconic American pastime that has become as appealing to me as dinner at other people's houses when I was a kid. I name brands in here because they are the ones I grew up with and combining them creates that flavor that makes old-school recipes taste just right. **MAKES 3 CUPS**

---

1 small head broccoli (about 12 ounces)
4 tablespoons extra-virgin olive oil
½ teaspoon cumin seeds
3 medium garlic cloves, grated
Kosher salt
¼ dry white wine
2 medium red onions, halved and sliced ¼ inch thick
4 ounces cream cheese, preferably Philadelphia
½ cup mayonnaise, preferably Hellmann's (or Best Foods west of the Mississippi)
½ cup sour cream, preferably Breakstone's
1 to 2 tablespoons red wine vinegar, preferably Regina

1. Prepare the broccoli: Cut the stem off the broccoli and peel it like a carrot. Cut a piece from the upper part of the stem and cut into small pieces until you have roughly ¼ cup. Discard the remaining stem. Cut the florets into small, bite-size pieces. You need 3 cups combined loosely packed broccoli florets and stem pieces.

2. Heat a large skillet over medium heat and add 2 tablespoons of the olive oil. When the oil begins to get hot, add the cumin seeds and broccoli stems. Stir and cook 2 minutes and then add the broccoli florets, garlic, and a pinch of salt, stirring so the garlic doesn't burn in the pan. Once the garlic starts to brown, add the white wine. Increase the heat slightly and cook the broccoli until tender, 5 to 8 minutes. The wine should be all but completely evaporated. Transfer to a baking sheet and refrigerate immediately to cool.

3. Cook the onions: Wipe the same skillet clean with a paper towel and, over medium heat, add the remaining 2 tablespoons olive oil and the onions. Season generously with salt. Cook, stirring regularly, until the onions caramelize, 15 to 20 minutes. Do not rush this step. It also gives you time to allow the broccoli to cool down. The more the onions taste like candy, the better the dip. Set aside to cool.

4. Make the dip: In a food processor, process the cream cheese until smooth. Add the mayonnaise and sour cream and process again until smooth. Season to taste with salt and vinegar. Pulse in the cooled broccoli until mixed but still somewhat chunky—about ten 1-second pulses. Transfer the dip to a bowl and stir in a little more than half of the onions. Put the remaining onions on top of the dip.

old-school tip

Let it rest. I find that making this dip and letting it sit overnight before eating is a game changer. I also know that you may struggle with making something so tasty and putting it away. So make it, have a taste, and then stash the rest. Take the dip out of the fridge a while before serving so you can loosen it up with a whisk and it won't be ice-cold when people dig in. You can also keep the cooked onions separate, warm them up at the last minute, and stir them into the dip. That addition of a warm ingredient just before serving will give the dip an even richer flavor.

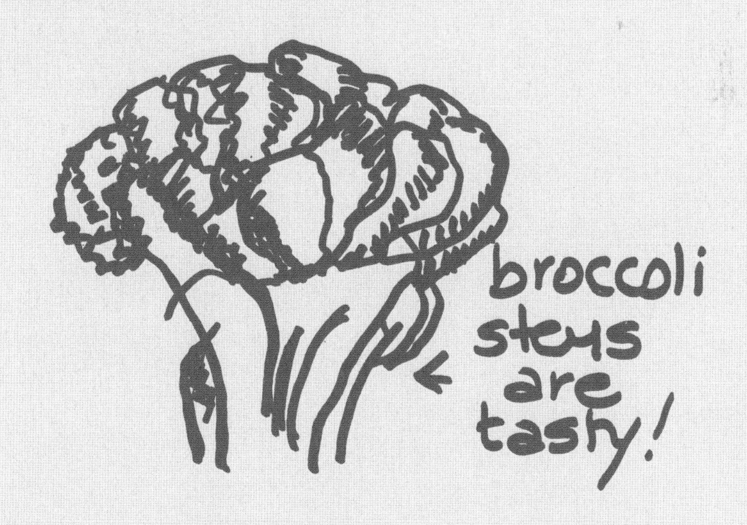

pickled grapes with prosciutto

The most important choice you can make here is a grape that you love to eat and one that is seedless. The seeds add bitterness and disrupt that wonderful "pop" that grapes have when you bite into a whole one. I look for ones about the size of a smaller cherry and find ½ pound is 20 to 24 grapes. To me, pickling these grapes leaves you with the right amount of raw fruity freshness and juice combined with the acidity from the vinegar. Wrapped in a slice of prosciutto, this is the type of nibble that makes you feel hungrier as you eat. **SERVES 8**

1½ cups white wine vinegar
¾ cup sugar
9 whole cloves
1 tablespoon mustard seeds
1 tablespoon black peppercorns
1½ teaspoons kosher salt
½ pound seedless red grapes (preferably medium to large)
1 garlic clove, lightly crushed
10 to 12 thin slices prosciutto, halved lengthwise
Extra-virgin olive oil, for drizzling

1. Make the pickling liquid: In a small nonreactive saucepan, whisk together the vinegar, sugar, cloves, mustard seeds, peppercorns, and salt and simmer over medium heat, stirring to dissolve the sugar and salt, 3 to 5 minutes. Remove from the heat and let stand for 5 minutes.

2. Pickle the grapes: Cut off the "belly button" at the top of each grape (where it connects to the stem), taking as little of the actual grape as possible, make a few shallow incisions in each grape, and put the grapes in a small bowl. Pour the pickling liquid over the grapes and let sit overnight in the refrigerator. These grapes keep for a long time, so make a jar and have them around for when you need them.

3. Serve the grapes: Rub the garlic over the prosciutto and wrap each grape in about 2 layers of the prosciutto and set seam side down on a serving platter. Secure the ham around each grape with a toothpick, if desired. When ready to serve, drizzle a little of the pickling liquid and a little olive oil over them.

old school variation

Alternatively, brown the grapes in a sauté pan in a thin layer of hot canola oil, turning them so the prosciutto crisps. Serve warm.

white mushrooms on toast

I cook the mushrooms and *then* make the toast. Of course, it would be more logical made in reverse so you could finish the mushrooms, spoon it on the waiting toast, and eat immediately. But toasting the bread gives the mushrooms a much-needed minute to cool and "gel" flavor-wise. I have a distinct memory of my mom patiently stirring these mushrooms and letting them cool slightly as she toasted slices of brioche under the broiler. The toast was always browned on both sides with the slightly cooled mushrooms spilling onto the toast. One of my original food memories.

MAKES 16 PIECES; SERVES 6 TO 8

---

3 tablespoons extra-virgin olive oil
1 small yellow onion, finely diced
Kosher salt and black pepper
2 small garlic cloves, minced
¾ pound white mushrooms, ends trimmed, wiped clean, and cut into ¼-inch slices
2 tablespoons dry Marsala
½ cup sour cream
1 tablespoon chopped fresh tarragon leaves
16 (½-inch-thick) slices baguette

1. Preheat the oven to 375°F.

2. Cook the mushrooms: Heat a large saucepan over medium heat and add 2 tablespoons of the olive oil. Once hot, add the onion, season with salt and pepper, and cook until tender, 3 to 5 minutes. Add the garlic, lower the heat, and cook for an additional minute. Add the mushrooms, season with salt and pepper, and cook until they have softened and the liquid they release has nearly evaporated, 8 to 10 minutes.

3. Pour in the Marsala and simmer until the flavor of the alcohol has mellowed considerably, 3 to 4 minutes. Add the sour cream and allow it to melt over the mushrooms. Season with salt and pepper. Add the tarragon. Bring to a simmer and then shut off the heat. Taste.

4. Toast the bread: Arrange the bread slices in a single layer on a baking sheet and brush them with the remaining 1 tablespoon olive oil. Bake until lightly browned and crispy, 6 to 8 minutes. Season with salt.

5. Serve the toasts: Arrange the toasts on a platter and top each one liberally with the mushrooms. If the creamy aspect of the mushrooms thickens too much when they cool slightly, don't be afraid to add a splash of lukewarm water and warm them up over low heat to loosen again before topping the pieces of toast.

roasted squash soup with popcorn

I have been serving this soup at Butter for about eight years. Some people take it pretty seriously. One night a sweet couple walked into the restaurant without a reservation and asked for two bowls of "the soup." Turns out, that day, I had made some roasted lentil soup with smoked ham hocks instead. When they heard that, they stood up, put on their coats, and told the waiter: "Give the chef a message: When she is ready to make the soup, we'll be back to eat it!" And they walked out! That sealed it into tradition.

So as soon as I feel that fall nip in the air, I head down to the farmers' market and buy some of my favorite squash from farmer Alex Paffenroth of Paffenroth Gardens. I am particularly in love with any type of squash with a dark green skin, such as kabocha. I also love combining kuri or Hokkaido squash with the old workhorse butternut. Go rogue at the supermarket. Try some squash you've never tried before. Squash are like people; each kind offers something special and unique. One note, though: This recipe changes depending on the squash you use. Don't be afraid to tinker with the flavor by adding more or less sugar or garlic or molasses accordingly.

SERVES 8 TO 10

---

6 pounds butternut or other winter squash (2 large or 3 medium butternut)
12 tablespoons (1½ sticks) unsalted butter
2 tablespoons packed dark brown sugar
3 tablespoons blackstrap molasses, plus more if needed
Kosher salt and white pepper
1 teaspoon ground ginger
½ teaspoon ground cinnamon
¼ teaspoon ground cloves
Grated zest and juice of 1 orange
2 tablespoons Worcestershire sauce, plus more if needed
2 garlic cloves, grated
2 cups skim milk
1 cup heavy cream
Juice of ½ to 1 lemon, to taste
1 to 2 cups freshly popped and salted popcorn

recipe continues

1. Preheat the oven to 375°F.

2. Prepare the squash: Put the squash on a cutting board and split them in half lengthwise. Scrape out the seeds and discard. Arrange the squash in a single layer, cut sides up, on 1 or 2 rimmed baking sheets.

3. Heat a small saucepan over medium heat. When it begins to smoke lightly, remove the pan from the heat and add 8 tablespoons (1 stick) of the butter. Swirl the pan to melt the butter and wait until it starts to turn a light brown color (return to the stove if needed). Immediately pour the butter liberally over the squash halves and into the cavities. Sprinkle the brown sugar and molasses liberally over the squash and into the cavities as well. Season with salt and pepper.

4. In a small bowl, mix together the ginger, cinnamon, and cloves. Transfer the spice blend to a small fine-mesh strainer and dust the squash halves and cavities with an even layer.

5. Cook the squash: Cover the squash halves somewhat snugly with foil and carefully put the baking sheet(s) in the oven. Add about an inch of water to the baking sheet(s) to create steam while the squash bakes in the oven. Bake for 1½ to 2 hours. To check for doneness, pierce one of the halves through the foil with the tip of a small knife. The knife should slide in and out easily. If at all firm, bake the halves for an additional 30 to 45 minutes. Remove from the oven. Carefully peel back the foil and set aside to cool.

6. Make the soup: Using a large spoon, carefully scoop the flesh from the squash into a large pot. Get all of the cooking liquid *inside* the squash, too, but avoid the skin and the liquid in the bottom of the baking sheet(s): Both will add unwanted bitterness to the soup. Put the pot over low heat. Add half of the orange zest, the orange juice, 2 tablespoons Worcestershire sauce, and the garlic. Stir to blend. Taste for seasoning. If the squash lacks sweetness, add a little molasses. If it lacks salt, add a little salt or Worcestershire sauce.

7. In a medium saucepan, heat the remaining 4 tablespoons (½ stick) butter over medium heat until it turns light brown and then pour it over the squash, stirring to blend. In the same pot, heat the milk, cream, and 2 cups water. Season the liquid with salt and pepper and bring to a simmer. Stir the milk mixture into the squash and bring a simmer.

8. Finish the soup: Puree the soup in small batches in a blender. Combine all of the batches and taste for seasoning, adding salt, orange zest, or pepper, as needed. If the soup is too thick, add an additional cup of water and blend. Stir in a little lemon juice to brighten the flavors. Serve the soup family style, or ladle the soup into individual bowls, with the popcorn on the side.

chilled cucumber soup with fiery yogurt sauce

I keep a little skin on the cucumbers because it deepens the flavor and color of this refreshing soup. My thoughts about chiles: Sometimes I'm in the mood for a mouth-numbing hit of heat and sometimes I want something milder. If you use a jalapeño and want to calm it down, remove the seeds and white "ribs" inside; that's where the spice really packs its punch. The flip side of the spicy flavor of a chile is the surprisingly floral notes the flesh contains. The honey in the yogurt sauce can pick up on the hint of honeysuckle that lurks beneath the heat of a jalapeño.

I add the lemon juice just before serving so the acid adds flavor without ruining the vibrant color. After blending this soup, let it sit in a bowl placed over an ice bath to chill it further. And put your serving bowls in the refrigerator so the soup stays cold even as you enjoy it! **SERVES 6 TO 8**

SOUP

4 hothouse cucumbers (3½ pounds total), 2 of them peeled and all cut into ½-inch rounds
2 to 3 cups ice water
Kosher salt and white pepper
1 to 2 teaspoons honey (optional)
2 small Kirby cucumbers, cut into small wedges for garnish
Juice of 1 lemon

SAUCE

1 small fresh chile, such as jalapeño or Scotch Bonnet, sliced (seeds and all) into ⅛-inch rounds
2 teaspoons honey
1 teaspoon hot Spanish paprika
1 teaspoon ground cumin
1 cup whole-milk yogurt
1 tablespoon red wine vinegar
Kosher salt

1. Make the soup: Put half of the hothouse cucumber slices in a blender and add 1 cup of the ice water. Blend on low speed (so as not to whip too much air into the soup as you blend it; the air makes the cucumbers taste less intense) until smooth. You may have to stop the blender to push the cucumbers down toward the blade. Add more water if the blender has trouble crushing up the cucumber. Season with salt, pepper, and a touch of honey, if a little sweetness is needed. Transfer to a large bowl and repeat with the remaining hothouse cucumber. Combine the two batches in the bowl and taste for seasoning. Put the bowl in an ice bath to chill it more quickly.

2. Make the sauce: In a small bowl, stir together the chile, honey, paprika, and cumin. Mash slightly with the back of the spoon so the ingredients meld together. (If you own a mortar and pestle, this is a great place to pull it out to blend these ingredients to a chunky paste.) Stir in the yogurt and vinegar. Season to taste with salt.

3. Serve the soup: Just before serving, season the Kirby cucumbers with salt, pepper, and a little lemon juice and add some to each soup bowl for garnish. Give the soup a final stir over the cucumber slices. Spoon a dollop of the yogurt sauce on top and partially swirl it into the soup. Serve immediately.

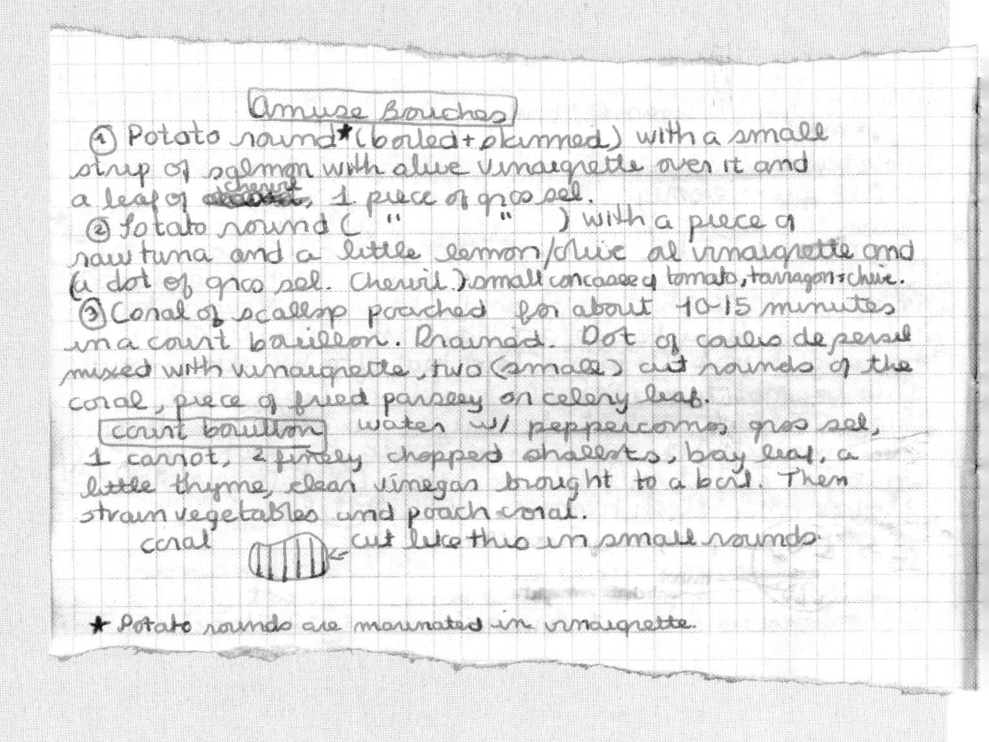
Amuse Bouches

(1) Potato round* (boiled + skinned) with a small strip of salmon with olive vinaigrette over it and a leaf of chervil, 1 piece of gros sel.

(2) Potato round (" ") with a piece of raw tuna and a little lemon/olive oil vinaigrette and (a dot of gros sel. Chervil.) small concassee of tomato, tarragon + chive.

(3) Coral of scallop poached for about 10-15 minutes in a court bouillon. Drained. Dot of coulis de persil mixed with vinaigrette, two (small) cut rounds of the coral, piece of fried parsley on celery leaf.

court bouillon: water w/ peppercorns gros sel, 1 carrot, 2 finely chopped shallots, bay leaf, a little thyme, clear vinegar brought to a boil. Then strain vegetables and poach coral.

coral — cut like this in small rounds

* Potato rounds are marinated in vinaigrette.

overnight garlic bread

I'll bet you've marinated plenty of chicken breasts, flank steaks, and vegetables, but how about garlic bread? I love to wrap this up, leave it overnight, and then just toss it in the oven for half an hour when people come over. Is it crucial to leave it overnight? No. Is the anticipation of having this ready to bake off in your fridge fun? Yes. The garlic flavor tastes baked through. I love that. Sometimes I make it when I'm at home with my daughter so we don't have to share with any guests! This gets even better when you add slices of mozzarella (you need about 12 ounces) and a sprinkle of red pepper flakes to make an addictive, melty snack. **SERVES 6 TO 8**

---

1 (13-inch) loaf Italian bread
7 medium garlic cloves, grated
⅓ cup extra-virgin olive oil
4 tablespoons (½ stick) unsalted butter, cut into 10 to 12 thin slices
1 tablespoon flaky sea salt, such as Maldon
1½ teaspoons cayenne pepper

1. Prepare the bread: Cut the bread in half lengthwise as if you were making an oversize hero sandwich. Mix the garlic with the olive oil and spoon over the length of the cut sides of the bread, using the back of the spoon to fully spread the garlic over the bread. Arrange the butter slices on the bottom half of the bread. Sprinkle with the salt. Use a small fine-mesh strainer to dust the cayenne evenly over the whole bread. Close up the bread and wrap it tightly in foil, sealing the ends. Refrigerate overnight.

2. Preheat the oven to 375°F.

3. Bake the bread: Put the bread in its foil wrapping in the oven and bake until it feels hot to the touch, 35 to 40 minutes. Transfer to a baking sheet and unwrap the foil carefully as hot steam will escape from the bread. Bake, unwrapped, until the exterior develops a little crispness, 10 minutes. Remove from the oven, slice, and serve immediately.

crispy squid with garlic, red pepper flakes, and basil

Squid, once cleaned, is a cheap date. It cooks quickly and has a rich flavor for its small price tag.

It took me a while to realize that when you cut the squid bodies into rings, they get considerably thicker once fried than they look in their raw state. So, if you are cutting squid into rings at home, use a sharp knife and cut them thinly. Cooking time is critical, too; squid needs to be cooked either very briefly or for a long time to be enjoyed tender. **SERVES 4 TO 6**

---

1 quart frying oil, such as canola
4 large eggs
3 cups coarse bread crumbs, preferably panko
1 pound small squid, cleaned, bodies cut into ¼-inch-thick rings, tentacles intact
Kosher salt
1 tablespoon extra-virgin olive oil
3 very yellow inner stalks of celery and the leaves, thinly sliced
1 teaspoon red pepper flakes
2 garlic cloves, minced
1 lemon, halved lengthwise, seeded, and chopped (skin, pith, and all) into small chunks
½ cup basil leaves, small leaves left whole and larger ones torn into pieces

1. In a large, deep, heavy-bottomed pot (or deep-fryer), heat the 1 quart frying oil slowly to 350°F. Monitor the temperature of the oil with a thermometer. Line a baking sheet with a kitchen towel to drain the squid once they are cooked.

2. Prepare the squid: Whisk the eggs in a medium bowl. Put 1 cup of the bread crumbs in another medium bowl. Arrange the squid rings and tentacles on a baking sheet and season lightly with salt. Dip one-third of the squid rings and tentacles into the egg to coat. Use a slotted spoon to remove them and allow any excess egg to drip off. Transfer the squid to the bread crumbs and toss to coat. Transfer to a baking sheet and arrange in a single layer to avoid clumping. Repeat twice more using the remaining bread crumbs

recipe continues

(they can get gloppy from the egg, which is why I like to start with a fresh bowl of them twice along the way) and squid. Refrigerate the squid while you make the sauce.

3. Make the sauce: In a medium bowl, combine the olive oil, celery, red pepper flakes, garlic, and lemon. Season with salt and stir to blend.

4. Cook the squid: When ready to serve, lower the squid, in small batches, into the oil. Fry, turning with a slotted metal spoon, until crisp, 2 minutes. Drain on the lined baking sheet and season each batch immediately with salt. When the last of the squid is almost crisp, toss in the basil leaves. Be careful because the basil leaves will splatter as they hit the oil so stand back after you toss them in. When the leaves look translucent, 30 seconds to 1 minute, remove and drain everything on the prepared baking sheet. Season immediately with salt.

5. Serve the squid: Toss the squid, fried basil leaves, and reserved basil in a bowl and serve with the lemon sauce drizzled over the top or on the side, if preferred.

grilled clams with charred zucchini and garlic

When I went to Charleston, South Carolina, a few years ago, I watched (I will admit, in horror) as a chef put whole oysters on a hot grill. He waited a few minutes and watched as they popped open as if they had some internal timer. He pulled one off the grill and handed it to me along with a lemon wedge. Having grown up in New York and eaten oysters raw my whole life, this was a sacred moment. The oyster was a little tough, but absolutely delicious—proving that there is no better thing than a food cooked in its own shell for deep, authentic flavor. Once home, I tried the technique with littleneck clams and found I like them even more than oysters. Be patient with the clams; sometimes they can take a few minutes to open on the grill. Just when you're ready to give up and turn your back on them, that's when they open!

Extra-honest confession that makes this recipe even more special to me: I'm not a grill gal at heart. Growing up in an apartment building in midtown Manhattan meant I literally never had grilled food. It is not a taste that hearkens back to anything for me—I almost filed it as overrated! This recipe is one of many that changed my mind. Grazing the shell exterior with your teeth and tasting a bit of the char is an amazing prelude to the flavors in this dish. **SERVES 6 TO 8**

---

3 tablespoons canola oil
3 tablespoons pine nuts
Kosher salt
2 garlic cloves, minced
3 medium zucchini (1¼ pounds total), cut lengthwise into ¼-inch-thick slabs
2 teaspoons red pepper flakes
2 tablespoons unsalted butter
3 dozen medium littleneck clams, thoroughly scrubbed of all sand and grit
1 lemon, halved

1. Preheat the grill.

2. Brown the nuts: In a medium skillet, heat 1 tablespoon of the canola oil over medium heat. When it gets hot, add the pine nuts. Season them lightly with salt and cook, stirring constantly, until golden brown, 2 to 3 minutes. Transfer immediately to a medium bowl so they don't get overly brown and bitter to cool. Stir in the garlic.

3. Cook the zucchini: In a bowl, toss together the zucchini and remaining 2 tablespoons canola oil. Sprinkle the red pepper flakes evenly over the zucchini slices (if you just dump them in, they tend to stick to only a couple of the zucchini slices). Season lightly with salt and mix gently. Arrange the zucchini in a single layer on the hottest part of the grill and cook until they are charred and can easily be pierced with a fork but not falling apart, 3 to 5 minutes. Use a pair of metal tongs to remove the zucchini from the grill and transfer to a cutting board. Stack the slices and cut them crosswise into ½-inch slices. Toss them in the bowl with the pine nuts.

4. In a medium pan, melt the butter.

5. Cook the clams: Scatter the clams on the grill in a single layer. Have a large platter ready. As the clams open, use tongs to remove them from the grill and put them on the platter. This may take from 1½ to 5 minutes. When they have all opened, squeeze the juice from the lemon into the melted butter and add the zucchini and pine nuts. Drizzle this mixture all over the clams, trying to get zucchini, nuts, and liquid inside the shells. Serve immediately.

Cleaning clams

Mollusks are best stored on a little ice and covered with a damp cloth. Because they filter salt water to live, fresh water produces the opposite effect. After scrubbing the shells under cold running water to remove grit, submerge the clams in a mixture of kosher salt (about 2 scant tablespoons) and cold water (about 2 quarts) for a few hours so they filter out any internal grit. Then cook immediately.

baked clams with bacon

I am a big fan of recipes that require a little cooking in advance so I can take off my apron and enjoy time with friends and family. This recipe lets me do just that: The clams get prepped ahead of time and then baked at the last minute. Try it with mussels as well, for something a little different. **SERVES 4**

---

20 medium littleneck clams, thoroughly scrubbed or all sand and grit
¼ cup dry white wine
4 slices bacon, cut into thin slices crosswise
4 tablespoons (½ stick) unsalted butter, at room temperature
2 scallions (green and white parts), thinly sliced
2 medium garlic cloves, finely chopped
Grated zest and juice of 1 lemon
Kosher salt and white pepper
½ cup plain dried bread crumbs
1 small bunch curly parsley, leaves finely chopped (1 heaping tablespoon)

1. Prepare the clams: Heat a large skillet over high heat and add the clams in a single layer. Add the wine and cook until the clams open, 5 to 8 minutes. Use kitchen tongs to remove the clams from the skillet as they open. Gather them in a large bowl. Allow them to cool for a few minutes and then twist off the top shell, leaving the clam in its bottom shell. Slide a paring knife under each clam to dislodge it from the shell but leave it inside the shell. Refrigerate until ready to cook.

2. Preheat the oven to 375°F.

3. Cook the bacon: Rinse and dry the large skillet and cook the bacon in it over medium heat until crisp, 5 to 8 minutes. Drain on a paper towel and reserve the bacon fat in the pan.

4. Make the bread crumb topping: Put the butter in a food processor and add the scallions, garlic, lemon zest, and half of the lemon juice. Pulse to blend. Transfer the mixture to a bowl and season with salt and pepper. Add the reserved bacon fat and the bread crumbs and stir to blend. Spoon a little of the bread crumb mixture on a baking sheet and cook in the oven until golden brown and bubbling, 3 to 5 minutes. Taste and adjust the seasoning, if needed.

5. Bake the clams: Remove the clams from the refrigerator and loosely mold some of the bread crumb mixture into each of the shells so the clam body is somewhat covered. Arrange them in a single layer on a baking sheet. Bake until the tip of a small knife inserted into a clam comes out warm to the touch, 10 to 15 minutes.

6. Remove from the oven and preheat the broiler. Broil the clams until well browned, about a minute, watching them constantly so they don't burn. Remove them from the oven. Squeeze a little lemon juice over each clam. Top each clam with some bacon and parsley. Serve immediately.

chicken wings with marmalade

This is the kind of recipe where I have no idea how to gauge the number of servings; in my family, we wouldn't dare think of any fewer than 6 to 8 wings per person. So take into account who the lucky people will be who will share this with you—if you are willing to share, that is. Either way, this method of cooking chicken wings is great for a small batch to enjoy solo or a larger batch for a crowd. People always marvel at the crisp exterior the cornstarch achieves and the texture the wheat germ adds. The marmalade comes from the single memory I have of my maternal grandmother cooking when I was a child. She roasted some chicken thighs and then glazed them with textured (not smooth) marmalade at the very last minute. Since it happened many years ago, I consider it a significant cooking (and flavor) memory.

SERVES 4 TO 6

---

2 quarts frying oil, such as canola
3 pounds chicken wings (12 to 14 full wings or 24 to 28 individual pieces)

SAUCE

½ cup chunky orange marmalade
1 teaspoon reduced-sodium soy sauce
1 teaspoon red wine vinegar
Kosher salt (optional)
1 jalapeño chile, thinly sliced into rounds (seeds and all)

FLOUR MIXTURE

1 cup all-purpose flour
2 tablespoons wheat germ
1 cup cornstarch
1 tablespoon kosher salt
½ teaspoon black pepper

Kosher salt

1. Preheat the oven to 300°F.

2. In a large, deep, heavy-bottomed pot (or deep-fryer), heat the 2 quarts frying oil to 360°F. Monitor the temperature of the oil with a thermometer. Place a rack in a baking sheet to drain the chicken pieces as they come out of the oil.

3. Let the chicken wings sit at room temperature while the oil heats. If the wings are straight from the cold fridge, the oil temperature will drop drastically when you fry them, resulting in a less crisp crust.

4. Make the sauce: In a small saucepan, combine the marmalade, soy sauce and vinegar. Heat gently to loosen the marmalade and then keep warm on the stove while you fry the chicken wings. Taste and add salt, if needed.

5. Make the flour mixture: In a paper bag (I think the bag gives it extra flavor), combine the flour, cornstarch, wheat germ, salt, and pepper. Shake to blend. Add the chicken pieces to the bag, close it, and shake until each one is fully coated with the flour mixture, shaking off any excess flour. Put the floured pieces in a single layer on a baking sheet.

6. Fry the chicken: Group your batches of chicken into similar-sized pieces so they are done cooking around the same time. Add a small batch of the wings, say 8 pieces, to the hot oil. Fry until they float to the surface and are golden brown, 3 to 5 minutes. Transfer to the rack and immediately season the pieces on both sides with salt. Keep an eye on the oil temperature because it will drop with each batch of chicken you fry. Take care the oil is hot enough before adding a new batch of chicken. Put the fried chicken on a baking sheet in the oven while you fry the rest. When all of the chicken pieces are fried, stir the jalapeño slices into the sauce. Use a pastry brush and brush each piece generously all over with the marmalade sauce. Taste for seasoning. Serve immediately.

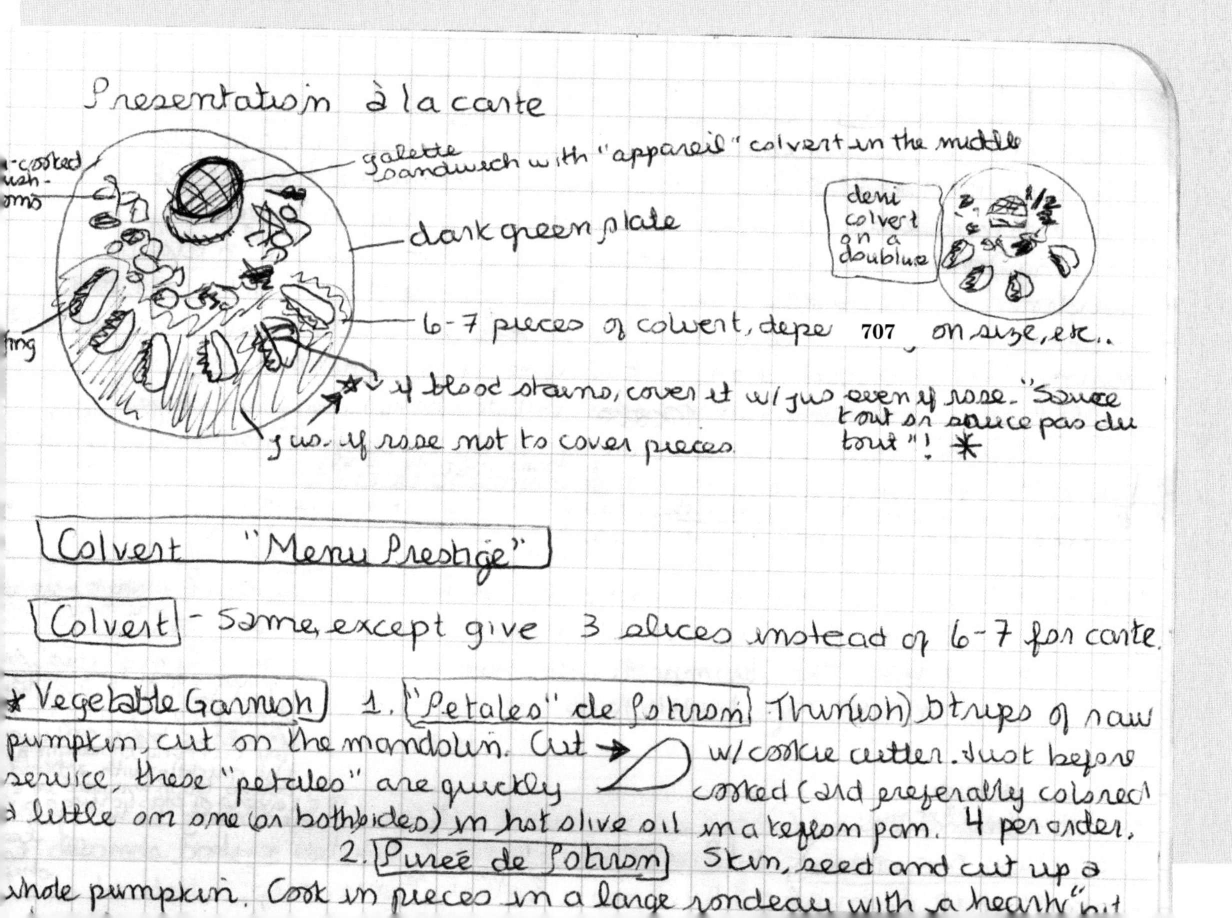

Presentation à la carte

-cooked
ush-
oms

galette sandwich with "appareil" colvert in the middle

dark green plate

demi colvert on a doublure

6-7 pieces of colvert, depe[nding] on size, etc..

ing

* if blood stains, cover it w/ jus even if rose. "Sauce tout or sauce pas du tout"! *

jus- if rose not to cover pieces.

Colvert "Menu Prestige"

Colvert - Same, except give 3 slices instead of 6-7 for carte.

* Vegetable Garnish 1. "Petales" de Potiron (Turkish) Strips of raw pumpkin, cut on the mandolin. Cut → [shape] w/ cookie cutter. Just before service, these "petales" are quickly cooked (and preferably colored a little on one (or both sides) in hot olive oil in a teflon pan. 4 per order.

2. Purée de Potiron Skin, seed and cut up a whole pumpkin. Cook in pieces in a large rondeau with a heav

little spare ribs

I consider my early food memories some of the most important because they are the ones that started it all for me. It's true that spareribs are great glazed with honey or deep-fried until crisp and served with some hot sauce. This recipe promises none of that. The ribs are almost steamed tender with clear flavors that coat the meat. My father used to make these and let them hang out in the pan on the stove until we were ready to eat. I wasn't tall enough to peer over the pan at first so I would root around, as if in the dark, looking to steal one before dinner. When I make them, the aroma of soy sauce and the cider vinegar takes this Italian-American gal to an oddly familiar place of comfort. I love these with some roasted garlic (page 199) on the side. **SERVES 4 TO 6**

---

6 tablespoons cider vinegar
2 tablespoons rice vinegar
¼ cup dark soy sauce
1 tablespoon sugar
3 pounds pork spare ribs, on the bone, cut into 1½-inch square pieces
2 tablespoons Dijon mustard
Coarsely cracked black pepper
Kosher salt (optional)

1. Cook the ribs: In a large saucepan, combine ⅔ cup water, the cider and rice vinegars, soy sauce, and sugar. Bring to a simmer, stir to dissolve the sugar, and add the spare ribs. Stir to separate the pieces so they are all coated with the liquid. Cover and simmer over low heat, stirring from time to time, until the meat is tender and starting to separate from the bone, 1 hour to 1 hour 15 minutes.

2. Finish the sauce: Scoop out the ribs to a serving bowl and keep warm. Add the mustard to the cooking liquid and simmer to reduce it until thickish, 5 to 10 minutes. Pour the sauce over the ribs and gently toss them in the sauce to coat each one. Taste for seasoning. Sprinkle with pepper (and salt, if needed), and serve immediately.

salads

for all seasons

leeks vinaigrette

chilled iceberg wedge with
blue cheese and leeks

baked potato salad

arugula and strawberry salad

greenmarket caesar salad with
quickie poached egg dressing

marinated asparagus spears

pea salad with tarragon
and pea shoots

farfalle pasta salad with beet
vinaigrette and parsley pesto

shrimp and cucumber salad

winter greens salad from the oven

To me, a salad is all about the choice of acid: vinegar, citrus— the salad's spark plug. It's a small part, but a car can't run without it!

I learned one of my most valuable lessons in the kitchen at Restaurant Daniel in New York. A seriously VIP chef came in for dinner and we all waited breathlessly to see what his table would order. We figured the squab terrine or the Jerusalem artichoke soup or the coveted end piece of a whole halibut. Instead, he ordered a mixed green salad and chicken! I was working the salad station at the time and was charged with the responsibility for his appetizer. I layered vinaigrette, salt, and pepper so carefully over different types of greens and arranged them on a plate so that each leaf looked perfect. Out the salad went. And a few minutes later, back it came!

"The monsieur says his salad is too salty," the busboy said as he ran out of the kitchen.

The whole staff was silent. Everyone knew I had made it and I was going to hear about it. Daniel took a bite of the lettuce and chewed thoughtfully. I didn't breathe.

"You didn't add too much salt," he began, "you just added too much vinegar and his palate mistook one for the other." He walked away and I remade the salad.

Acid can be as powerful as salt in cooking. Especially in a salad.

leeks vinaigrette

I did eat this dish in a Parisian bistro. What a cliché, I know. What remains the strongest part of this particular food memory was the unique texture of the leek with the richness of the chopped egg, the zing of mustard, and the crunch of bread crumbs. Leeks are underloved, often used as a supporting cast member to give soups body and flavor. But they come to life in this dish, a celebration of their many inner layers, which are enhanced by a tasty vinaigrette falling into all those wonderful crevices. Cook the leeks ahead—they can hang in the dressing for a while in the fridge—and top with the egg and bread crumbs at the last minute. **SERVES 6 TO 8**

VINAIGRETTE

¼ cup Dijon mustard
Juice of ½ lemon (about 2 tablespoons)
2 tablespoons red wine vinegar
1 teaspoon capers, roughly chopped, plus 1 teaspoon of their brine
Kosher salt and white pepper
⅔ cup extra-virgin olive oil
1 small bunch fresh tarragon, leaves finely chopped (about 2 tablespoons)

4 large eggs
8 to 10 leeks (4 to 4½ pounds)
Kosher salt
2 slices sourdough bread
1 tablespoon extra-virgin olive oil
10 to 15 yellow celery heart leaves and 2 to 3 very yellow inner stalks, thinly sliced
White pepper

1. Make the vinaigrette: In a medium bowl, whisk together the mustard, lemon juice, and vinegar. Add the capers, caper brine, and a pinch each of salt and pepper. Slowly whisk in the olive oil and then stir in the tarragon. Taste for seasoning.

2. Hard-boil the eggs: Put the eggs in a saucepan large enough to hold them in a single layer and cover them with cold water by 2 inches. Bring the water to a boil, remove from the heat, cover, and let steep for 8 minutes. Drain the water from the eggs and cover them with cold water to stop them from cooking. Swirl the pan around a few times so the eggs knock against the sides of the pan, lightly cracking the shells. It will make them easier to peel. Before serving, peel and finely chop the eggs.

3. Prepare the leeks: Trim the root end and slice off the dark green from each leek. Peel off one or two of the tough outer layers. Split the leeks in half lengthwise but not all the way to the end;

recipe continues

the leeks should remain in one piece. Wash the insides of each leek thoroughly under running cold water, separating the layers. Leeks are very dirty and the slightest bit of dirt in the leek results in a mouthful of grit when eating this dish. After each leek is washed, do your best to close them up as if they hadn't been cut.

4. Cook the leeks: Bring a large skillet of water to a boil. Season it amply with salt and taste: It should taste like seawater. Plunge the leeks in the boiling water and simmer until a knife can easily be inserted and removed from a leek, 6 to 8 minutes. The leeks should be tender but still retain their shape and not feel mushy. Use tongs to remove the leeks from the water and transfer them to a cutting board. Dry them thoroughly with a kitchen towel, cut them in half, and put them, cut side down, in a single layer on a kitchen towel. This drains any excess liquid. This is the most important step because water in the leeks will dull the flavor of the dressing and leeks. Refrigerate until cold, or overnight.

5. Make the bread crumbs: Stack the slices of bread on top of one another and use a serrated knife to cut them into small random pieces each about the size of a pea. Heat a small skillet over medium heat and add the olive oil. Add the bread crumbs and toast, stirring, until browned, 3 to 5 minutes. Season with salt.

6. Serve the leeks: Put 2 to 3 leek halves on a plate and spread their layers gently apart. Drizzle the vinaigrette over the leeks, taking care that the dressing oozes into the crevices. Sprinkle with some of the celery stalks and leaves, some of the egg, and some of the bread crumbs. Season with salt and pepper, if needed.

Celery Hearts

Nothing is more old school to me than using the very inner yellow leaves and stalks from the heart of a head of celery. I love the taste—somewhere between a spice (like celery seed) and an herb (parsley or tarragon). Break away the green stalks (which I often nibble on to avoid eating everything I'm cooking) and pull out a couple of those tiny yellow stalks and yellow leaves. Not light green; that won't do. Dig deep in the heart and get those inner bits. They have the most intense flavor.

cheese

After I completed the program at La Varenne and got my cooking school diploma, I spent a few months working in a restaurant down by the French Alps, home of the most intoxicating cheese I had ever eaten: Beaufort. This cheese is made simply by pouring cooked milk into a mold and allowing it to age for an average of 5 to 12 months. Essentially a one-ingredient food, wonderfully nutty and often dotted with salty crystals (which are actually milk crystals), it is a must for any cheese lover.

We cooks shared a house and a car, a Renault 4L (Quatrelle), with a gearshift you had to pull in and out of the dashboard as you changed speeds. It was like a beer can held together by two pieces of dental floss with a tube of toothpaste as the engine. I charted the course and nabbed a fellow cook. "C'mon," I said, grabbing him as if we had been hired by the CIA to scope out the next evil dictator.

We boarded the tin can and gunned it (42 mph) the 16 miles to Beaufort. The highway was empty except for a few cars and a small truck directly in front of us. The air was fresh. We were in the country, the land of cheese, and I could smell it in the air! And with each passing minute the smell of Beaufort, that heavenly mix of barnyard and rich milk with salty touches, intensified.

"Can you smell the Beaufort?!" I shouted to my copilot, who was half asleep. He nodded wearily. "I mean, isn't it amazing?" I marveled.

"I think what you're smelling is that." He pointed to the truck that had been in front of us for the whole drive.

I squinted to catch a better look.

It was filled with cow manure.

chilled iceberg wedge with blue cheese and leeks

There are a few touches to this salad that I love. Chilling the iceberg makes the texture and temperature of the lettuce incredibly refreshing. I like to leave the blue cheese in little chunks so there are little creamy bites of cheese meandering through the dressing. Speaking of the dressing, two things to note: It benefits from sitting in the fridge overnight if you have the luxury of time on your side. Also, this makes an obscene amount of dressing, but I like it very much. If you have extra, use it on steak or roasted chicken. The chopped leek? I like to use raw leek the way I might use a raw scallion or raw onion; it's surprisingly strong and stands up to the blue cheese better than scallions. **SERVES 8 TO 9**

---

3 large heads iceberg lettuce
1 cup mayonnaise
½ cup sour cream
Juice of 1 lemon (about ¼ cup)
2 tablespoons red wine vinegar
2 garlic cloves, finely grated
7 to 8 splashes (or a scant tablespoon) Worcestershire sauce
2 splashes Tabasco sauce
Kosher salt and coarsely ground black pepper
8 ounces blue cheese, crumbled into chunks
4 slices bacon, cut into 1-inch pieces (optional)
1 leek (white and light green part only), finely chopped and well washed

1. Prepare the lettuce: Trim the stem end from each head of lettuce, remove the outer leaves, and cut each head into 3 wedges. Transfer to a small platter and put in the refrigerator for at least 1 and up to 4 hours.

2. Make the dressing: In a medium bowl, whisk together the mayonnaise, sour cream, lemon juice, vinegar, garlic, Worcestershire sauce, and Tabasco. Taste for seasoning, adding salt and pepper, if desired. Vigorously stir in half of the blue cheese so it blends in but also remains in visible pieces.

3. Cook the bacon: In a small skillet, cook the bacon with ¼ cup water over medium heat until all of the water evaporates and the bacon becomes crisp, 5 to 8 minutes. Use a slotted spoon to transfer the bacon to a paper towel to drain.

4. Serve the salad: When ready to serve, remove the iceberg from the fridge, arrange it on a serving platter, and coat each wedge with a generous amount of the dressing. Top with the remaining blue cheese, the chopped leek, and the bacon pieces, if using. Sprinkle with coarsely ground black pepper and serve immediately.

baked potato salad

I really love baking potatoes to make potato salad. It avoids the waterlogged factor and makes the process so much simpler. When you peel the skin from half of the baked potatoes, chop up the potato skin, pan-fry it until crisp, and then put it back over the potato salad at the last minute for an interesting garnish out of something that would otherwise end up in the garbage. I also find warm potatoes delicious sponges for flavor. Drop the potatoes in with the dressing, toss, and take a "nosebath" over the bowl. You'll want to dive in. **SERVES 4 TO 6**

---

2 pounds Idaho potatoes (about 3 large), scrubbed
Kosher salt and white pepper

PESTO

1 small bunch flat-leaf parsley (about ½ ounce), with about 1 inch of stems still attached, roughly chopped
1 small bunch basil (about ½ ounce), with about 1 inch of stems still attached, roughly chopped
Kosher salt and white pepper
3 tablespoons extra-virgin olive oil

DRESSING

2 tablespoons red wine vinegar
1 shallot, sliced into thin rounds
1 tablespoon Dijon mustard
2 teaspoons chopped capers, plus 1 teaspoon of their brine
4 cornichons, quartered lengthwise and sliced into ¼-inch pieces, plus 1 tablespoon of their brine
⅓ cup extra-virgin olive oil

1. Preheat the oven to 400°F.

2. Bake the potatoes: Arrange the potatoes in a single layer on a baking sheet. Bake until the potatoes are tender and yielding when pierced in the thickest part with the tip of a knife, about 1 hour. Remove from the oven and allow to cool for a few minutes.

3. Make the pesto: Meanwhile, in a food processor or blender, combine the parsley and basil. Season with salt and pepper, add 2 tablespoons water, and blend. With the machine running, pour the olive oil through the top of the food processor in a slow, steady stream. The texture should be a little rustic and chunky. Taste for seasoning.

4. Make the dressing: In a bowl large enough to hold the potatoes, whisk together the vinegar, shallots, mustard, capers and brine, and gherkins and brine with 1 tablespoon water. Whisk in the olive oil. Taste for seasoning.

5. Finish the salad: Once the potatoes are cool enough to handle, peel half of them. (Some potato skin is a nice flavor in the salad.) Put the potatoes in the large bowl with the dressing and lightly crush them with the tines of a fork. Season lightly with salt and pepper and toss them in the dressing. Drizzle with the pesto and stir to blend. Serve warm or at room temperature.

Basil and Parsley Stems

I am a serious nibbler when I cook. I think it's because the aroma of food gets my stomach juices flowing. The other day, I tasted a basil stem. The upper half (closest to the leaves) was surprisingly juicy and had great flavor. I cut it into thin rounds and stirred it into my dressing. Parsley stems, more grassy than sweet, meld well with the basil stems and somehow intensify the flavor of the potatoes in this recipe. Don't be so quick to throw all of those herb stems away!

arugula and strawberry salad

Every year, the Bishop family of Mountain Sweet Berry Farm in Roscoe, New York, has a picnic shindig on their front lawn. One year, a bunch of us chefs sat in awe as Rick Bishop drove us around the property and pointed out all of the wondrous things growing there. He had twenty-four types of potatoes growing last time I checked. The real revelation? The salad. I am not one who likes to put things like strawberries in salad. To me they belong in ice creams, shortcakes, and tarts. This salad changed my mind. With arugula, this dressing, and the poppy seeds, another side of strawberries comes out to play. They are green tasting, almost grassy, and their seeds combine with the poppy seeds to create a great texture. **SERVES 4**

DRESSING
3 tablespoons mayonnaise
2 tablespoons sherry vinegar
1 teaspoon honey
3 tablespoons extra-virgin olive oil
1 tablespoon canola oil
¼ teaspoon kosher salt

SALAD
1 generous pint of fresh strawberries, hulled and halved lengthwise
A sprinkle of poppy seeds
2 cups arugula leaves

1. Make the dressing: In a large bowl, whisk together the mayonnaise, sherry vinegar, and honey. Whisk in the olive oil, canola oil, and salt.

2. Assemble the salad: Toss the strawberries and poppy seeds in the dressing. Add the arugula and gently mix. Serve immediately.

greenmarket caesar salad with quickie poached egg dressing

Quick-poaching the eggs for the dressing avoids the raw-egg issue and adds a more unusual flavor to this salad. There's something more luscious about the taste of the egg; in fact, this dressing can easily be interpreted as a souped-up mayonnaise. I also love that the poached eggs leave me utterly at ease for keeping this dressing in the fridge for a couple of weeks. Another note: Canned tuna gives the dressing that anchovy flavor but also adds body without making the dressing heavier. And please make sure you fully dry your lettuce. There's nothing worse than water on your salad diluting the flavors of your beautiful dressing!. **SERVES 4**

DRESSING

3 garlic cloves, peeled
1 teaspoon kosher salt
2 large eggs
1 tablespoon fresh lemon juice, plus more as needed
1 tablespoon red wine vinegar, plus more as needed
1 tablespoon caper brine
1 tablespoon Worcestershire sauce
½ teaspoon Tabasco sauce
1 (2.8-ounce) can tuna packed in oil, drained
¼ cup extra-virgin olive oil

CROUTONS

6 tablespoons (¾ stick) unsalted butter
3 cups (¾-inch) cubed sourdough bread
Kosher salt
¾ cup freshly grated Parmesan

2 heads romaine lettuce, outer leaves removed, sliced into 1-inch rounds
Cracked black pepper
½ cup grated Parmesan cheese

1. Make the dressing: Use a mortar and pestle to grind the garlic cloves and the salt to a paste. (Alternatively, this dressing can be made entirely in the food processor by initially processing the garlic and salt, and then adding the other ingredients.)

2. Quick-poach the eggs: Bring a small, shallow pan of water to a boil. The water should be deep enough to submerge the eggs but not so much that they have to fall several inches in the water to land on the bottom of the pan. Crack each of the eggs into a small cup or bowl. Lower the heat and bring the water to a gentle simmer. Salt the water. Carefully submerge the eggs into the water. Cook for 2½ minutes. Use a slotted spoon to remove them, one at a time, from the water and transfer to a food processor or blender. They don't have to be perfect.

3. In the bowl of the food processor, combine the lemon juice, vinegar, caper brine, Worcestershire sauce, Tabasco, tuna, and olive oil. Pulse a few times to blend. Overblending changes the flavor. Taste for seasoning. Do not overblend. The dressing is more flavorful if left with a little texture. Taste for seasoning. Transfer to a bowl. Stir in the garlic paste.

4. Make the croutons: In a large skillet, heat the butter over medium heat. When the butter begins to froth, add the bread. Season with salt. Toss and cook over medium-low heat until the bread browns and crisps, 5 to 8 minutes. Use a slotted spoon or spatula to remove the croutons from the pan and drain and arrange them in a single layer on a paper towel. Season with the Parmesan. Set aside to cool.

5. Serve the salad: Put some of the dressing in the bottom and on the sides of a large bowl. Add the lettuce and season with pepper. Toss the romaine, gathering dressing slowly from the sides and toss in the croutons. If the lettuce is dry, add some more dressing. If the salad needs more zing, add a tiny splash of vinegar or another squeeze of lemon. Top with the remaining Parmesan. Serve immediately.

marinated asparagus spears

Sesame oil is an intense flavor I have to be in the mood to eat. I love how rich and roasted tasting the oil can be, and something green and crispy, like asparagus, is the perfect partner for it. The sesame seeds are plentiful on purpose in this dressing because they add crunch. I love tasting the asparagus and then grinding a few of the seeds between my teeth. Though I am definitely a fan of quickly roasting vegetables in the oven or pan-roasting them on the stovetop in a little oil and a splash of water, all that goes out the window here. Blanching the asparagus is like getting the perfect mud mask; it rehydrates the asparagus and makes them juicy. **SERVES 4 TO 6**

---

1 tablespoon honey
2 tablespoons white wine vinegar
3 tablespoons sesame oil
2 tablespoons reduced-sodium soy sauce
¼ teaspoon red pepper flakes
Kosher salt
1 pound fairly thin "pencil" asparagus, ends trimmed, cut into 2-inch pieces
¼ cup sesame seeds, toasted

1. Preheat the oven to 350°F.

2. Bring a large pot of water to a rolling boil.

3. Make the dressing: In a small pan, heat the honey over medium heat until it froths and turns golden brown, 2 to 3 minutes. Remove from the heat and carefully pour the vinegar over it. Return to the heat and simmer to reduce for an additional minute. In a bowl, whisk together the sesame oil, soy sauce, and red pepper flakes. Season with a pinch of salt. Whisk in the honey mixture.

4. Cook the asparagus: Prepare an ice bath: Fill a large bowl halfway with ice cubes and add some cold water. Set a colander squarely inside the ice bath. The colander will keep you from having to pick ice out of the asparagus later. Add salt to the boiling water until it tastes like seawater. Add the asparagus and cook until bright green but still crunchy, 1 minute for thin spears and 1½ to 2 minutes for medium ones. Use a slotted spoon to remove the asparagus from the water and transfer them to the colander inside the ice bath. Move them around gently to accelerate the cooling process. Vegetables take longer than you think to cool, so allow them to sit for a few minutes in the ice water. Hold a piece of the asparagus in your hand for a few seconds to assure that it's really cool (even in the center). Lift up the colander to drain the asparagus and then spread them out on a kitchen towel. If the asparagus are still wet, pat them dry thoroughly with another kitchen towel, or even allow them to air-dry and chill in the fridge before adding the dressing.

5. Finish the salad: Toss the asparagus, sesame seeds, and dressing together and refrigerate for an hour or until ready to serve.

pea salad with tarragon and pea shoots

I used to buy a lot of different baby greens from the market and make a huge mix to sprinkle on most of my dishes at the restaurant. I felt as if it added that fresh element that so much food needs. Now I like to add just one green, a single clear flavor, to make a statement. Pea shoots have always been one of my favorites because they make peas, frozen or fresh, taste like an amplified, improved version of themselves. They take peas from coach to business class, and the dressing upgrades them all the way to first. The sugar in the cooking water and on the peas themselves also intensifies flavor while the mustard adds a little bite. I like to use superfine sugar because it dissolves easily. Don't freak out if you can't find every type of pea; a few different types will do just fine. **SERVES 6 TO 8**

DRESSING

1 tablespoon plus 2 teaspoons Dijon mustard
Juice of ½ lemon
1 tablespoon sherry vinegar
½ teaspoon capers, roughly chopped, plus 1 teaspoon of their brine
Kosher salt and white pepper
⅓ cup extra-virgin olive oil
8 sprigs fresh tarragon, leaves chopped

PEAS

Kosher salt
Sugar
¾ pound sugar snap peas, ends trimmed
¾ pound snow peas, ends trimmed
1 cup shelled peas
White pepper
¼ cup pea shoots

1. Make the dressing: In a medium bowl, whisk together the mustard, lemon juice, and vinegar. Add the capers and brine, and a pinch each of salt and pepper. Slowly whisk in the olive oil and add the tarragon. Taste for seasoning.

2. Cook the peas: Bring a large pot of water to a boil. Prepare an ice bath: Fill a large bowl halfway with ice cubes and add some cold water. Set a colander squarely inside the ice bath. The colander will keep you from having to pick ice out of the peas later. Add salt to the boiling water until it tastes like seawater. Add a generous pinch of sugar. Add the sugar snap peas and cook until bright green and crisp-tender, 2 minutes. Use a strainer

recipe continues

to remove the peas from the water and transfer them to the colander inside the ice bath.

3. Bring the water back up to a boil and add the snow peas and shelled peas. Cook until they float back to the surface, 1 minute. Use the strainer to remove the peas and plunge them into the ice bath with the sugar snaps. Allow them to sit in the ice water for a couple of minutes to ensure they have cooled thoroughly.

4. Lift up the colander to drain the peas and then spread them out on a kitchen towel. Use another kitchen towel to gently pat them dry and then let them air-dry. Water on the peas will dilute all of the good flavors.

5. Serve the salad: Transfer the peas to a medium bowl and season with salt, pepper, and a sprinkle of sugar. Stir to blend. Toss with the dressing and pea shoots. Taste for seasoning. Serve immediately.

Sugar

I can't tell you how many times a tiny pinch of sugar or drizzle of honey makes a difference in cooking. Don't think of sugar as just adding sweetness; think of it as something that will also turn up the volume on acidity (from the lemon) and saltiness (from the capers). I love to "sugar" tomatoes, beets, green beans, asparagus, and corn, along with peas.

Tartare de Betterave

Finely chop 2-3 shallots.
Finely chop 2-3 branches of celery
finely chop bunch of parsley.
finely chop bunch of capers.

When these 4 tasks are completed, mix the four components together.

Take 3 beets, peel them, and get 'em chopped finely in The Robot. Mix into above mixture and season with generous-ish amounts of olive oil, s/p and Tobasco. Amuse bouche: Flat layer in little white molds, small leaf of chervil and a dot of good olive oil.

farfalle pasta salad with beet vinaigrette and parsley pesto

This pasta represents a collision of the two types of flavors I always crave with pasta. On the one hand, there is the grassy, earthy flavor of the parsley. To me it tastes almost like that intense waft of freshly cut lawn we've all gotten through the open window of a car zipping down a suburban street. On the other hand, I always want a little richness and sweetness, combined with a hint of acidity. Tossing pasta in a vinaigrette of any kind was not always my first instinct, but the more I cook and the more I eat, the more the rule book goes out the window. This recipe is fun because the beets play a sweet supporting role in the pasta salad. I love golden beets the most so, if they look the best, go for it. Otherwise, pick a classic red beet, sweet and earthy. **SERVES 6 TO 8**

PARSLEY PESTO

Kosher salt

2 cups loosely packed curly parsley leaves

½ teaspoon sugar

½ cup extra-virgin olive oil

1 cup thinly sliced scallions (green and white parts)

BEET VINAIGRETTE

8 small red beets (about 1¾ pounds total), peeled and quartered

Kosher salt

2 teaspoons capers, drained and coarsely chopped

2 tablespoons red wine vinegar

4 tablespoons extra-virgin olive oil, plus more if needed

PASTA

1 pound farfalle pasta

1 tablespoon unsalted butter

¾ cup shaved Parmesan

1. Make the parsley pesto: Bring a large pot of water to a rolling boil. Prepare an ice bath: Fill a large bowl halfway with ice cubes and add some cold water. Set a colander squarely inside the ice bath. The colander will keep you from having to pick ice out of the parsley later. Add salt to the boiling water until it tastes like seawater. Add the parsley and cook for 1 minute. Use a slotted spoon to transfer the parsley to the colander

recipe continues

inside the ice bath and allow to cool for 3 to 5 minutes. Drain the leaves slightly and then put them in a blender with the sugar and olive oil. Blend until smooth. If the mixture is too thick, add some water to facilitate blending. Taste for seasoning. Transfer to a bowl large enough to hold the pasta and stir in the scallions. Keep the pot of water for the pasta.

2. Make the beet vinaigrette: Put the beet pieces in a medium saucepan and add enough cold water to cover the beets about three-quarters of the way. Bring to a rolling boil over high heat. Allow the water to reduce almost completely. Add another cup of water and reduce again until there is about ½ cup liquid. In addition to vibrant color, you are looking to extract earthy and sweet flavors from the beets. Season with salt. Remove from the heat, strain, pushing some solid through the strainer. Combine the beet liquid with the capers, red wine vinegar, and olive oil. Stir to blend. Taste and add more oil or salt if needed. Discard the beet solids.

3. Cook the pasta: Return the pot of water to a rolling boil. Add the pasta to the pot and cook, stirring occasionally with a slotted spoon to make sure it doesn't clump or stick to the bottom as it cooks, until al dente, 8 to 10 minutes. Drain the pasta in a colander, reserving some of the cooking liquid.

4. Finish the dish: Pour the pasta into the bowl with the parsley pesto, add the beet vinaigrette and butter, and toss to blend. Add some of the reserved pasta water if the mixture seems dry. Top with the cheese and serve immediately.

shrimp and cucumber salad

I love this salad because it's so clean and healthy on the one hand but packs the punch of something more naughty when you eat it. Hothouse (or English) cucumbers are sold both waxed and unwaxed. The unwaxed ones usually come tightly wrapped in plastic. Go for those. Pick firm ones without any discoloration (such as inconsistent light colored streaks) or soft spots. These cucumbers also have very small seeds and they don't need to be scooped out. Keeping the center of the cucumber makes them a juicier choice than using regular cucumbers, where you have to scoop out the seeds. Yes, hothouse cucumbers are more expensive but they are worth it. For added punch, smear shrimp with chili-garlic paste (page 282) before broiling. **SERVES 8**

---

2 hothouse cucumbers: 1 peeled, 1 unpeeled
Kosher salt
6 tablespoons rice vinegar
1 (2-inch) knob fresh ginger, peeled
2 pounds (12- to 15-count) shrimp, peeled and deveined
1 tablespoon extra-virgin olive oil, plus more for the rack
1 lime, halved
1 medium avocado, preferably Hass, halved and pitted
Pinch of flaky sea salt, such as Maldon
4 sprigs fresh cilantro, finely chopped, stems and all

1. Preheat the oven to 375°F.

2. Marinate the cucumbers: Cut the cucumbers into ¼-inch-thick rounds. Consistent seasoning is important here, so arrange the cucumber slices in a single layer on a baking sheet. Season them lightly on both sides with kosher salt. Transfer to a bowl (large enough to hold the shrimp) and toss with 4 tablespoons of the vinegar and the ginger and refrigerate.

3. Cook the shrimp: On the same baking sheet, arrange the shrimp in a single layer and season both sides with a good sprinkle of kosher salt and the olive oil. Toss the shrimp in a bowl and put a rack over the baking sheet. Lightly oil the rack to prevent any sticking and arrange the shrimp (without crowding) in a single layer. Roast the shrimp until they feel fairly firm and are pink, 8 to 10 minutes.

4. Serve the salad: Remove the shrimp from the oven, squeeze lime juice over them, and immediately add them—along with any of their cooking juices—to the bowl with the cucumbers. Use a tablespoon to scoop out the avocado in bits. Season with the sea salt and the remaining 2 tablespoons rice vinegar. Put the cilantro in the bottom of 8 bowls. Top with the shrimp and avocado and stir to reveal the cilantro. Serve immediately.

winter greens salad from the oven

My favorite thing about this recipe is putting the salad into the oven and lightly wilting it just before serving. I got the idea from a salad we used to make at Guy Savoy's eponymous restaurant in Paris. We would spend half an hour arranging a plate of lamb's lettuce into a perfect pile of leaves and then transform it by covering the whole dome of salad with a tent of paper-thin black truffle slices. Just before sending it out to the guest, the salad would go under a low broiler for a few seconds to warm and wilt slightly. "Makes the truffle aroma and flavor more intense," Guy Savoy explained as I watched in wonder.

Years later, when conceiving the menu for my first cooking show, I had to share this idea in an American salad. I love the idea that the last step could intensify the flavors in such a simple way. The bourbon, the nuts blended into the dressing—these are American flavors done with a French flair. **SERVES 8**

APPLES

1 tablespoon bourbon, preferably Knob Creek

1 tablespoon extra-virgin olive oil

3 medium apples, such as Empire or Braeburn (1 to 1¼ pounds), cored and sliced ¼ inch thick

Kosher salt and cracked black pepper

DRESSING

2 tablespoons cider vinegar

2 teaspoons honey

Juice of 1 lemon

Kosher salt and cracked black pepper

¾ cup extra-virgin olive oil

¾ cup pecan halves, toasted and roughly chopped

GREENS

2 heads radicchio, cored, leaves torn into bite-size pieces

2 heads Belgian endive, cored, leaves separated

1 cup arugula leaves

1 cup torn escarole leaves

1. Preheat the oven to 300°F.

2. Marinate the apples: In a small bowl, combine the bourbon and olive oil. Toss the apple slices in the bowl and season with salt and pepper.

3. Make the dressing: In a food processor, combine the vinegar, honey, and lemon juice and season with salt and pepper. Pulse a couple of times to blend. Pulse in the olive oil. Transfer to a bowl, stir in the pecans, and season with salt and pepper.

4. Serve the salad: In a bowl, combine the radicchio, endive, arugula, and escarole and toss with the dressing to coat the greens. Transfer the salad to a large, wide ovenproof platter and put the platter in the oven with the door ajar until the greens wilt ever so slightly, 1 to 2 minutes. Rotate the platter halfway and leave for 1 minute. Pull the apple slices from the bourbon, leaving any excess bourbon behind in the bowl, and arrange on top of the salad. Serve immediately.

Bitter Greens

This salad belongs in its own category because the flavors are robust—the vinegar and bourbon, in particular. But the greens I chose also have a lot of texture and some bitterness. That bitterness is interesting to me against the richness of the pecans and the sweetness the honey offers in the dressing. You can vary the bitterness by swapping in other greens. I think the radicchio, endive, and arugula are great together but you can blend in another mellower green in place of the escarole, like Bibb lettuce, if you want to tamp down the bitter aspect. To me, this salad can also work as a side dish or served with roasted chicken.

meat
my favorite
all-american recipes

beef meatballs and sauce with rigatoni

double-decker cheeseburgers
with roasted mirepoix

roast beef with small potatoes, pan drippings
and Sichuan peppercorns

mom's meatloaf

seared hanger steak with
marinated broccoli and
balsamic-raspberry vinaigrette

braised short rib french onion soup

slow-cooked brisket, cider-glazed
parsnips, and celery

porterhouse with melted maître d'butter

roasted "bistro" leg of lamb with
crispy rosemary

pasta with spicy lamb sausage
and yellow tomato sauce

spice-rubbed rack of pork with
a side of harissa

bacon-wrapped pork chops with apple
and brussels sprouts

I feel like people are always talking about their mothers and grandmothers in the kitchen. What about that unsung culinary hero, Dad? Mine is, to this day, a smart shopper. He keeps his eye out for the good stuff and pounces when he finds it. When I was growing up, he would come home with a plastic bag and pull out anything from a few heads of broccoli from the supermarket to shrimp and black beans from Chinatown.

He is a real wizard at the stove. One night he would make spaghetti and meatballs and the next some steamed rice and pork dumplings. I learned from my father that a meaty main course doesn't have to be a classic meat, potatoes, and green vegetable affair. It can be a satisfying bowl of pasta with some meat, it can be dumplings, and it can be any cut of meat, large or small.

He's also a risk-taker. Once, he set up a portable grill on the fire escape outside our kitchen window in Manhattan and began grilling a large steak. Our upstairs neighbor panicked at the sight of the smoke and called the fire department. After a visit from several firemen (axes and all), my dad grudgingly reeled in his little grill. But that steak was delicious!

My dad always says: "If it's delicious, you won't hear a question or a complaint, just the sound of forks and slices of bread scraping plates." It's your money and your time, so spend it on what you want and make what you feel like cooking!

beef meatballs and sauce with rigatoni

This recipe is a complete throwback to my childhood. I can't tell you how much I enjoy a dish of dried pasta with these meatballs, sauce, and cheese. I think if you make your own meatballs, you get a pass on making pasta from scratch. The al dente rigatoni has got that wonderful texture against the tender meatballs.

One of my favorite things to do with the leftover meatballs and sauce is to pop the bowl in the fridge and wait for it to cool completely. Usually, in the middle of the night, I will wake up and unearth a meaty boulder from its nap in the sauce and dig in. What is it about eating standing with the fridge door open that makes food taste incredible? Maybe it's because we're being bad and eating when we aren't supposed to, but I think it's also the effect this delicious sauce has on me. **SERVES 4 TO 6**

SAUCE

3 tablespoons extra-virgin olive oil
2 medium yellow onions, halved and thinly sliced
5 garlic cloves, halved and thinly sliced
Kosher salt and white pepper
6 plum tomatoes (1 to 1¼ pounds), cored, halved, and diced
1 teaspoon sugar
1 teaspoon dried oregano
1 (28-ounce) can whole peeled tomatoes, broken into smaller pieces, with their liquid

MEATBALLS

1 pound ground beef, 85% lean, preferably sirloin
1 teaspoon kosher salt, or more if needed
½ cup plain dried bread crumbs, plus more if needed
½ cup freshly grated Parmesan
⅓ cup finely chopped curly parsley
⅛ teaspoon red pepper flakes, or more if needed
1 large egg, lightly beaten, plus an extra if needed

½ cup canola oil
Kosher salt
¾ pound dried rigatoni pasta
1½ to 2 cups grated Parmesan, to taste

recipe continues

1. Fill a large pot with water and bring it to a rolling boil.

2. Make the sauce: In a large wide, saute pan, heat the olive oil over medium heat. Add the onions and garlic and season with salt and pepper. Cook until the onions are tender, 10 to 15 minutes, and then add the plum tomatoes, sugar, and oregano. Stir to blend and then pour in the canned tomatoes and their juices. Cook, stirring from time to time, until it comes to a simmer, about 5 minutes, to allow the ingredients to meld together. Taste for seasoning. Lower the heat and let the sauce continue to cook as you make the meatballs. Season to taste with salt and pepper.

3. Make the meatballs: Put the beef in a large bowl and spread it all over the bottom of the bowl and up the sides a little. This will help you to distribute the seasoning evenly over the meat. Sprinkle the meat with the salt and add the bread crumbs, Parmesan, parsley, and red pepper flakes. Use your hands to mix all of the ingredients together. Work in 1 of the eggs with your hands. Roll 1 small ball (about 1½ to 2 inches in diameter).

4. Taste test: In a small skillet, heat 1 teaspoon of the canola oil over high heat. When the oil begins to smoke lightly, shut off the heat (to avoid splattering), and add the meatball. Put the heat back on high and brown on all sides for a few minutes until cooked but still pink in the middle. Taste for seasoning and texture. If too moist, add more bread crumbs. If too dry, add another beaten egg or a splash of water. Adjust the salt and red pepper flakes, if needed, as well. Roll the remaining meat into 1½-inch diameter meatballs; you should have about 20.

5. Cook the meatballs: Heat a large skillet over high heat and add the remaining canola oil. When the oil begins to smoke lightly, shut off the heat and add the meatballs in a single layer, spreading them apart somewhat so they have a chance to brown instead of steaming. Put the heat back on high and turn the meatballs to brown them on all sides. Cook to medium-rare, 3 to 5 minutes. Squeeze the sides of 2 meatballs between your thumb and index finger to make sure they are still tender in the center. Use a slotted spoon or spatula to remove them from the pan and transfer them to a tray lined with a kitchen towel to drain any excess grease.

6. Cook the pasta: Season the boiling water with salt until it tastes like seawater. Bring the water back up to a boil. Add the pasta to the pot and cook, stirring occasionally with a slotted spoon to make sure it doesn't clump or stick to the bottom as it cooks, until al dente, 8 to 10 minutes. Drain the pasta in a colander, reserving about 1 cup of the cooking liquid.

7. Serve the meatballs: Meanwhile, once you drop the pasta in the water, add the meatballs to the sauce and simmer over very low heat, 3 to 5 minutes. Shut off the heat and allow the sauce and meat to rest as your pasta finishes cooking. Pour off any excess grease in the skillet used to brown the meatballs, add a ladle of sauce, and warm the pan over low heat. Stir to catch any browned bits of meat in the skillet. After a few minutes, pour that sauce back in with the rest. Stir in a little of the reserved pasta cooking liquid if needed to thin. Transfer the sauce and meatballs to a large bowl and toss in half of the cooked pasta. Add about ¾ cup of the Parmesan cheese. Stir in the remaining pasta. Serve with the remaining cheese in a bowl on the side.

Old-school tip

Why did our grandmothers stew the sauce and meatballs on the stove all afternoon? It does enrich the sauce when the meat stews in it all afternoon but the meatballs are always way more cooked than need be. I like to cook my meatballs the way I eat my hamburgers, medium-rare to medium. Also, why put the pasta in a bowl and then ladle the sauce over the top? Stirring the sauce and pasta together first allows the pasta to absorb the flavors of the sauce. So, if you can resist temptation, let the pasta sit in the sauce, heat off, for a few minutes before digging in.

double-decker cheeseburgers with roasted mirepoix

The condiment I like most on my burger was introduced to me by one of my friends and colleagues, Ian Halbwachs. He spread out a classic mirepoix (chopped carrot, celery, and onion) on a baking sheet and roasted it until it resembled the vegetables at the bottom of a roasting pan with a large cut of meat. They were almost candied. To me, they give a burger a slight roast beef quality. I also stir some chopped pickle into the mirepoix for acidity.

It's unfortunate that American cheese gets no respect in the cheese world. I lived in France for years and have had the privilege of eating many an incredible morsel of cheese. I just don't think of American cheese as cheese: I think of it as the perfectly melty addition to make a hamburger be all that it can be. I've served burgers with aged cheddar from all corners of the world, crumbled the finest blue cheese on top of others, and served melted Swiss and caramelized onions with bacon poured over burgers. All of those are sublime and have their time and place. But when I want to dig into an old-school classic, this is how I serve my burgers. **SERVES 4**

VEGETABLES

1 small carrot, chopped into ½-inch pieces
1 small red onion, chopped into ½-inch pieces
1 small celery stalk, chopped into ½-inch pieces
2 tablespoons canola oil
Kosher salt and black pepper
1 large "half-cooked" pickle or ⅓ cup dill pickle chips, chopped into ¼-inch pieces

SPICY MAYONNAISE

¼ cup mayonnaise
1 tablespoon Sriracha hot sauce, or to taste
Splash of pickle juice

BURGERS

1½ pounds ground beef chuck, 80% lean
Kosher salt and black pepper
¼ cup mayonnaise
4 tablespoons canola oil
4 seeded hamburger buns (I'm partial to potato rolls, split
8 slices American cheese

1. Preheat the oven to 375°F.

2. Roast the vegetables: In a food processor, combine the carrot, onion, and celery. Pulse 15 to 20 times, stopping to scrape down the sides, until the vegetables are in small pieces. Stir in the oil and season with salt and pepper. Spread the vegetables on a baking sheet and roast until caramelized and tender, 30 to 35 minutes. Note: If the vegetables start to get dark, lower the oven to 325°F to finish cooking. Transfer the vegetables to a bowl and set aside to cool. Stir the chopped pickle into the vegetables. (Leave the oven on.)

3. Make the spicy mayonnaise: Meanwhile, in a small bowl, whisk together the mayonnaise, Sriracha, and pickle juice. Add the Sriracha gradually to get your desired heat level.

4. Make the burger mix: In a medium bowl, spread the beef all over the bottom of the bowl and up the sides a little. This will help you to distribute the seasoning evenly over the meat. Season liberally with salt and pepper. Stir in the mayonnaise. Divide the meat into 8 parts (about 3 ounces each) and roll each into a ball. Use the palm of your hand to gently flatten each ball into a small patty that's 2½ to 3 inches across and between ¼ and ½ inch thick.

5. Cook the burgers: Once the vegetables are cool, heat 2 large skillets over high heat and add the oil (or work in batches if you have only 1 pan). When the oil begins to smoke lightly, remove the skillets from the heat and add the burgers in a single layer (without crowding). Make an indent in the center of each burger. The burgers will puff in the middle as they cook and the indent will help keep the thickness even. Return the pans to high heat. Cook, undisturbed, for about 1 minute. Use a metal spatula to flip them over and then put a slice of cheese on top of each burger to allow it to melt as the burgers finish cooking. Cook for an additional 1 to 2 minutes for rare to medium-rare.

6. Assemble the burgers: Put the bun halves cut sides up on a baking sheet and toast in the oven until light brown, 2 to 3 minutes. Remove from the oven and add a dollop of spicy mayonnaise to each bottom, but don't spread it around. Put a burger on top of the mayo. Spoon a hearty spoonful of the vegetables and a little more mayo on top of each burger. Top with a second burger and a hearty tablespoonful of the vegetables. Top with the other half of the bun. Serve immediately.

old-school tip

Use the method for testing meatballs on page 96 to test your burger mix for seasoning, too.

roast beef with small potatoes, pan drippings, and sichuan peppercorns

There's a time for a fancy cut of meat like filet mignon, rib-eye, or strip steak. I imagine drawing a horizontal line across the middle of a cow. I call it the Mason-Dixon Line. Above the Mason-Dixon are all those fancy, expensive cuts that take a relatively short time to grill, sear, or roast. Below the line are all the cuts—short ribs, shanks, and brisket—that require slow, low-temp cooking. But what about top round, a.k.a. roast beef? Where does that live? It's kind of in no-man's-land with the tail and the shanks. It has minimal intramuscular fat (marbling) so it can cook more quickly than you think. It's definitely special, its unique flavor harnessing both the deep, beefy richness of a stew and the wonderful brown candy flavor of a seared strip steak. I love it on sandwiches or sliced and served really hot with some mashed potatoes. **SERVES 10 TO 12**

---

1 large (8- to 10-pound) beef top round roast
1 tablespoon Sichuan peppercorns, lightly crushed
Kosher salt
4 pounds small potatoes, preferably new potatoes or fingerlings
1 tablespoon Dijon mustard
½ cup dry Marsala
2 cups low-sodium beef broth
Juice of ½ lemon

MY DEAR FRIEND AND MEAT GURU, PAT LAFRIEDA

1. Preheat the oven to 500°F.

2. Prepare the roast beef: Season the roast on all sides with salt and the Sichuan peppercorns. Put it on a roasting rack. Put the potatoes in the bottom of a roasting pan and season them with salt. Put the rack in the pan directly over the potatoes.

3. Cook the beef: Roast, undisturbed, for 10 minutes. Lower the temperature of the oven to 350°F. Roast for about 10 minutes per pound (1 hour 20 minutes to 1 hour 40 minutes) and then begin testing the internal temperature. The

recipe continues

thermometer should read about 130°F for medium-rare. Remember that carryover cooking (which happens while the roast rests after it comes out of the oven) will mean the temperature will increase a few degrees to a true medium-rare after the roast is removed from the oven. If it's undercooked, you can always cook it more, but if overcooked, there is no fixing it! Transfer the roast beef to a cutting board and the potatoes to a serving platter; at this point, the temperature should be about 130°F for medium rare. Bear in mind, roast beef ends can be 140°F while the middle is 120° to 125°F, so there will always be varying degrees of doneness. Keep both warm while you make the sauce.

4. Make the sauce: If there is an excess of grease in the roasting pan, pour or spoon it off and reserve it separately without losing too much of those precious bits or juices from the bottom. Add the mustard, Marsala, and stock to the juices in the roasting pan. Bring the liquid to a boil, lower the heat, and simmer to reduce the liquid, scraping any bits of meat from the bottom, until the liquid cooks down and forms a loose sauce, 3 to 5 minutes. Taste for seasoning. Add the lemon juice. Finish by stirring in some of the excess reserved grease, to taste.

5. Serve the roast: Carve the roast in the kitchen or at the table and serve with the potatoes and sauce.

staff meal

This chapter is about real family eating. There is also family eating at any restaurant. Ah, the romance of "staff meal" (cleverly dubbed "family" meal), which has been trumped up in cookbooks. I have seen many a glossy photo of the happy chefs and owners in crisp blue linen shirts on the terraces of Michelin-starred restaurants. They are invariably holding glasses of wine and smiling fondly at the staff around them as everyone tucks into platters of grilled fish and vegetables or salads of fresh fruit. Pitchers of water and silverware litter the table.

My experience? You work in a restaurant and you're starving.

My two solutions to this problem at Restaurant Guy Savoy:

Strategy #1: I kept a quart of heavy cream stashed in the walk-in behind the lemons. I would take a swig of it whenever needed.

Strategy #2: The cheese fridge. There were a lot of scraps from the cheese board that weren't pretty enough for the customers. Edges of the most beautiful wheels of Camembert, Beaufort from the Savoie that screamed of hazelnuts and barnyard, a Reblochon that I imagined melted over potatoes, bacon, and onions. These cheeses, with a baguette I'd pick up for a few francs around the corner, and I was set.

And you know what?

I kind of enjoyed being hungry and not really having enough to eat; it somehow both fueled and matched the drive I felt to learn how to cook. Like coal in a furnace.

Worst staff meal I ever had? Easy: some undercooked and unseasoned couscous and the "raft" from a consommé. Yes, that mass of egg whites (and some shell bits) and ground meat that pools and forms at the top of a boiling broth. The raft is like the Coast Guard, sitting atop the broth, catching all impurities and imparting flavor. It wasn't pretty. But it was good for the restaurant's bottom line.

Best staff meal? I have a Colombian gentleman, Alvaro Buchelly, who has been cooking with me for more than ten years. The day I confirmed I was pregnant with my daughter, I strolled in the back door of Butter and practically fell into a bowl of his spicy chicken and orzo soup laced with cilantro and sliced poblanos. We stood right by the stove, eating this soup, listening to the background music of stocks bubbling and chickens roasting. It was magical.

Ask any cook how many bowls of overboiled (and yet somewhat lovingly made) pasta with greasy ground beef and not enough tomato they have had in their lives. But the camaraderie they enjoyed while eating it is priceless.

mom's meatloaf

On the corner of my block was this old Irish bar, Mulligan's. Sometimes I would see the cooks there slicing big thick wedges of meatloaf and it made me want to grab two oversize slices of crusty bread and make a sandwich. My mother's tiny meatloaf paled in comparison the first time I saw her pull it from the oven. It didn't have that oversize look, but I smiled politely as she cut me a small slice. Then I took a bite. Ketchup? Yes. Tarragon and sour cream? Strokes of genius. My meatloaf allegiance was forever changed. If you have time, grind your own beef, using brisket and chuck, and your own pork, using a shoulder cut. I will admit that I get a meatloaf that is slightly lighter and the meat is easier to work with. **SERVES 6 TO 8**

---

2 teaspoons canola oil, plus more if needed
2 small yellow onions, minced (about 1 cup)
2 garlic cloves, minced
Kosher salt
1 pound ground beef (preferably 8 ounces ground sirloin and 8 ounces ground chuck)
¾ pound ground pork (preferably shoulder)
1 teaspoon hot paprika
1 teaspoon black pepper
1 cup plus 2 tablespoons plain dried bread crumbs, plus more if needed
⅔ cup ketchup, plus more for brushing, preferably Heinz
1 cup sour cream
1 medium bunch curly parsley, leaves chopped (¼ cup)
1 medium bunch fresh tarragon, leaves chopped (2 tablespoons)
3 large eggs, lightly beaten, plus another as needed

1. Preheat the oven to 400°F. Line a baking sheet with parchment paper.

2. Make the meatloaf mix: In a medium skillet, heat the canola oil over medium heat. Add the onions and garlic, season with salt, and cook, stirring from time to time, until translucent, 3 to 5 minutes. Scrape into a bowl and set aside to cool. Reserve the pan; do not wipe it out.

3. Put the beef and pork in a large bowl and gently knead them together with your hands. Spread the meat out on the bottom and the sides of the bowl and season with 2 teaspoons salt. Add the paprika, the pepper, bread crumbs, ketchup, sour cream, parsley, tarragon, the onion mixture, and 3 of the eggs. Mix to blend.

4. Taste test: Heat the skillet over medium heat; if there isn't a sufficient layer of fat left in the pan, add a little more oil. When the pan is hot, lower the heat and add a small piece of the meatloaf mixture. Cook until cooked through, 1 to 2 minutes per side. Remove from the pan and taste. If too moist, add more bread crumbs. If too dry, add another egg.

5. Cook the meatloaf: Mold the meat mixture into the shape of a rectanguler loaf pan, roughly 9 × 5 inches, and place it on the parchment-lined baking sheet. The meat will feel slightly wet. It should form into a ball but still stick to your hands slightly. Bake for 15 minutes.

6. Brush the meatloaf with additional ketchup and lower the oven temperature to 350°F. Bake until the meat is firm when touched or when it has an internal temperature of 150°F, 30 to 35 minutes more. Remove from the oven, pour off any excess grease, and allow the meatloaf to rest for 10 to 15 minutes before slicing and serving. Brush again with ketchup, if desired.

Old-school tip

Ever bite into meatloaf and end up with a piece of undercooked onion or a chunk of raw garlic? I find adding them raw to meatloaf sometimes results in steamed (read: tasteless) or even crunchy bits of vegetable. By cooking them on their own first, the garlic and the onion meld more into the meat.

seared hanger steak with marinated broccoli and balsamic-raspberry vinaigrette

Broccoli has been eclipsed lately by its foxier counterpart, broccoli rabe. But they are totally different vegetables! Broccoli rabe is bitter and has a rougher texture. I really like it profoundly overcooked, charred on the edges, with an obscene amount of garlic. Broccoli needs different treatment and I have to say no one makes it better than my dad. He always makes it "al dente" with a super tasty, super vinegary dressing.

One of the secrets to making broccoli become something even better is by using some of the stem and not just the floret. The stems absorb flavors so well and remind me of sweet cabbage. The combination of tangy balsamic with floral raspberry vinegar makes the broccoli in this recipe take on an almost nutty quality. It's also that this recipe leaves the broccoli chilled and refreshing while the seared steak and pan drippings are hot from the pan; the temperature contrast adds more to the experience of eating it. I serve them side by side on platters so the chilled platter doesn't cool down the steak. I am a firm believer in getting a good sear on steak but also in turning the meat a few times to move the blood back and forth from one side of the steak to another. I like to call it "internal basting." **SERVES 4**

---

2 medium heads broccoli, with stems (about 1¼ pounds total)
Kosher salt
½ cup Balsamic-Raspberry Vinaigrette (page 283)
2 tablespoons canola oil
2 pounds hanger steak, trimmed of any sinew
Black pepper

1. Marinate the broccoli: Cut the broccoli lengthwise into smaller pieces. The goal is to create "stalks" of broccoli with the florets on top, kind of like oversize asparagus spears. In a large pot, bring 4 quarts water to a boil. Stir in a handful of salt. You want the water to taste like seawater. When it comes back to a boil, plunge the broccoli into the water and cook for 2 to 3 minutes, stirring from time to time. Drain the broccoli on a kitchen towel. Arrange the spears on a platter and drizzle them liberally with the balsamic vinaigrette. Refrigerate the platter.

2. Cook the steak: Heat a large cast-iron skillet over high heat. Add the oil. Season the steak on all sides with salt and pepper. When the pan begins to smoke lightly, use a pair of metal tongs to gingerly place the steak in the hot oil. Cook to medium-rare, 5 to 6 minutes on each side. The total cooking time will be 10 to 12 minutes for medium rare (or an internal temperature of 130°F. Remove the steak and allow it to rest on a cutting board for 10 minutes.

3. Serve the steak: Slice the steak against the natural grain (or lines) in the meat. This will make the meat more tender for chewing. Taste for seasoning. Arrange it on its own platter. Serve the broccoli straight from the refrigerator, tossing it to recoat with the dressing.

braised short rib french onion soup

Short ribs. What a trusty cut of meat: marbled, tender once cooked, and flavorful, so flavorful! This is one of those cuts below the Mason-Dixon Line (see page 101) that work overtime to hold the cow upright. I often liken them to my friends. Some people I have met made the worst first (and even second) impression—all gruff exterior. It didn't seem like we would ever be friends. The short ribs, when you first get them, will feel somewhat tough and unyielding in your hand. Don't be deceived. As you brown them and let them bubble gently in the oven, you will watch a metamorphosis take place. Some of those people, with another look, wound up becoming some of my closest friends—utter softies. Like them, this meat is totally worth the wait!

As a general rule, I rarely cook with broth or stock. I am a big fan of using water and allowing the natural flavors—whether meat, fish, or vegetable—to come through. I never understood, for example, why pumpkin soup should be made with chicken stock. I say, cook with water and add more pumpkin to get an intense version of the flavor you set out to create! This rule, however, goes out the window in this recipe. You want to make beef taste beefier than ever and for that you need to end up with flavorful meat and a good beef broth. **SERVES 8**

About 5 pounds "flanken cut" beef short ribs, cut through the bone into 2½- to 3-inch-thick pieces
Kosher salt and black pepper
⅓ cup canola oil
3 medium yellow onions (1¾ pounds total), halved and sliced ½ inch thick
10 garlic cloves, roughly chopped
1 tablespoon packed dark brown sugar
3 cups dry red wine
2 quarts low-sodium beef broth
3 bay leaves
2 tablespoons Dijon mustard
1 tablespoon whole-grain mustard
1 bunch scallions (light green and white parts), sliced into ½-inch rounds
½ cup dry Marsala
8 (¾-inch-thick) slices sourdough bread
12 ounces Gruyère, grated (about 5 cups)

1. Season the short ribs: I don't trim the short ribs; they have glorious marbling that acts like an internal baster, providing moisture and oozing collagen (a great natural thickener) to leave you with a rich, flavorful cooking liquid. Season the ribs generously on all sides with salt and pepper and allow them to sit at room temperature for at least 30 minutes before cooking to allow the seasonings to penetrate. The short ribs will also come closer to a temperature that makes the stovetop browning less of a shock compared to the cold world of your fridge where they were napping quietly just moments before.

2. Preheat the oven to 350°F.

3. Brown the short ribs: Set a large cast-iron skillet over high heat and add the canola oil. When it begins to smoke, add the short ribs in a single layer, leaving room between them, and brown on both sides, 2 to 3 minutes per side. To avoid overcrowding, the short ribs can be cooked in two pans instead of one. Transfer the short ribs in a single layer to a Dutch oven off the heat and set aside. Pour off and discard all but 1 tablespoon of excess grease from the skillet.

4. Cook the onions: Add the onions and garlic to the skillet, season with salt, and cook over medium heat to brown the onions (be careful not to burn them), 5 to 8 minutes. Sprinkle with the brown sugar and stir until melted. Scrape into a saucepan and set aside.

5. Braise the short ribs: Off the heat, pour the wine into the same skillet. Place over low heat and simmer until there is a scant ½ cup liquid left. Pour the reduced wine into the Dutch oven over the ribs and add the broth and bay leaves. Bring the liquid to a simmer and then transfer to the oven. Cook for 1 hour.

6. Finish the soup: Stir the two kinds of mustard into the saucepan of onions and simmer the mixture for a few minutes over medium-low heat.

7. Braise the short ribs, uncovered, until tender, 2½ to 3 hours. Check periodically to make sure the broth isn't boiling; it should never rise above a gentle simmer. If it does, lower oven to 325°F. Remove from the oven. (Leave the oven on for toasting the bread.)

8. Meanwhile, use a pair of tongs and a slotted spoon to gently remove the meat from the broth. Use a ladle to skim the grease from the surface of the broth. Simmer the broth on the stove over medium heat until there is only 3 to 4 cups of liquid remaining, 15 to 20 minutes. Stir in the scallions and Marsala. Put the short ribs on a flat surface and slice them against the grain. Season again with salt. I like to keep some of the bones for that rustic bone sucking that I love, but you can opt to leave them out, if desired. Taste for seasoning. Return the meat to the onion mixture.

recipe continues

9. Arrange the bread slices on a baking sheet and toast on both sides in the oven until dry and crisp, 8 to 10 minutes total.

10. Preheat the broiler.

11. Serve the soup: Put some of the Gruyère in the bottom of ovenproof bowls and ladle in a little of the broth, onions, and meat. Top each with 1 slice of the bread and ½ cup cheese. (Yes, ½ cup.) Put the bowls on a rimmed baking sheet (to catch any dripped cheese) and slide under the broiler until the cheese is bubbling and melted. Top with black pepper and a touch of salt. Serve immediately.

Old-school tip

It doesn't matter what you put in this dish (or any meat dish for that matter) if you aren't going to take the courageous plunge and season the meat the way it should be. Meat needs more salt than you can imagine. I count a heaping teaspoon of kosher salt (Diamond Crystal brand) per pound of meat. That means, for this recipe, you should be using close to 2 tablespoons salt to coat all sides of the meat before cooking. Finish by cracking black pepper on all sides as well. Beef and black pepper make the world spin.

Basics

Beef Stock
30-40l without cover

4 queue de boeuf, entier (oxtails) } raw
3 pied de veau (veal's feet)

fill 1/3 of the way (more to cover the meat) with hot/water and keep it on the lowest setting for heat intensity. Bring to a boil (~1 ½ hrs! it took), skim of all foamy residue and then fill the basin completely with hot water. Add about - 1 tbsp. tomato concentrate
- 8-10 burned onions (16 halves). The onions are burned by laying tinfoil on the flat top, laying the onion halves down and cooking them into blackness.
- 2 well-bound bouquet garni. leek whites w/ thyme and bay leafs
- parsley stems
- 1/3 bac of cooked red wine

Let cook uncovered a while, then skim again, put on cover and let cook undisturbed

slow-cooked brisket, cider-glazed parsnips, and celery

There are two distinct parts of brisket: the first and second cuts. The first is very lean while the second is loaded with fat marbling. This makes cooking a whole brisket something of a felony, since the two parts need wildly different cooking methods to fulfill their delicious destinies. Better to have just the fatty, flavorful second cut, in my opinion—even in several pieces—than one big ol' brisket. So when you buy it, ask your butcher if it's possible to get all second cuts. If faced with only a whole brisket, have your butcher at least separate the first and second cuts. You will immediately see how much less fat marbling is in the first cut of meat. You will want to cook the two pieces separately, allowing for a longer cooking time on the second cut.

As far as companions for this meat go, I like to cook brisket with some of the humblest vegetables: earthy yet underrated parsnips and celery hearts, which almost act like an herb would in this recipe, with hints of anise and a pleasant bittersweet quality like arugula or radicchio. **SERVES 6 TO 8**

---

3 tablespoons canola oil
1 (3½- to 4-pound) brisket, preferably second cut, untrimmed
Kosher salt and cracked black pepper
2 teaspoons cumin seeds
2 teaspoons coriander seeds, lightly crushed
3 pounds small parsnips, peeled and halved lengthwise
1 cup apple cider
¼ cup blackstrap molasses
¼ cup cider vinegar
2 cups low-sodium beef broth, plus more, if needed
3 to 4 inner yellow stalks and leaves from the center of 1 head celery, sliced in ¼-inch half moons

1. Preheat the oven to 350°F.

2. Brown the brisket: In a Dutch oven or large ovenproof pot, heat 2 tablespoons of the canola oil over high heat. Season both sides of the brisket pieces with salt,

recipe continues

pepper, and the cumin and coriander seeds. When the oil begins to smoke lightly, use metal tongs to add the meat to the pot. If the brisket you have cannot fit in the pot in a single layer, brown it in batches. Cook, undisturbed, until browned on one side, 5 to 8 minutes. Turn onto the other side and brown for 5 to 8 additional minutes. Remove the meat from the pot and put it on a rimmed baking sheet to rest.

3. Cook the parsnips: In the same pot, over low heat, add the parsnips and sprinkle generously with salt. Cook until browned, 3 to 5 minutes. Stir in the cider, molasses, and vinegar and simmer until the liquids reduce and start to coat the parsnips, an additional 5 to 10 minutes. Simmer over very low heat. Pour the parsnips and the cooking liquid into a bowl. If the cooking liquid is watery, reduce for a few additional minutes and pour it back over the reserved parsnips.

4. Braise the brisket: Return the brisket to the pot and pour in the beef broth. Bring to a gentle simmer over medium heat. Transfer to the oven, cover, and braise, for 2 hours. Add the parsnips and their liquid and continue to braise uncovered until the meat is tender when pierced with a fork, an additional 45 minutes to 1 hour. If the meat looks dry or begins to get overly browned as it cooks, add additional beef stock and cover the pot with a lid or a layer of foil.

5. Finish the dish: Remove the pot from the oven and allow the meat to rest for 10 to 15 minutes. Transfer the meat and parsnips to a serving platter. It should be fork-tender without being dry. If the cooking liquid is too thin, simmer it on the stove over medium heat. Taste for seasoning. Pour the sauce over the meat and sprinkle with the celery. Serve immediately.

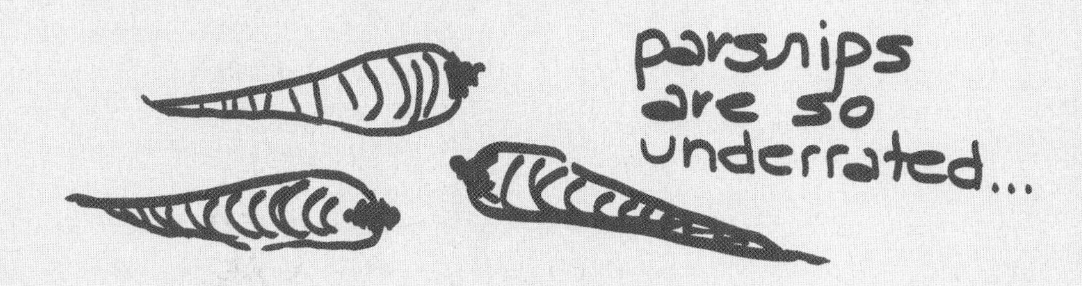

porterhouse with melted maître d' butter

This steak is a splurge and an indulgence. When I hit the supermarket or butcher's shop, I take a purchase like this seriously. My goal is always to honor the meat by keeping the preparation as simple as possible. A flavorful butter—in this case the classic French maître d'hôtel butter, which is studded with shallots, parsley, and lemon zest—is my favorite companion. Please note that because the "strip" side cooks longer than the "filet" side, this steak will vary in doneness. **SERVES 2 TO 4**

---

5 tablespoons unsalted butter, at room temperature
2 to 3 medium shallots, minced (about ½ cup)
Kosher salt
1 teaspoon green peppercorns, chopped
1 teaspoon Dijon mustard
Pinch of grated lemon zest
½ teaspoon fresh lemon juice
1 tablespoon Worcestershire sauce
Coarse sea salt, such as fleur de sel
1 tablespoon chopped flat-leaf parsley leaves
1 porterhouse steak, about 2½ pounds and 2½ inches thick
Black pepper

1. Make the butter: In a medium skillet, heat 1 tablespoon of the butter over medium heat. Add the shallots, season with kosher salt, and cook until translucent but not browned, 3 to 5 minutes. Transfer the shallots to a medium bowl. Whisk in the green peppercorns, mustard, lemon zest, lemon juice, and Worcestershire sauce. Use a fork to blend in the remaining 4 tablespoons butter. Season with sea salt to taste and stir in the parsley. Roll the butter into a 1-inch cylinder (like cookie dough) in plastic wrap or parchment paper and refrigerate until ready to use.

2. Preheat the broiler.

3. Cook the steak: Heat a cast-iron skillet over high heat until it begins to visibly smoke. Use a kitchen towel to blot any excess moisture from both sides of the steak and season both sides liberally with kosher salt and pepper. Shut the heat off underneath the skillet and then use a pair of tongs to add the steak to the pan. Return the heat to high and brown the steak on the first side for 3 to 5 minutes. Resist the temptation to move it as it cooks. Lower the heat to medium and cook for an additional 8 to 10 minutes. Flip the steak, raise the heat to high, and brown for 3 to 5 minutes. Lower the heat to medium-low and cook for an additional 8 to 10 minutes, flipping it again every few minutes. Turn the steak on the edge with the fat cap, holding it with tongs, and brown that over medium-high heat for 3 to 5 minutes. Lower the heat and allow the steak to cook for an additional 3 to 5 minutes on each side.

4. Test for doneness: The simplest way to check for doneness is to make a small incision by the center bone in the thickest part of the steak. It should be a little less cooked than you would like, which allows for carryover cooking and the finishing touch of running the steak under the broiler. For rare, a 2½-inch porterhouse steak will take 30 to 35 minutes to cook total and look rosy inside. Add about 4 minutes for medium-rare with a rosy red center and another 4 for medium. If using a meat thermometer, take your steak out of the pan between 125° and 130°F for rare, 130° and 135°F for medium-rare, and 135° and 140°F for medium. The smaller filet piece will cook faster so test that piece for doneness. Better to slightly undercook than overcook (and ruin!) this piece of meat. Remove the steak from the pan and set aside to rest for 10 minutes.

5. Finish the steak: Slice the maître d' butter into thin (⅛-inch) rounds. Slice both the tenderloin and strip sides of the steak and transfer to a heatproof platter with the meat still tightly arranged around each side of the center bone. Top the steak with a single layer of the butter slices and put under the broiler until the butter softens, 30 to 45 seconds. If the butter doesn't melt into the meat, spread it a little with a knife to speed the process and avoid overcooking the meat. Serve immediately.

roasted "bistro" leg of lamb with crispy rosemary

There are a few things I have always done a certain way because I was told it was the best way and I never asked questions. I fell in love with this cut of meat watching one spit-roast for hours in a French bistro. This is a recipe where I had to wade through a few clichés and some mechanical thinking to get to a good place:

- First up: bone in or out? I vote in. The bone adds flavor and moisture and acts like an internal heating rod as the meat cooks. Plus, it also provides something sturdy to hold on to as you carve the meat. It also gives the meat a French bistro feel.
- Number one flavor cliché on my list? Lamb and rosemary together: really worth it? Hell yes. The two are like cornflakes and milk or peanut butter and jelly. What I object to, though, is the classic way we combine these two ingredients. Poor rosemary does not benefit from being cooked for hours; you want that aromatic rosemary we all love without the cough syrupy, stemmy flavor that comes from stewing it to death.
- What about "studding" the meat with garlic cloves? I love this idea. Garlic belongs here as much as rosemary. But going to all the trouble of studding the leg isn't worth it, in my opinion. Instead, you can grate a few large cloves of garlic, spread over the meat just as it comes out of the oven, and baste the garlic with the hot pan drippings. That will remove the raw taste of the garlic while still leaving you with its fresh flavor.
- Salt the meat ahead or just before you cook it? I am going to say do it in advance. I do firmly believe that you get the best results if you remove the lamb from the fridge and let it come up to room temperature before cooking it—especially with a fairly large cut like a leg. So why not salt it at that point, too? That will give the salt a chance to permeate the meat.

OK, I think we're ready now. One final note before you dig in: Only carve what you think you will eat. Cutting the meat off the bone only as you need it will keep it from drying out. Try a salsa or herb pesto with leftover lamb slices. This also makes great sandwiches, whether warm on a toasted roll with the drippings or cold with mayonnaise and slices of fresh chile. **SERVES 6 TO 8**

---

2 tablespoons kosher salt
2 tablespoons cracked black pepper
1 tablespoon packed dark brown sugar
1 tablespoon ground cumin
1 tablespoon smoked paprika
1 (6- to 7-pound) bone-in leg of lamb, trimmed of any excess fat on the edges
2 tablespoons extra-virgin olive oil
8 garlic cloves, minced
2 tablespoons Dijon mustard
½ cup dry white wine
2 tablespoons canola oil
6 to 8 sprigs rosemary

1. Season the lamb: In a small bowl, mix together the salt, pepper, brown sugar, cumin, and paprika to create a dry rub. Rub the exterior of the lamb leg with the olive oil, and then coat the leg in the seasonings. Let sit at room temperature for 1 hour.

2. Preheat the oven to 350°F. Get out a shallow roasting pan or rimmed baking sheet that can hold the leg of lamb without too much excess space. Fit either type of pan with a roasting rack to elevate the meat and therefore allow hot air to circulate around the meat as it cooks.

3. Cook the lamb: Put the lamb leg on the rack on the roasting pan and put it in the oven. Cook, undisturbed, for 45 minutes. If the drippings start to burn add ½ cup of water to the bottom of the pan.

4. Use a thermometer and take the temperature of the thickest part of the leg meat. It should register 90° to 100°F. Lower the oven temperature to 325°F and continue to roast the lamb for an additional 30 to 45 minutes. Ideally, the temperature of the thickest part should now be at about 118°F, which, after resting, will be medium-rare. Transfer to a cutting board to rest for 15 to 20 minutes.

5. Use a large spoon to scoop up and discard any fat from the top of the pan drippings but keep the actual cooking juices in the pan. Put the pan on a burner over low heat. Stir in the garlic, mustard, and wine and bring to a simmer. Cook until the wine tastes cooked and integrated with the mustard, 3 to 5 minutes.Taste for seasoning. Spoon some of this sauce over the lamb as it rests.

recipe continues

6. Fry the rosemary: Heat a medium skillet over medium heat and add the canola oil. When the oil begins to smoke lightly, shut off the heat, step back (because the oil will splatter when you add the herbs), and toss the rosemary into the oil. When the sputtering dies down, allow the rosemary to fry in the oil for another 5 to 10 seconds or so. Use a slotted spoon to extract the sprigs and put them on a kitchen towel to drain. Season immediately with salt.

7. Carve the meat: Observe that the meat has lines almost like the grain of a piece of wood. Starting at the loin (skinnier) end of the leg, aim the blade of your knife at a right angle to the grain and slice thin pieces. The slices will not all be the same size, some big and some small, but if they are all relatively the same thickness, you will get that consistent mouthfeel. Because this cut can be tough, even when properly cooked, I find thinner slices allow you to enjoy the flavor without being interrupted by toughness. Arrange the slices on a platter, garnish with the rosemary, and spoon any remaining pan sauce on top.

Leg of Lamb

When buying a leg of lamb, you may find you can get it with the shank (lower leg) attached or removed. Whenever possible, buy it with the shank attached. In France, that calf muscle on the shank, known as the souris *(mouse), is the prized piece to nab. Juicy and tender, it's like the "oyster" on the underside of a chicken or that little crispy, cheesy edge of macaroni and cheese. In plain terms, if you are roasting and carving this leg of lamb, the souris is yours for the nibbling as you carve and present the rest of the leg to friends or family. You've earned the best piece of the meat for yourself in exchange for the labor of love that went into cooking.*

pasta with spicy lamb sausage and yellow tomato sauce

How does a tomato sauce actually come along and change everything? I had used the same basic tomato sauce recipe that I learned from my parents for as long as I can remember. And then I wanted something a bit different—a way to do justice to fresh tomato sauce. The answer turned out to be simple enough: This is more of a vinaigrette than a sauce. The thick texture comes from blending the oil and flesh of the fresh tomatoes. This is one of the few recipes that I cook both at the restaurant and at home. It has this bizarre addictive quality! I have been making this dish for years and I would still happily walk into the back door of the kitchen at Butter and eat an enormous bowl of it. Probably the thing I like most is how much this sauce departs radically from the sauce I ate growing up, and that my parents can appreciate the change. In fact, my mom tackled this recipe a few weeks ago and my dad only gave me one sidelong glance as we ate. Pretty good! **SERVES 4 TO 6**

SAUCE

Kosher salt
5 large yellow beefsteak tomatoes (about 3 pounds total)
¾ cup extra-virgin olive oil
10 garlic cloves, thinly sliced
3 large shallots (about 5 ounces), thinly sliced
¼ teaspoon red pepper flakes
1 tablespoon dried oregano
1 teaspoon sugar
2 to 3 tablespoons rice vinegar, to taste

PASTA

1 pound dried pasta, such as penne or cavatappi
1 tablespoon extra-virgin olive oil
1 tablespoon canola oil
1 pound spicy lamb sausage, such as merguez, casings removed
Grated Parmesan

1. **Make the sauce:** Bring a large pot of water to a boil and salt the water generously. Core the tomatoes and, with the knife, make a small "x" in the bottom of each. Use a slotted spoon to plunge

recipe continues

the tomatoes into the boiling water until the skins show evidence of peeling away (slightly) from the flesh of the tomatoes, 1 to 2 minutes. Use a slotted spoon to remove them from the water and drain them on a kitchen towel.

2. In a medium skillet, heat 2 tablespoons of the olive oil over low heat and add the garlic, shallots, and red pepper flakes. Season with salt. Stir in the oregano and sugar. Cook until the shallots and garlic are tender and translucent, about 5 minutes. Add a splash of water, if needed, to prevent browning.

3. Meanwhile, once the tomatoes are cool enough to handle, peel off and discard the skin and then quarter each tomato. Add the tomatoes to the skillet and stir in about 1 tablespoon salt. Turn the heat to medium and cook until the tomato quarters start to lose their shape, 8 to 10 minutes. Add ½ cup water and simmer, smushing the tomatoes with the back of a spoon to break them up, until the tomato sauce is soft and blender-ready, 15 to 20 minutes. Taste for seasoning.

4. Cook the pasta: In a large pot, bring 6 quarts water to a rolling boil. Season the water with salt until it tastes like seawater. Bring the water back up to a boil. Add the pasta to the pot and cook, stirring occasionally to make sure it doesn't clump or stick to the bottom as it cooks, until al dente, 8 to 10 minutes. Drain the pasta in a colander, reserving some of the cooking liquid in case you need it later.

5. Transfer the tomato sauce to a blender and puree until smooth. With the machine running, slowly add the vinegar through the top of the blender. Next, pour the remaining olive oil (½ cup plus 2 tablespoons) through the top in a slow, steady stream. Taste for seasoning.

6. Cook the sausage: Heat a large skillet over medium heat and add the canola oil. When the oil begins to smoke lightly, add the lamb sausage, breaking it into small pieces as it falls into the skillet. Cook, stirring from time to time, until the sausage browns and crisps and is cooked through, 8 to 10 minutes. Taste for seasoning.

7. Assemble the dish: Transfer the pasta to a large skillet and gradually add sauce. (You will end up with extra sauce. It freezes nicely.) Toss to blend with a wooden spoon. If the sauce is too thick, add a little of the reserved pasta water to thin it out. Drain any excess grease from the sausage and stir it into the pasta. Taste for seasoning. Sprinkle with Parmesan and serve.

old school variation

You can make this dish without the sausage but lower the amount of vinegar in the sauce. Without the richness of the meat, the acidity of the sauce needs to be dialed down for balance.

Rice Vinegar

I always read recipes for fresh tomato sauces and imagine myself skipping down the path from the garden with an apronful of tomatoes straight from the vine. I lovingly wash and cook them down with just the perfect amount of garlic, onions, olive oil, and oregano. After watching it bubble on the stove, I taste it only to discover that the freshness of the tomatoes is gone and I am left with something pretty watery. This recipe omits the dependence on an A-plus performance from the tomato and gives it a needed boost with the mellow acidity of rice vinegar and the punch from a pinch of red pepper flakes. Let a bottle of rice vinegar become your secret weapon in the kitchen. It's great for pickling vegetables, smoothing a rough, acidic edge in a salad dressing, and turning this sauce into a home run.

spice-rubbed rack of pork with a side of harissa

Harissa, a North African condiment, is one of my favorites to have on hand for those spicy moments; I think it makes the perfect companion to a beautiful cut of meat like pork loin. And while a standing beef rib roast or a rack of lamb is something that we immediately know to roast whole, what about a pork rack? The layer of fat that surrounds each chop is so much more satisfying when the rack is roasted whole. That way it doesn't need bacon or other companions—just a dollop of harissa to add a bit of kick, and maybe some smoky shallots (page 196). **SERVES 8 TO 10**

---

1 (8- to 10-pound) whole pork rack
2 tablespoons canola oil
1 medium bunch thyme, stemmed (about ¼ cup)
2 teaspoons ground allspice
2 teaspoons fennel seeds
1 teaspoon cumin seeds
Flaky sea salt, such as Maldon
1 lemon, quartered
Harissa (page 285)

1. Preheat the oven to 450°F. Let the pork rack sit at room temperature to take the chill off.

2. Make the spice rub: In a small bowl, mix together the thyme, allspice, fennel seeds, and cumin seeds.

3. Cook the pork: Heat a heavy-bottomed roasting pan large enough to hold the pork rack over medium heat. Add the oil. Season the pork on all sides with sea salt and the spice rub and cover the ends of the bones with foil to prevent burning. When the oil begins to smoke lightly, put the pork, fat side down, in the hot pan. Brown it for 3 to 5 minutes and then turn it on its second side, and brown for an additional 3 to 5 minutes. Put the rack skin side down in the pan and put the pan in the oven. Cook for 10 minutes.

4. Lower the oven temperature to 325°F, remove the foil from the bones, and roast until the meat has an internal temperature of between 145° and 150°F, an additional 50 to 60 minutes. Transfer the pork to a cutting board to rest for 10 to 15 minutes.

5. Serve the pork: Slice the pork into chops, allowing 1 bone per portion. Arrange them on a platter, squeeze a bit of lemon juice on top, and season with additional salt, if desired. Serve immediately, with harissa.

bacon-wrapped pork chops with apple and brussels sprouts

In 1999, I made pea soup at Restaurant Daniel for the first time. There were sugar snap peas, snow peas, fresh English peas, frozen peas, and pea shoots in the recipe. As I stirred five versions of the same vegetable I realized the recipe was harnessing all the power of the main ingredient in its many forms. Why not employ the same idea and gussy up pork with more pork? I love how the bacon crust forms like a suit of armor over these pork chops. What I love even more is that this recipe addresses the fact that pork chops are a surprisingly lean cut of meat without any marbling meandering through them. Enter bacon, the universal cure-all for problems in matters of taste, texture, and richness. **SERVES 4**

---

4 center-cut pork chops, preferably bone-in, each 1½ to 2 inches thick (about 3 pounds total)
Kosher salt and black pepper
12 thin slices bacon
1 tablespoon canola oil
12 Brussels sprouts, leaves separated
1 to 1½ tablespoons sherry vinegar
1 apple, preferably Braeburn or Macoun, cored, quartered, and thickly sliced

1. Preheat the oven to 375°F.

2. Prepare the chops: Season the pork chops generously on both sides with salt and pepper. Lay 3 slices of bacon, slightly overlapping, on a flat surface. Put a chop in the middle of the bacon and fold the ends of the bacon up tightly over the center part of the chop. Repeat with the other 3 chops.

3. Cook the chops: Heat a large cast-iron skillet over medium heat and add the oil. When the skillet is good and hot (I wait for some light visual signs of smoke), add the chops in a single layer. Cook the chops on their first side for 3 to 5 minutes, depending on thickness. Turn them on their second side and transfer the skillet to the oven. Cook for an additional 8 to

10 minutes or an internal temperature of about 148°F. Flip them onto a warm platter and let rest for 5 minutes. Turn them on their other side and season lightly with salt and pepper.

4. Serve the chops: While the pork chops are resting, pour off all but 2 tablespoons grease from the skillet, put it back on the stove over medium heat, and allow the drippings to get hot. Stir in all of the Brussels sprout leaves, tossing them in the grease, and cook until lightly crisped, 3 to 4 minutes. Season the leaves with salt and add the vinegar.

5. Serve the pork: Transfer the pork to a serving platter and spoon any cooking juices over the chops. Toss the apple pieces with the vinegar and sprinkle over the chops. Top with the Brussels sprouts leaves. Serve immediately.

bacon

I grew up eating mostly the pre-sliced bacon you can get at a supermarket. It cooks easily, whether on a rack in the oven or in a pan on top of the stove. While I will freely admit that I only really eat Canadian bacon when on a diet or with poached eggs from time to time, I have rarely met bacon I don't like. The question is where to use which kind. Slab bacon, which is generally sold thickly cut (or in an actual slab), needs that tough outer skin removed and is great for cutting into "lardons" (½-inch-thick strips) that are then cooked crisp and tossed with bitter greens and a bright acidic dressing for an amazing salad. They are also great with roasted chicken or dropped last minute into a braise or soup. I use presliced, whether thin or thick, for a lot of other things. For my spice-rubbed bacon (page 269), I use thin slices so it crisps up more easily in the oven. For wrapping these pork chops, I would opt for something thicker that can withstand the cooking time of the pork chops. I personally enjoy my bacon smoky and salty but there are so many to choose from. I've found my favorites through trial and error. Experimenting with bacon is always fun.

Cuisinart®

poultry

a love affair

brined and roasted whole chicken

flattened chicken breast with
pickled red onions and bay leaf

breaded chicken with mustard and dry sherry

braised chicken legs and thighs
with ginger and tomato

cornish hen on the grill

thanksgiving turkey with
miles standish stuffing

roasted turkey wings with honey and garlic

turkey breast that reminds
me of thanksgiving

whole duck with
green peppercorn glaze

fried duck hearts with golden
raisins and serrano chiles

Growing up just a few blocks from Radio City Music Hall in Manhattan, I really wanted to be a Rockette. To prepare for this, my best friend and I would dance to various disco themes in my parents' living room. We were, at age seven, planning to get an apartment in the area and become the two best Rockettes ever. Rehearsal was critical to our success.

At this time, my father was developing his hobby of cooking Chinese food. He pored over thick volumes while stirring various bowls of soy sauces, dried mushrooms, and rice vinegars. One of my favorite things he ever made was a roast duck that required three to four days of preparation. First the duck was hung to dry for three days, then marinated, and finally roasted. Once the duck was cooked, you could eat "super crispy duck, bones and all," my father explained excitedly.

On day three, as the duck hung from the ceiling in the small space between the dining room and living room, my friend and I emerged from my bedroom in tutus and cut off T-shirts, a Donna Summer double album tucked under my arm. I twirled and twirled to Donna's lyrics, imagining that each turn was a little straighter and more like that of a true Rockette. I reached my arm up as I twirled and my hand bumped against the hanging duck, catching some random grease from the bird. It woke me from my dance reverie, for sure, but, to this day, I wonder if that duck wasn't trying to tell me something deeper—something about what profession I would eventually choose . . .

Poultry is a topic I hold dear to my heart.

brined and roasted whole chicken

I am not a person who brines poultry on a regular basis, but I do so when I want a change of pace. Keep in mind that brining comes with built-in risks, namely oversalting—either of pan drippings and gravy or the meat itself. Done right, however, brining keeps turkey and chicken from drying out and is a chance to season the meat deeply. I love the flavors here—particularly the molasses and dried sage—that summon Thanksgiving and fall but are ones I like in subtle ways all year round. I call my brine recipe the full spa treatment for poultry. First, you brine the bird like a mud mask. Then, just after roasting, you rub the white meat with a lemon butter (like a post-mud-mask moisturizing treatment) to make the meat flavorful and moist. **SERVES 3 TO 4**

---

8 ounces (3 cups) Diamond Crystal kosher salt
1 cup honey
½ cup blackstrap molasses
½ cup reduced-sodium soy sauce
1½ teaspoons red pepper flakes
1½ teaspoons chopped dried sage
5 to 6 sprigs fresh thyme
1 head garlic, broken into individual cloves and smashed
2½ pounds ice cubes
1 (3- to 4-pound) whole chicken
10 tablespoons (1¼ sticks) unsalted butter: 2 tablespoons melted and 8 tablespoons at room temperature
Grated zest of 1 lemon

1. Make the brine: In a large deep pot, bring 6 cups water to a boil. Remove from the heat, add the kosher salt, and stir until it dissolves completely. Add an additional 6 cups water and allow to cool for a few minutes.

old-school tip

Instead of heating the entire amount of liquid for the brine and then waiting for it to cool, I heat just the amount of liquid needed to combine and dissolve all of the ingredients and then add the rest of the water in ice cube form. This cools the brine as the ice cubes melt in the hot liquid and brings the liquid to the level you need.

2. Stir in the honey, molasses, soy sauce, and red pepper flakes. Pour the mixture into a cooler large enough to hold the brine and the chicken (at least 7 quarts) and stir in the sage and thyme. Use a large whisk to blend all of the ingredients. Add the garlic and ice cubes.

3. Brine the chicken: Submerge the chicken in the brine. Cover the cooler and allow the bird to sit in the brine overnight or for about 12 hours. Do not exceed 14 hours or the bird will be too salty.

4. An hour before cooking, remove the chicken from the brine, rinse it under cold water, and dry it thoroughly with kitchen towels. Discard the brine.

5. Preheat the oven to 400°F.

6. Roast the chicken: Put the chicken, breast side up, in the center of a shallow roasting pan (a large cast-iron skillet is great) or a rimmed sheet pan fitted with a rack. Brush the breast meat with the 2 tablespoons melted butter. Put the chicken in the oven and roast until the juices run clear or a thermometer inserted into the thickest part of the thigh registers 160°F. I count about 12 to 15 minutes per pound of bird. For a 3-pound bird, I check the juices and temperature after 30 minutes of cooking. Remove from the oven and allow it to rest for at least 10 minutes before transferring it to a cutting board.

7. When you remove the bird from the pan, gently put it breast side down on the board so the juices can flow through the breast meat as it rests for an additional 10 to 15 minutes. Then turn it breast side up. In a medium bowl, mash together the 8 tablespoons butter with the lemon zest.

8. Serve the chicken: Carve the chicken by removing the wings and legs first. Cut the drumstick from the thigh. Then cut the breasts off the bone and slice ½ inch thick. Spread some of the lemon butter on the flesh of the chicken while it's still hot. Arrange the pieces on a platter and serve immediately.

old-school variation

Double the brine ingredients (and the amount of water) to make enough for 1 (14- to 18-pound) turkey or 2 to 3 (3- to 4-pound chickens). For chicken, I never exceed 14 hours in the brine and for a turkey, no more than 24 hours. For instructions on how to cook turkey, see pages 145–149.

flattened chicken breast with pickled red onions and bay leaf

Butterflying these chicken breast halves is one of those small gestures that takes chicken from just everyday to special. The edges of the breast are thinner than the meatier part closer to the wing bone. By butterflying them, you level the playing field and prevent the thinner part from overcooking before the thicker part of each breast is cooked through. I really love when a chicken breast is just cooked and still so juicy. Not only is the texture improved but those chicken juices amplify the flavor so much. **SERVES 2**

PICKLED ONIONS

1 medium red onion, halved and cut into ⅛-inch slices
⅔ cup cider vinegar
¼ cup sugar
1 small garlic clove, smashed and peeled
1 dried bay leaf
12 black peppercorns
1 teaspoon mustard seeds
1 whole star anise

CHICKEN

2 (10-ounce) "airline" skin-on chicken breast halves (small wing bone intact)
1 tablespoon fresh thyme leaves
1 bay leaf, cut into thin (⅛-inch) strips
3 tablespoons canola oil
Kosher salt and black pepper

1. Pickle the onion: Put the onion in a quart-size, nonreactive heatproof container with a lid. Combine the rest of the ingredients in a small saucepan and bring to a boil, stirring to make sure the sugar has dissolved. Cool slightly and then pour the mixture over the onion.

2. Butterfly the chicken: Put the chicken breasts skin side down on a cutting board. Use a large knife to make a lengthwise but horizontal cut through the upper quarter of the meat and towards the wing, but cutting only halfway through the meat. Pull your knife out and use your hand to fold the cut section of the thicker part of the breast (and the little "tender" on top of it) over. The result should be a breast that is much flatter. It should even

recipe continues

the meat out and flatten it at the same time.

3. Cook the chicken: Heat a cast-iron skillet large enough to hold the chicken breasts in a single layer over medium heat and add the oil. Season the chicken generously on both sides with salt and pepper. Rub 1 tablespoon of the canola oil on the breasts and spread the thyme leaves and bay leaf strips on the flesh side of each. When the oil begins to smoke lightly, shut off the heat and add the breasts, skin side down, to the pan. Turn the heat back on to medium, cover the breasts with a piece of foil just large enough to cover them, and top with a smaller heavy pan, such as cast iron, with something heavy in the center to weight the meat down as it cooks. Cook, undisturbed, until browned, about 10 minutes. Resist the urge to check it or fuss with it. Remove the weight from the chicken breasts and flip them to the other side. Reduce the heat to medium-low and allow the breasts to finish cooking gently until the meat near the wing bone reaches 155°F, 3 to 5 minutes more. Season them again with salt, if needed.

4. Serve the chicken: Transfer the chicken breasts to a platter or individual plates and top with some of the pickled onions and a little of the pickling liquid. Serve immediately.

Old-school tip

Sometimes I want to have a dressing or sauce with a thick consistency without being heavy. It's nice when vegetables (in this case, onions) can act as the thickeners. Instead of just topping the chicken with onions and some of the pickling liquid, combine in a blender ¼ cup boiled chicken stock, a little of the pickling liquid, a handful of the onions, and the pan drippings from cooking the chicken and blend on low speed until smooth. Taste for seasoning and add a little extra-virgin olive oil through the top if the sauce needs some additional richness. Put some of that under the chicken breast like a sauce, so you bite into the crispy skin and then dig into the meat mixed with the delicious sauce underneath!

butterflying chicken breasts:

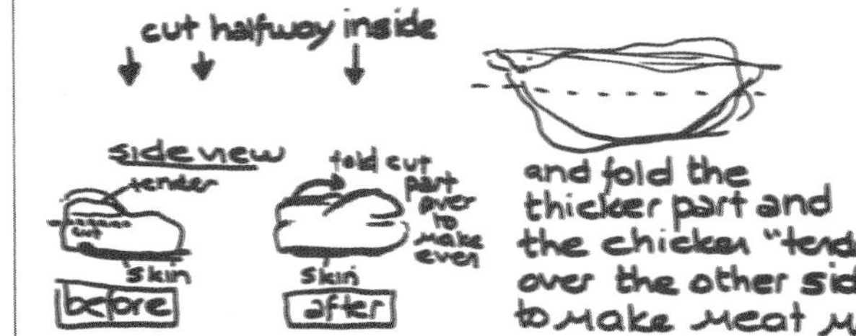

and fold the thicker part and the chicken "tender" over the other side to make meat more even. Like flattenin a bump in the roa

breaded chicken with mustard and dry sherry

I'd say to my mother while I was growing up, "Can you make THE chicken tonight for dinner?" and she'd know I meant this recipe. I had never experienced another recipe that so deeply bumped up the flavor of chicken. But it's more than that. There is no other recipe I would even consider that calls for (shocking!) skinless chicken. In fact, don't tell anyone that you got this recipe from me because no self-respecting professional chef would willingly remove the skin before cooking chicken. But here is my exception to the rule.

If you're like me (I am the queen of substitutions for recipes), you're standing at your kitchen counter wondering if you can substitute sherry vinegar for the dry sherry and grainy mustard for the Dijon and so on. The answer is no. But, you can cheat and marinate the chicken for only an hour or so and still get decent results (though if you really want to get the full effect, give it at least a few hours or overnight to work its magic). **SERVES 4**

½ cup reduced-sodium soy sauce
½ cup dry sherry
1 tablespoon Worcestershire sauce
1 tablespoon Tabasco sauce
2 tablespoons Dijon mustard
¼ cup canola oil
1 (3½- to 4-pound) whole chicken, cut into 8 pieces: each breast half split into 2 even pieces with the wings still attached, 2 drumsticks, and 2 thighs
1½ cups plain dried bread crumbs
5 tablespoons unsalted butter, melted
Kosher salt
Lemon wedges

1. Marinate the chicken: In a large bowl, whisk together the soy sauce, sherry, Worcestershire sauce, Tabasco, mustard, and canola oil. With the exception of the wings, remove the skin from the chicken. Submerge all the chicken pieces in the marinade. Don't be afraid to get your hands dirty: Turn the chicken pieces around in the marinade so that each piece is coated on all sides. Put a piece of plastic wrap on top of the chicken and add a heavy weight, such as a small plate, to ensure the chicken is submerged in the marinade. Refrigerate for 3 hours or overnight.

recipe continues

2. Preheat the oven to 400°F.

3. Cook the chicken: In a medium bowl, mix together the bread crumbs and butter. Season with a few large pinches of salt. Remove the chicken pieces from the marinade, allowing any excess liquid to drip off, and roll them in the bread crumbs. Take care to bread all sides of each piece. Arrange them in a single layer (without crowding) on a baking sheet with a fitted rack. Elevating the chicken will help avoid a soggy underside on your chicken. Bake until the pieces are cooked through (internal temperature of 155° to 160°F) and the bread crumbs are golden brown, 25 to 30 minutes.

4. Preheat the broiler.

5. Put the chicken under the broiler for a minute or two, watching, to further brown the bread crumbs. Serve with lemon wedges.

Old-school tip

The bread-crumb market has become considerably more crowded since the days when my mom used to send me to the store to buy them. I can remember just picking between 4C and Progresso. Both have a relatively fine and pleasantly sandy texture. For this recipe I'd recommend picking up a tin of plain dried Progresso bread crumbs. And what about chicken? There are a lot of choices to make and, to be honest, while I pinch pennies in many places, spending some extra cash on all-natural or organic chicken is worth it. I am a big fan of Murray's and Bell & Evans brands in particular.

braised chicken legs and thighs with ginger and tomato

This is a chicken cacciatore with a little twist on the flavor, and is really representative of the melting pot of flavors I experienced during my childhood. My mom, ever the Italian, made braised chicken with tomato. She also edited an amazing Indian cookbook that made her revise the chicken tomato combo and add hauntingly flavorful spices like cinnamon, which evokes the sweetness of the tomatoes. The red pepper flakes (in place of black or white pepper) wake the chicken up and accentuate the richness that lives naturally in the dark meat. The most important step to respect is when you add the white wine. Let it simmer around the chicken for a few minutes to ensure that the raw alcohol taste cooks off. I love this with rice pilaf (page 212). **SERVES 6 TO 8**

---

3 tablespoons canola oil
6 large whole skin-on chicken legs, thighs and drumsticks separated
Kosher salt
1 teaspoon red pepper flakes
1 teaspoon cumin seeds
2 large white onions (about 1¾ pounds total), halved and thinly sliced
1 (2-inch) knob fresh ginger, peeled and grated (1 tablespoon)
3 garlic cloves, smashed and peeled
1 cinnamon stick
2 dried bay leaves
2 cups dry white wine
1 (28-ounce) can whole peeled tomatoes with their juice
2 tablespoons unsalted butter

1. Brown the chicken: Heat a large skillet over high heat. Add 2 tablespoons of the canola oil. Arrange the chicken in a single layer on a baking sheet and season the pieces with salt and half of the red pepper flakes. Turn the pieces on their other side and season with more salt and the remaining red pepper flakes. When the oil begins to smoke lightly, carefully add the pieces to the oil. Do not overcrowd the pan; work in batches if necessary. Resist the temptation to move or turn the chicken and allow the pieces to brown on their first side, 5 to 8 minutes. Use tongs to flip the pieces over and brown, 3 to 5 minutes more. Transfer the chicken pieces to a large plate or baking sheet.

2. Make the sauce: In the same skillet, strain off the oil and wipe out any burnt bits. Add the remaining 1 tablespoon canola oil over medium heat. When the oil begins to smoke lightly, add the cumin and stir rapidly to give the seeds a quick roast, 5 seconds. Add the onions. Season with salt and cook, stirring frequently, until they turn light brown, 5 to 8 minutes. Stir in the ginger and garlic and add the cinnamon and bay leaves. Pour in the white wine and gently boil until reduced by half to allow the raw taste of the alcohol to cook out before adding any other ingredients, 8 to 10 minutes. Add the tomatoes and their juices and simmer to allow the flavors to come together, 10 minutes.

3. Cook the chicken: Add about 1 cup water to the skillet and arrange the chicken pieces in the sauce. Use a wooden spoon to break up the tomatoes. Keep the heat low and simmer until the pieces are cooked through and the meat can be pulled off with a fork, 30 to 45 minutes. If the sauce gets too thick or begins to stick to the bottom of the skillet, add a little more water. If it's too thin, transfer the chicken to a tray, bring the sauce to a boil, and simmer until thick enough to coat the chicken. Stir the butter into the sauce. Return the chicken to the sauce, if need be. Discard the cinnamon and bay leaves before serving.

Old-school tip

I would be lying if I said I didn't fix many crises in the kitchen with a pinch of butter. It's one of the ultimate chef's crutch ingredients to correct sauces that need richness or soups that taste bitter; butter arrives on the scene and is that great diplomat. But the more I cook, the more I see butter (and its caloric implications) as something I add for its actual flavor to shine through. In my opinion, one of those places is whenever tomatoes are the driving force in a recipe. Butter gives those sweet-tart tomatoes a shoulder massage and lets them know everything is going to taste wonderful.

cornish hen on the grill

I love what yogurt does to tenderize and add richness to hens or chickens. I have marinated the game hens in this recipe for as little as a few hours and as long as a day and a half before cooking. When this tenderizing technique, stolen brazenly from Indian cooking, is combined with the charred flavor of the grill, the result is a pleasantly tangy, smoky, and tender hen. I usually marinate something like this on a Sunday or Monday so I have them to cook early in the week when I am least likely to cook an elaborate meal. This pairs nicely with Braised Savoy Cabbage with Jalapeños (page 194) **SERVES 4**

¾ cup plain whole-milk yogurt
1 small (1-inch) knob fresh ginger, peeled and grated (1 tablespoon)
1 teaspoon ground cumin
½ teaspoon red pepper flakes
2 (1½- to 2-pound) Cornish hens
Kosher salt
2 tablespoons canola oil
1 lemon

1. Make the marinade: In a large bowl, whisk together the yogurt, ginger, cumin, and red pepper flakes.

2. Marinate the hens: Put the hens, breast side down, on a cutting board. Use a strong pair of scissors to cut through the hens along one side of the backbone. Cut along the other side of the backbone to remove it. Without the backbone, the hens will, in essence, be flattened, and will cook evenly when grilled. Make sure the hens can lie flat once opened, for even cooking. Slather the hens on the flesh side only with the yogurt mix and put them, flesh side down, on a large plate or platter. Cover with plastic wrap and refrigerate for a couple of hours or overnight.

3. Grill the hens: Preheat half the grill over high heat. Take care that the cooking grates are super clean to prevent the hens from sticking. Put a large double layer of foil on the cooler half of the grill.

4. Remove the hens from the yogurt, using a kitchen towel to wipe off any excess. Season them generously on both sides with salt and drizzle with the oil. Lay the hens, skin side down, on top of the foil. You want to roast them slowly on the grill, not scorch them over intense heat, which would dry them out. Cook, covering the grill with the lid, for 8 to 10 minutes. Take care that they are not cooking too rapidly. Then, use a pair of tongs to rotate them 180 degrees and cook until a thermometer inserted into the thigh registers between 150°F and 155°F, 10 to 12 minutes more.

5. Turn the hens skin side down directly on the grill and above the fire and cook, uncovered, until the skin is charred and a thermometer inserted into the thigh registers 160°F, a few minutes.

6. Remove from the grill and allow to rest for a few minutes. Squeeze lemon juice on top and cut into smaller pieces or serve whole, family style. Serve immediately.

Old-school tip

All this work in fancy restaurants had me forever avoiding the pith (that layer of white bitterness between the rind and the flesh) of citrus fruits. Sometimes, it's fun to embrace it instead. Take a whole lemon and chop it up into smallish pieces. As you chop, weed out and remove any pits. Slice one fresh jalapeño (seed it if you don't want it to be super spicy) and stir it together with the chopped lemon, a pinch of sugar, and a splash of olive oil. Chill it in the fridge while the hens cook. The charred meat against this chilled lemon mixture is a great contrast of flavors and temperature. I also like it with squid (page 51).

thanksgiving turkey with miles standish stuffing

This is a family recipe from my father's side. "This is a traditional American stuffing," he says with a sly grin. "Of course they had mozzarella cheese and pepperoni on the *Mayflower*." The cheese melts into the stuffing, acting like a glorious goopy glue, the pepperoni adds a little spice, and the breakfast sausage brings the hints of sage and onion and toasted bread out in the open. Every other year, my mother would experiment with some fancy stuffing from an issue of *Gourmet* magazine and we referred to those as the "charming" but "off" years for stuffing. **SERVES 12 TO 14**

STUFFING

8 to 10 tablespoons (1 to 1¼ sticks) unsalted butter, as needed
3 medium yellow onions (about 1¼ pounds total), halved and thinly sliced
8 celery stalks, thinly sliced
Kosher salt and white pepper
8 slices white sandwich bread
2 tablespoons fresh thyme leaves
10 fresh sage leaves, cut into thin strips (1 tablespoon)
1 teaspoon dried rosemary
1 turkey heart (if available), cut into small pieces
1 turkey liver (if available), cut into small pieces
1 pound bulk spicy pork breakfast sausage (or regular sausage mixed with ½ teaspoon red pepper flakes)
10 ounces pepperoni (not sliced), casing removed, cut into ¼-inch cubes
1 pound whole-milk mozzarella, cut into ¾-inch cubes
½ to 1 cup low-sodium chicken broth

THE BIRD

1 (14- to 16-pound) turkey, giblets and neck removed and reserved
Kosher salt and white pepper
4 tablespoons (½ stick) unsalted butter, melted

GRAVY

Turkey neck (if available)
7 cups low-sodium chicken broth
Kosher salt and white pepper
1 tablespoon Dijon mustard
½ cup dry Marsala or sherry
2 tablespoons all-purpose flour

Cranberry Sauce (optional; page 146)

recipe continues

1. Preheat the oven to 400°F.

2. Make the stuffing: In a large skillet, melt 2 tablespoons of the butter over medium heat. Add the onions and celery and season with salt and pepper. Cook the vegetables until translucent, 5 to 7 minutes. Transfer the onion mixture to a bowl. Wipe the pan clean.

3. Arrange the bread slices in a single layer on 2 baking sheets and toast on both sides until light brown, 8 to 10 minutes. (Alternatively, brown them in a toaster.) While the bread is still hot, lightly butter both sides of each piece using 4 to 6 tablespoons of the butter. Cut into ½-inch squares and transfer to a large bowl. Toss with salt, pepper, the thyme, sage, and rosemary.

4. In a small skillet, heat 1 tablespoon of the butter over high heat. Quickly sauté the heart and gizzard pieces for 30 seconds. Season with salt and pepper. Remove from the heat and add them to the bowl of celery and onions. Stir to blend. Use the same pan to cook the pork sausage. Set a large skillet over medium heat, crumble in the sausage meat, and allow it to cook over medium heat until brown and fully cooked, 5 to 7 minutes. Transfer the sausage and any cooking juices to the bowl with the onion mixture.

5. Wipe the skillet clean and set it over high heat. Add the remaining 1 tablespoon butter. Add the pepperoni pieces and cook, stirring, over high heat for 2 to 3 minutes. Drain on a paper towel.

6. Add the pepperoni, onion mixture, and mozzarella to the bowl containing the toasted bread. Mix to blend and add just enough chicken broth to moisten all of the ingredients.

7. Stuff the bird: Put the turkey on a flat surface, season generously with salt and pepper inside and out, and stuff the cavity with the stuffing. Wrap any remaining stuffing in foil, making a package like a large envelope, and refrigerate. Tie the turkey's legs closed with a strong piece of kitchen twine or string by wrapping them around and around the drumsticks and pulling them closed like you're tying a shoe. Transfer the turkey breast side up to a roasting pan fitted with a roasting rack.

8. Roast the bird: Soak a large double-layered piece of cheesecloth large enough to cover the turkey in the butter and cover the breasts with the cheesecloth to prevent the top skin from burning before it is cooked. Reduce the oven temperature to 350°F and put the roasting pan in the oven. Roast, basting periodically, for about 12 minutes per pound of turkey, or 2 hours 45 minutes to 3 hours 15 minutes for a 14- to 16-pound bird.

9. After the turkey has been in the oven for about 2 hours, remove the roasting pan from the oven, remove the cheese-cloth from the top of the breasts, and return the turkey to the oven. Add the foil package of stuffing to the oven, too, and let it heat up for about 45 minutes.

10. Start the gravy: Meanwhile, about 30 minutes before the turkey is done, combine the neck and broth in a saucepan and simmer gently on top of the stove as the turkey finishes cooking. The broth should reduce by about half. Season with salt and pepper, if desired.

11. Test the bird: The temperature of the thigh (where the meat is thickest and takes the longest time to cook) should register 155° to 160°F. As a precaution, take the temperature of the stuffing as well. It should register a similar temperature to the meat. If the bird is fully cooked and the stuffing a little lower, you can remove the stuffing from the cavity and cook it more while you carve the turkey and make the gravy. Remove the turkey from the oven, transfer to a cutting board or serving platter, and allow it to rest for 20 to 30 minutes.

12. Make the gravy: If the bottom of the roasting pan is burned, wipe away the burned bits. Remove any excess grease. Put the roasting pan over the burners of the stove over low heat, add the mustard and Marsala to the pan and scrape the bottom to get the drippings and tasty bits as the Marsala simmers and reduces. Pull the neck out of the hot broth and pour about ½ cup into a small bowl. Whisk the flour into the bowl, taking care there are no lumps. Once the Marsala has almost completely evaporated, about 8 to 12 minutes, pour the hot broth and the flour mixture into the roasting pan. Whisk to blend. Taste for seasoning. Reduce until the mixture thickens to a gravy consistency, 30 to 35 minutes.

13. Serve the bird: Remove the stuffing from the turkey and combine with the foil package of stuffing in a large serving bowl. Carve the turkey and serve with the gravy on top or on the side and a bowl of cranberry sauce.

cranberry sauce

I make this every year and serve it alongside a can of Ocean Spray cranberry sauce. There's something so endearing to me about the imprint of the can on the sauce next to this homemade version. **MAKES ABOUT 2½ CUPS**

1 pound fresh cranberries
1½ cups sugar
½ cup orange juice, such as Tropicana
1 cinnamon stick
½ teaspoon ground allspice
¼ teaspoon ground nutmeg
Grated zest and juice of 1 orange

1. In a medium saucepan, combine all of the ingredients and bring to a simmer over medium heat. Simmer to incorporate the flavors and cook the cranberries 8 to 10 minutes.

2. Strain out the cranberries and transfer them to a bowl. Pour the liquid back into the saucepan and simmer to reduce it by half so it's more syrupy, about 15 minutes. Stir everything together and allow to cool before serving. Remove the cinnamon stick.

While the turkey is roasting, make yourself a holiday cocktail to get in the mood . . .

cranberry kir

I love to use cranberry juice and a little cranberry sauce mixed together to replace the classic cassis for a Kir Royale. You don't need an expensive sparkling wine here. In fact, the cheaper the better, as long as it is dry, not sweet. **SERVES 4**

¼ cup chilled cranberry juice, or more if needed
1 tablespoon jellied (smooth) cranberry sauce
2 teaspoons honey
Juice of ½ lemon
16 ounces (2 cups) chilled Champagne or dry sparkling wine

1. Make the cranberry blend: In a small bowl, combine the cranberry juice and cranberry sauce and whisk until fully blended. If too thick to mix with the sparkling wine, thin it out slightly with a little more cranberry juice. Stir in the honey and lemon juice.

2. Make the cocktail: Divide the cranberry mixture among 4 glasses and pour in the sparkling wine, stirring with a spoon as you pour so the cranberry integrates and doesn't just sit on the bottom of the glasses. Serve immediately.

turkey cheat sheet

How much turkey per person? I count 1 pound per person and 1½ pounds if you're a leftovers type.

One big bird or two smaller ones? I always prefer two smaller ones. If one cooks nicely and the other doesn't, you have two chances of having juicy turkey. I also find a large bird so much more difficult to deal with—from physically fitting it into my oven to carving it, too.

Brining? Variety is the spice of life. If you feel like mixing it up, try my brine (page 130). The risk of overly salty drippings and gravy looms on the horizon but the flavor is always good. For the most part, I'm a purist: I put the bird in the oven with my mother's buttered cheesecloth on the white meat and am done with it.

How to get crispy skin? I sometimes use a technique employed when making traditional Peking duck. Fill a large pot (one that will hold your turkey with room to spare) halfway with water. Bring the water to a boil and season it with salt and pepper. Submerge the turkey in the water for 1 minute. If the water is not high enough to completely submerge the bird, use a ladle to pour hot water from the pot over the exposed part. Remove the turkey from the water and allow it to rest in the refrigerator for 12 hours (or overnight) before stuffing and roasting. Alternatively, remove the turkey from its plastic wrapping and let it dry out in the refrigerator, uncovered, for the whole night before roasting.

Stuffing in or out of the bird? In. It adds moisture, slows cooking, and, in my opinion, is generally conducive to a juicy turkey.

If I stuff the bird, what do I do if all the stuffing doesn't fit? My father always wrapped the excess stuffing in foil and placed it in the bottom of the roasting pan so the turkey drippings would hit it as it cooked. I simply add the foil packet to the oven to cook alongside the turkey.

Basting? Everyone thinks something different. My feeling is this: Everyone checks on the turkey at some point in the cooking process, maybe once or twice. So when you naturally check on the turkey to make sure all is good, give it a baste with the pan drippings.

How long to cook it? I generally follow the rule of 12 minutes per pound if the bird has stuffing in the cavity. A little less if no stuffing is involved.

Pop-up thermometer? Cute, aren't they? A little insurance policy, or so it would seem. But those suckers don't pop up until way past 165°F, so you will get a dry turkey along with the pop-up. Use a thermometer.

Carve at the table or in the kitchen? I'm all about the turkey wing. So I never carve the turkey in front of other people because I want to be able to gnaw on a wing with wild abandon while my guests are in the other room. Carving is messy, too. Better to leave the mess in the kitchen and serve the carved bird at the table.

roasted turkey wings with honey and garlic

You can't be in a hurry when you make this recipe because, while it is simple, it takes time for the wings to cook, especially if they are big. The good news is that I find it hard to overcook them. They are not always easy to find so halve the recipe and roast only a few if you want. The cooking time and amount of garlic paste can vary.

SERVES 4 TO 6

---

6 turkey wings, ranging anywhere from 8 to 12 ounces each
⅓ cup canola oil
Kosher salt and white pepper
6 garlic cloves, peeled
2 tablespoons honey
2 tablespoons extra-virgin olive oil
2 tablespoons rice wine vinegar
1 tablespoon Worcestershire sauce
1 teaspoon mild curry powder, lightly toasted
Red wine vinegar (for sprinkling)

1. Preheat the oven to 375°F.

2. Cook the wings: Toss the turkey wings in a bowl with the canola oil and season allover with salt and pepper. Arrange them in a single layer on 2 racks, each set over a baking sheet. Roast until they are golden brown with crispy edges, 1 hour 30 minutes to 1 hour 45 minutes.

3. Make the seasoning paste: In a food processor, pulse the garlic until finely chopped. Add the honey, olive oil, rice wine vinegar, Worcestershire sauce, and curry powder. Blend until smooth. A few minutes before the wings are finished, spoon or brush the wings with the garlic paste and then finish cooking them. Sprinkle with some additional salt and a little red wine vinegar before serving.

roasted turkey breast that reminds me of thanksgiving

The hint of spice on the meat and the herbs are reminiscent of Thanksgiving stuffing. I have served this with mashed sweet potatoes (page 206) and constructed, the next day, a sublime sandwich with warmed leftover sweet potatoes and slices of this turkey with the bacon and cooking juices spread on the bread. **SERVES 4 TO 6**

---

1 (6½- to 7-pound) whole bone-in turkey breast
Kosher salt
3 garlic cloves, minced
2 tablespoons extra-virgin olive oil, plus more if needed
Pinch of grated nutmeg
Pinch of ground allspice
1 tablespoon chopped fresh sage leaves
1 tablespoon chopped fresh thyme leaves
2 cups dry white wine
4 thin slices bacon

1. Preheat the oven to 375°F.

2. Prepare the turkey: Generously season the turkey on all sides with salt. In a small bowl, combine the garlic, olive oil, nutmeg, allspice, sage, and thyme. Mix to blend. Put the turkey breast skin side down on a flat surface. Spread half of the garlic on the flesh side.

3. Cook the turkey: Put the turkey breast, breast side up, on a rack in a roasting pan. Pour 1 cup of the wine into the bottom of the pan and transfer the pan to the oven. Roast for 15 minutes.

4. Lower the oven temperature to 325°F and roast the turkey for 1 hour. Spread the remaining garlic mixture on the skin and then finish cooking until the internal temperature of the thickest part registers 155 to 160°F, an additional 30 minutes to 1 hour. Check the temperature where the meat is thickest and then test in a couple of other places to get an idea of the overall temperature. Because this meat is on the bone, it will continue to cook once out of the oven—even more so than a boneless cut. If the skin starts to overbrown, cover the breast loosely with a piece of cheesecloth moistened with olive oil. Remove the turkey from the oven and allow it to rest for at least 20 minutes before slicing.

5. Meanwhile, cut the bacon lengthwise into ⅛-inch pieces. Cook in a medium skillet over medium heat until crisp. Set aside to drain on a kitchen towel.

6. Make a little "jus": Pour off any excess grease from the roasting pan and put the pan on top of the stove. Turn the heat to low and add the remaining 1 cup wine. Stir to blend and allow it to simmer gently over medium heat until almost all of the wine evaporates, 5 to 8 minutes. Scrape the bottom of the pan with a heatproof rubber spatula to gently extract the sugars and any little bits of turkey that got lost along the way. Pour into a small bowl. Taste for seasoning.

7. Serve the turkey: Use a sharp knife to cut the turkey into fairly thick slices. Spoon the jus over it and top with the bacon. Serve immediately.

Cooking Wines

The debate about what kind of wine to use when cooking continues, from "cook with what you drink" to "don't waste your money on something fancy." For me, the choice is simple: I just get the driest and cheapest white or red I can get my hands on. And while I'm cooking, I pour myself a glass of the "good stuff"—often a nice Grüner Veltliner or Chardonnay, two of my faves—to drink while I watch the cheaper wine reduce in the pan. I am also not above using the remains of that mystery bottle hanging out in the door of my fridge from who-knows-when. In a recipe like this, the complexities of the wine (and most of the alcohol) will cook away.

Poularde de Bresse, purée à la truffe

Roasted, whole in the oven. It is emptied normally but the claws are kept on (black). It is trussed with the claws on, upright. While it is in the oven, tinfoil covering is placed over the black claws so that they remain unharmed while it cooks. Trussed so that the wings are underneath equally on both sides. This gives the bird height for presentation.

When it is basted, the juices are lifted out w/ a ladle (and re-placed over the body of the bird) and w/ a strainer (small-holed). This way all the small shit doesn't get tossed over the bird again.

Purée Potatoes, washed, cooked to death w/ skin. When they are cooked, and red hot, they are peeled and quickly passed thru a tamis w/ a corne. The passed potatoes are then dropped in hot milk and stirred in a casserole w/ a wooden spoon. Then butter, s/p are incorporated. When reclaimed, the purée is reworked - heated w/ a bit of butter, chopped truffle and truffle juice

whole duck with green peppercorn glaze

Take a leap of faith and give roasting a whole duck a try. Yes, it looks seriously daunting and a whole duck is not cheap. I find those to be natural deterrents to giving duck a whirl. And yes, you must give in to the fact that the thighs and breast are never going to cook at the same rate. But the rewards are many: The thighs can be reserved and used on a salad, the breast meat is so juicy, and the skin so tasty. And all of that rendered grease in the bottom of the pan is great for cooking anything from pieces of fish to croutons. Be brave. Embrace a duck! **SERVES 4**

---

1 (4- to 4½-pound) whole Long Island (Pekin) duck, trimmed
Kosher salt
1 cup reduced-sodium soy sauce
⅔ cup honey
2 scant tablespoons (about 1 ounce) green peppercorns, plus 2 tablespoons of their brine
¼ cup champagne vinegar
1 teaspoon red pepper flakes
16 to 18 white or red cipollini or pearl onions, peeled (6 to 7 ounces total)
1 tablespoon canola oil

1. Prepare the duck: Remove the giblets and reserve them for another recipe, if desired (see page 155). Remove any loose pockets of fat surrounding the cavity. Season the inside of the duck with salt.

2. The night before, in a Dutch oven or wide saucepan large enough to hold the duck, combine 3 cups water, ¾ cup of the soy sauce, and ⅓ cup of the honey. Bring to a simmer. Lower the heat and submerge the duck in the mixture. Simmer for 1 minute and then turn the duck on its other side. Remove the duck to a rimmed baking sheet or platter and pat it dry with a kitchen towel. Ideally, the duck should sit uncovered overnight in the fridge to allow the flavors to meld with the duck and for the skin to dry out. This will mean a crispier skin once the duck is cooked.

3. Preheat the oven to 450°F. Remove the duck from the refrigerator to allow it to come to room temperature.

4. Prepare the glaze: In a medium saucepan, combine the green peppercorns and their brine with the vinegar, red pepper flakes, remaining ¼ cup soy sauce, and ⅓ cup honey. Bring to a boil. Lower the heat and simmer gently until reduced by half and the honey foams when you

recipe continues

gently swirl the pan, 8 to 10 minutes. Taste for seasoning. Set aside to cool.

5. Cook the duck: Put the duck in a roasting pan fitted with a rack, which will allow hot air to circulate around it as it cooks. Toss the onions in the canola oil and scatter them in the bottom of the pan. Roast in the oven, undisturbed, for 15 minutes. Stir the onions to assure they aren't burning on the bottom. Cook for an additional 15 minutes.

6. Lower the oven temperature to 400°F. Remove the duck from the oven and use a turkey baster to baste with the drippings from the bottom of the pan. Season the outside with salt. Return the pan to the oven and cook until the duck registers about 120°F when a thermometer is inserted into the breast meat, 5 to 10 minutes. Transfer the duck to a platter and pour the glaze over the breast and thigh meat. Arrange the onions around the bird. Allow the bird to rest for about 15 minutes.

7. Carve the duck: You can carve a duck like you would a turkey, slicing thin pieces off the breast and thigh meat and arranging it on a serving platter. Or, you can carve it like you would a whole chicken: cut off the two legs and the two breasts, detach the thighs from the drumsticks, and slice the breasts in half.

cipollini onions

My grandfather's favorite snack was a bowl of cippolini cooked tender with a little sugar and vinegar. They are hard work in terms of prep but worth the taste. A shortcut for peeling them? There isn't one. It helps to soak them in warm water for a few minutes before peeling to loosen their skins. When you peel them, try to avoid cutting away a lot (too much of the onion). I make an incision from top to bottom with a paring knife and peel the onion from its cozy jacket with my fingers.

fried duck hearts with golden raisins and serrano chiles

Every self-respecting chef should have knowledge of offal and how to use it. But the home cook? Why expand much more beyond the turkey gizzards at Thanksgiving and the occasional party mousse made from chicken livers? Because these parts have so much flavor! And they're cheap! This is especially true when it comes to duck hearts. I know, eating the heart of an animal seems so serious to some. But it's even more serious to butcher an animal and not enjoy all of its delicious parts. And duck hearts are at the top of my list. I've had them cooked with a little Cognac, shallots, and cream, the classic French way. Or you can deep-fry them. How can that be bad? It took a few tries and the help from my colleague Ian Halbwachs to make this nibble be all that it can be. These are insanely good. **SERVES 6 TO 8 AS AN APPETIZER**

---

1 pound duck hearts
1 quart buttermilk
⅓ cup golden raisins
½ cup champagne vinegar
½ cup apple juice
1 serrano chile
Kosher salt
2 quarts canola oil
4 large eggs
2 cups coarse bread crumbs, preferably panko

1. Prepare the duck hearts: Put the duck hearts on a cutting board and examine them: There should be a thin, clear membrane surrounding each one. Make a small, shallow incision in each and peel away that membrane. Transfer the duck hearts to a large bowl and pour the buttermilk over them. Take care that they are submerged. Refrigerate for 45 minutes.

2. Make the sauce: Combine the golden raisins, vinegar, and apple juice in a small saucepan and simmer over low heat until there's only about ⅛ cup liquid left, 10 to 12 minutes.

3. Cut each chile into thin rounds, seeds and all, and put in a bowl. Alternatively, to reduce the heat, clean out the ribs and

recipe continues

seeds. Take care to wash hands, knife, and board thoroughly. Sprinkle the chile slices over the sauce. Season all with salt.

4. Pour the canola oil into a medium pot and bring to 350°F over low heat. Monitor the temperature of the oil with a thermometer.

5. Bread the hearts: In a medium bowl, whisk the eggs. Pour half of the bread crumbs into a second bowl. Drain the duck hearts (discard the buttermilk), season them with salt, and drop them, in small batches, into the eggs. Extract them with a slotted spoon and scatter them over the bread crumbs. Add more bread crumbs when they start to become wet. Toss until each heart is coated with crumbs. Put the breaded hearts on a baking sheet.

6. Cook the hearts: Line a baking sheet with a kitchen towel and have ready a serving platter. Working in small batches, drop the duck hearts into the oil and fry until the exterior becomes crispy, 2 to 3 minutes. Remove them from the oil with a slotted spoon and transfer to the kitchen towel. Season immediately with salt. Skewer them individually, if desired, and coat with a little of the raisin-chile mixture. Serve immediately.

duck fat

What more sublime thing is there than duck fat? To me, precious little. Even bacon fat is a runner-up. Duck fat seemingly holds up better at hot temperatures than bacon grease, making its use even more versatile. It imparts some flavor and richness but is otherwise pretty neutral. Like if someone just took your hand and brought you from your seat in the back of the plane (right by the toilets) and wordlessly whisked you into first class. Sear a piece of fish in some duck fat? Yum. How about toasting some croutons for a goat cheese salad? It gives people my favorite reaction of all: They take a bite, sometimes a slight double take, and then a "What's in here?" facial expression. I just smile and say, "It's just goat cheese." Let that be our little secret.

When you buy a whole duck, you can remove the excess fat (it's hard to miss) around the cavity and just put that in a saucepan over low heat. The fat will melt down, leaving you with a little solid (which you discard) and perfectly wonderful liquid fat to use for other purposes. When you roast a whole duck, you will collect additional fat in the bottom of the roasting pan as well. Duck is the gift that keeps on giving. . . . Store it all in the fridge and melt it as needed.

And last but not least . . .

duck livers

Duck livers are incredibly rich and I cook them just as I would chicken livers; they make a delicious spread for toast. But if you buy a whole duck, then you only have 1 liver to work with. What to do? Try it in your sauce or gravy. When I was thirteen years old and fresh off a slice of airport pizza, my parents took me to the famed Michelin three-star restaurant La Tour d'Argent in Paris. What a contrast! This restaurant has such a tradition with duck. The carcass is essentially crushed (in a beautiful metal contraption) and the blood extracted to become part of the sauce for the meat. The ultimate carnivore's moment. Sans duck press at home, you can use the liver to get some of that fantastic flavor: Remove the outer membrane from the liver, chop the liver finely, and stir it into your sauce or gravy. It can even go into a honey or orange glaze.

fish
is easier to make
than you think

fresh clam chowder

mussels with white mushrooms
and hazelnuts

scallop gratin with scallions

angel hair pasta with caviar
and lemon

papillote of striped bass and herbs
with quick aioli

blackened salmon

roasted whole mackerel

broiled bluefish with corn and bacon

Learning how to select, cut, and cook fish is a lifelong process.

Pretending you already know how is even worse.

Chef de cuisine, Guy Savoy, Paris, France, 1993: "You know how to fillet fish, right?" he asked sternly.

"Of course," I answered, smiling, pretending the question was absurd. I had removed the bones from canned sardines before. How much harder could cleaning an actual fish be?

Oh boy.

I found myself downstairs with a mountain of fish. There was a 35-pound turbot, a bunch of skate wings, 2 large cod (with their heads still on), 2 salmon, and half a dozen dorade (similar to snapper).

"Allez là!" he shouted when he saw me standing there staring at the cases in awe. (That's French for: move your ass.)

I grabbed a dorade (because they were the smallest) and slowly began removing the first fillet. My knife was brand-new and super sharp but it doesn't matter how sexy the sports car if you don't know how to drive. I bumbled my way through the fillet, my fingers clumsily trying to trace the outline of the fish with my knife.

After a few fish, I started to get the hang of it and the fillets looked pretty good. In fact, they were beautiful. I love this! This is like painting! I feel like an artist! I trimmed a ragged edge from the tailpiece. But then the other side looked uneven, so I trimmed some from there as well. And I kept trimming . . .

Ever get a haircut where they keep telling you they need to "even out" one side or the other and you wind up unintentionally going from long hair to a pixie cut?

That's what happened to these fillets.

I knew the dorade was the lunch special and if we sold one, my mangled fish patty was not going to be a big hit at the county fair. Lunch was slow that day. Every time the chef called out an order, my heart stopped until I heard what was ordered. Not one of these fish was sold.

After lunch, we always had a break before dinner. I made a beeline to the fish store at the local market a block away. Could I really pull this off? I frantically searched the cases and found some dorade. I bought six fish and had them filleted. I dashed the new fillets back to the restaurant and replaced my mangled patties with the new ones. Phew.

"Ordering 4 dorade," the chef shouted in my direction. I pulled them out, seasoned them, and placed them in a large pan with some smoking hot oil.

The chef stood nearby, usual scowl in place.

"I think the fish down the block at the market is pretty good. Have you seen it?" I inquired timidly, almost wanting to reveal what I had done.

"Are you kidding?" he bellowed. "They are nothing in comparison to the fish we buy for this restaurant. Just look at these beautiful fillets!" he shouted, gesturing to the dorade in the pan—the very fillets I had secretly bought down the street.

I smiled and breathed a sigh of relief.

fresh clam chowder

I like watching this recipe build, in layers, on top of the stove. It begins innocently with some clams and becomes a naturally sweet and vegetal soup that satisfies as a main course—especially with a few pieces of toasted bread on the side for dipping. The Aleppo pepper (see Sources) is a critical component because it is smoky but also has a heat that grows without overpowering. Though this is a cream soup, don't be afraid to add a squeeze of lemon or a small splash of red wine vinegar at the end. The acidity can really brighten the flavors and, if stirred in quickly, won't hurt the texture of the cream. Also, when tasting this chowder, don't be afraid to season with a pinch of sugar to highlight the natural sweetness. **SERVES 6 TO 8**

---

5 pounds littleneck clams, well scrubbed with a brush under cold water
4 ounces thick-cut bacon, cut into ¼-inch pieces
2 teaspoons Aleppo pepper or other smoky dried pepper
2 tablespoons unsalted butter
2 celery stalks, sliced into ½-inch pieces
Kosher salt
2 small, thin leeks (white and light green part only), diced and well washed
2 garlic cloves, minced
1 cup dry vermouth
4 medium Yukon Gold potatoes (1 pound total), cut into ½-inch cubes
2 cups heavy cream, plus more if needed
2 bay leaves
1 tablespoon chopped fresh thyme leaves
Worcestershire sauce
Tabasco sauce
2 tablespoons chopped fresh tarragon leaves
2 tablespoons dry Marsala
Baked Bread for Clam Chowder Dipping (optional; recipe follows)

1. Cook the clams: Put a large sauté pan on the stove and add 1 cup water. Bring to a boil over high heat and add the clams. Stir the clams gently as they cook because the shells are fragile and break easily. Cook until they all open, 5 to 8 minutes. Put the clams in a colander and reserve the cooking liquid. Shell the clams, discarding the shells, and reserve the clams and cooking liquid separately.

2. Cook the bacon: Wipe out the sauté pan and cook the bacon over medium heat until crisp, 5 to 8 minutes. Use a slotted

recipe continues

spoon to remove the bacon to a paper towel and dust with the Aleppo pepper.

3. Cook the vegetables: Add the butter to the bacon fat in the pan and quickly sauté the celery over medium heat for 1 minute. Season with salt. Remove with a slotted spoon to a bowl. Add the leeks and garlic to the pan and season with salt. Cook until they become tender and translucent, 3 to 5 minutes. Add the vermouth and simmer until almost all of the liquid has evaporated, 8 to 10 minutes.

4. Cook the potatoes: Meanwhile, in a large saucepan, combine the potatoes, 2 cups cream, the bay leaves, and thyme. Bring the mixture to a gentle simmer and cook until the potatoes are tender, 5 to 8 minutes. Season with salt. Add a splash each of Worcestershire sauce and Tabasco. Stir to blend. Taste for seasoning.

5. Finish the chowder: There is a good chance there will be grit in the clam cooking liquid, so strain it and avoid the sediment at the bottom when adding it to the leek mixture. Stir in the celery. Taste for seasoning, adding more Worcestershire and Tabasco as needed. Pour the leek mixture into the potato mixture. Add the clams and tarragon. Discard the bay leaves. Add the Marsala and taste for seasoning. Add more cream and/or water, if needed, to thin. Top with the bacon just before serving, with baked bread, if desired.

baked bread for clam chowder dipping

I woudn't personally risk adding fresh dill to the soup but some dill seed on the toasts to go with it? It's a nice flavor with the clams and Vermouth in the chowder. Of course, toasts on the side of soup are about the crispy texture enhancing the soup experience but they are even better when they have a little personality of their own, too. **MAKES 8 PIECES**

---

8 (¾- to 1-inch-thick) slices from a round or oval loaf sourdough bread
4 tablespoons (½ stick) unsalted butter
3 medium garlic cloves, halved lengthwise and thinly sliced
Kosher salt
1 teaspoon Aleppo pepper
1 teaspoon dill seeds or fennel seeds

1. Preheat the oven to 350°F. Arrange the bread slices on a rimmed baking sheet in a single layer.

2. In a small skillet, melt the butter over low heat, add the garlic, and season with salt. Heat gently for 1 minute and then use a pastry brush to coat the bread slices with the garlic butter. Pour any remaining butter into the bottom of the baking sheet and dust the bread with the Aleppo pepper and dill seeds.

3. Bake until the slices are crisp, 12 to 15 minutes. Remove and allow to cool for a minute before serving alongside the soup.

a day in the life of a food dreamer

When I get out of bed in the morning, the first food thought I have is ____________ ____.

I love a breakfast that ____________________________________ because it is my favorite meal of the day.

During breakfast, I am thinking about ________________________________ because ____.

Lunchtime rolls around and I decide to make my favorite salad. It is something I often make and enjoy. It is salad made up of ____________________________, ____________________________, and ____________________________.

Midday dreams of naughty snacks include ____________________________ with ____.

Dinnertime. After a long day's work, I love to cook ____________________________ ____________. I especially enjoy watching ____________________________ eat.

For dessert, I love ____________________ but find myself daydreaming about ____________________________ with ____________________________.

ANSWER KEY

When I get out of bed in the morning, the first food thought I have is **what's for breakfast, lunch, and dinner today?**

I love a breakfast that **reminds me of my childhood** because it is my favorite meal of the day.

During breakfast, I am thinking about **what I am going to have for lunch** because **food is my profession and hobby.**

Lunchtime rolls around and I decide to make my favorite salad. It is something I often make and enjoy. It is salad made up of **buttery avocado slices with a squeeze of lemon juice, flaky sea salt and cracked black pepper, icy cold iceberg lettuce,** and **crumbled American blue cheese, pleasantly creamy and super tangy.**

Midday dreams of naughty snacks include **anything from brownies with crispy edges and gooey centers to toasted pumpkin seeds with red pepper flakes to raspberry sorbet floats** with **club soda and a squeeze of fresh orange.**

Dinnertime. After a long day's work, I love to cook **something quick and satisfying like a tasty stir-fry.**

I especially enjoy watching **my daughter or my hard-working cooks take a moment and** eat.

For dessert, I love **fresh fruit like chilled mangoes, pineapples, or watermelon** but find myself daydreaming about **really rich, eggy dark chocolate ice cream** with **toasted, slivered almonds and salty caramel.**

mussels with white mushrooms and hazelnuts

I really love the combination of hazelnuts with white mushrooms and mussels. For me, it's my down home (and affordable version of) surf and turf. The mushrooms are earthy, the hazelnuts rich, and the mussels sweet. You don't need many more elements to make a simple dish with complex taste. Because I find that mussels can vary in size and flavor, you may want to fiddle with the cooking time and the acidity of the sauce when you make this dish. I sometimes think we perceive seafood as exempt from seasoning, but a pinch of salt or a squeeze of lemon may be all you need to finish this dish. Sometimes I stir in some coarsely chopped arugula to add a peppery note as well. **SERVES 4 TO 6**

1½ pounds mussels, scrubbed and debearded
½ cup dry vermouth, preferably Noilly Prat
4 tablespoons (½ stick) unsalted butter
2 medium shallots, thinly sliced
¾ pound white button mushrooms, ends trimmed, wiped clean and quartered
Kosher salt
¼ teaspoon red pepper flakes
2 tablespoons blanched whole hazelnuts
Juice of 1 to 2 lemons, to taste
Grilled bread

1. Cook the mussels: Heat a skillet large enough to hold the mussels in a single layer over high heat for 1 minute. Remove from the heat and add the mussels and ¼ cup of the vermouth. Return the skillet to the stove and cook for 1 minute. Add about ¾ cup water. The mussels shouldn't take long to cook, about 2 minutes. Take care to stir the mussels from time to time so they cook as evenly as possible. Use tongs to pluck the mussels from the pan as they open. When all of the mussels are open, remove them and strain the liquid, reserving it for the sauce. Remove the mussels from their shells. Discard the shells.

2. Cook the mushrooms: Rinse the skillet and return it to high heat until it smokes lightly. Remove the pan from

recipe continues

the heat, add 1 tablespoon of the butter, and swirl the pan until the butter turns a light brown color. Return the skillet to the heat and immediately add the shallots and mushrooms. Season lightly with salt and the red pepper flakes. Cook the mushrooms until they start to give up liquid and brown, 3 to 4 minutes. Add the remaining ¼ cup vermouth and cook for 1 minute. Season to taste with salt.

3. Toast the hazelnuts: Meanwhile, in a small skillet, melt 1 tablespoon of the butter over medium heat and add the hazelnuts. Season them lightly with salt and toast them over low heat until they turn light brown, 5 to 7 minutes. Use a slotted spoon to remove the hazelnuts and transfer them to a cutting board. Roughly chop the hazelnuts.

4. Make the sauce: Transfer the mushrooms to a plate using a slotted spoon. If there is any cooking liquid from the mushrooms, combine it with the mussel cooking liquid in a small saucepan. Simmer over low heat for 1 minute. The sauce may need a pinch of salt. The flavor should be an initial taste of sweet mussel followed by an undertone of earthiness from the mushroom. Swirl in 1 tablespoon of the butter and a touch of lemon juice. Keep warm.

5. Assemble the dish: Heat a large skillet over high heat until hot, 2 minutes. Remove from the heat and add the remaining 1 tablespoon butter. When it turns light brown, return the skillet to the burner and add the mussels and mushrooms in a single layer. Cook for 1 minute without stirring them. They should be browned on their first side before you stir them slightly, with a wooden spoon, and leave them to brown for an additional minute. Stir in the sauce. Taste for seasoning. Toss in the hazelnuts. Serve immediately on a platter, family style, with slices of grilled bread.

Cleaning Mushrooms

While I was working at Guy Savoy in Paris, I learned to wipe each mushroom clean with a damp cloth. Mushrooms are sponges and submerging them in water, especially for a longer period of time, dilutes their flavor. For white mushrooms, I trim the very bottom of the stem (it's often coated in soil) and wipe the whole thing clean. If they are especially dirty? Rinse them briefly in cold water and then cut and cook them immediately after.

scallop gratin with scallions

Scallops with cheese? In this case, yes. My mother makes this as a holiday staple and I can still remember the first time I ate it as a kid. She ran out of the kitchen with the large scallop shells, sizzling, filled with this recipe. These are delicious, and the portion so small that it leaves you wanting more. Be warned: People may leave the table, shells in hand, to go somewhere and lick the crust of bread crumbs and leftover sauce from the shells in private. I also recommend some bread for sopping up the juices. **SERVES 4**

BREAD CRUMBS

2 tablespoons unsalted butter, at room temperature
¾ cup coarse bread crumbs, preferably panko, toasted
¾ cup thickly grated Gruyère
½ cup freshly grated Parmesan
1 tablespoon fresh thyme leaves, chopped
¼ teaspoon kosher salt
1 teaspoon black pepper

SCALLOPS

2 tablespoons canola oil
16 medium dry diver sea scallops, each halved down the middle
Kosher salt and black pepper
2 shallots, minced
2 garlic cloves, minced
½ pound small white button mushrooms, thinly sliced
¼ cup dry vermouth, preferably Noilly Prat
1 cup heavy cream
Juice of ½ lemon, plus 1 additional lemon for optional garnish
3 scallions (white part only), thinly sliced

1. Preheat the broiler.

2. Make the bread crumb topping: In a bowl, combine the butter and bread crumbs. Use a rubber spatula to mix them until they form a paste. Stir in the Gruyère and Parmesan cheeses. Mix in the thyme, salt, and pepper.

3. Cook the scallops: Heat a large skillet over high heat and add the canola oil. Season the scallops with salt and pepper. When the oil begins to smoke lightly, add them to the pan. Cook for 30 to 45 seconds until the edges brown and then quickly remove them to a plate using tongs.

4. Cook the mushrooms: Add the shallots and garlic to the pan and season with salt and pepper. Cook over medium heat until translucent, 2 to 3 minutes. Add the mushrooms and cook until they soften and brown lightly, 2 to 3 minutes. Add the vermouth and simmer until virtually all of the liquid has evaporated, 2 to 3 minutes. Add the heavy cream, stirring gently, and simmer until the mixture thickens, 5 to 7 minutes. Do not boil vigorously or the mixture risks separating. Taste for seasoning. Stir in the scallops, lemon juice, and scallions. Remove the pan from the heat.

5. Broil the scallops: Transfer the sauce and scallops to a shallow ovenproof dish (or into clean scallop shells, if desired). Sprinkle the bread crumbs over the top and broil until browned, 1 to 2 minutes. The time may be slightly longer or shorter depending on how quickly the top browns. Watch carefully! Serve immediately.

angel hair pasta with caviar and lemon

Domestic caviar is something that can be had for a good price, and only a small amount is needed to make a statement. Whenever I do buy it (which is admittedly rare), I find myself almost at a loss for how to honor it with an unusual preparation. Let's face it: Straight out of the little glass jar on toasted brioche with a schmear of crème fraîche is a great way to go. I also love it with smoked salmon. But it is such an unusual food that I searched high and low for a recipe that could do justice to it. This is a dish that came to me by way of exploration. I was cooking for a colleague and wanted to serve caviar—but I wanted the caviar to be a surprise. I twirled a forkful of this pasta, dripping with cream, over a little mound of caviar in a bowl. It looked so plain and simple—until he dug in and found the caviar lurking beneath! This dish is also nice made with trout or salmon roe.

A word on taste: I feel like a recipe that charts unfamiliar ground (in this case caviar) often doesn't instruct on the simplest thing: How is this dish supposed to taste? I wish you could provide aroma and taste on a page. The caviar is always salty but the pasta needs to be seasoned in its own right. The pepper illuminates the salt of the caviar. The lemon zest is floral and adds lightness to the flavor; the lemon juice adds some needed acidity along with sour cream. The cream comes in to temper everything and make sure the dish rides the line between acidic and rich.

SERVES 4 AS AN APPETIZER

---

1 cup heavy cream

1 cup sour cream
Kosher salt and black pepper
A few grates of zest and juice of ½ to 1 lemon
4 ounces dried angel hair pasta
1½ to 2 ounces American caviar or trout roe
1 small bunch chives, minced

1. Make the sauce: In a large skillet, whisk together the heavy cream and sour cream. Season with salt and pepper. Simmer the cream mixture over medium heat to reduce it, whisking until it thickens and all of the sour cream melts,

recipe continues

2 to 3 minutes. Add the lemon zest and some lemon juice. Taste for seasoning. At this point, the sauce should be thick enough to coat the pasta.

2. Cook the pasta: In a large pot, bring 6 quarts water to a rolling boil. Add 2 tablespoons salt and bring the water back up to a boil. Add the pasta to the pot and cook until al dente, stirring occasionally to make sure it doesn't clump or stick to the bottom as it cooks, for about 2 minutes. Drain the pasta in a colander, reserving ½ cup of the cooking liquid.

3. Add the pasta to the skillet and toss to coat with the cream. Shut the heat off and allow the pasta to rest in the sauce for 2 minutes, tossing to coat from time to time. If the sauce is too thin, simmer over low heat for 2 additional minutes. If it is too thick, simply thin it out with some of the reserved pasta water. Taste for seasoning. Add more salt or lemon if needed.

4. Serve the pasta: Spoon a small amount of caviar in the center of 4 serving bowls. Use a fork to twirl the pasta and make a large forkful. Use your index finger to gently coax the pasta off the fork and on top of the caviar in the plate. Ideally, the pasta should hide the caviar. Spoon any leftover sauce over the pasta. Repeat with the remaining plates. *Note:* The sauce thickens quickly so keep it loose with a little pasta water, if needed, as you plate. Sprinkle with the chives, a touch more grated lemon zest, and serve immediately.

papillote of striped bass and herbs with quick aioli

I like this dish because it makes for a flavorful and dramatic presentation. A papillote is a small, hermetically sealed envelope that allows the fish to steam in its own juices. It requires very little fat for cooking and the flavors are always very clean. The papillotes can be assembled in advance and the fish cooked at the last minute before serving. Now that we have got papillote down, what is aioli? Don't be daunted by the fancy term or worry about pronouncing it properly. Aioli is a sauce traditionally made with garlic, olive oil, and egg. Here I add hot baked potato to the mix because I feel like (even if it isn't true) the hot potato flesh cooks the egg slightly and I really love the texture it gives the sauce. **SERVES 2**

AIOLI

1 small Idaho potato (about 7 ounces), scrubbed
1 large egg yolk
1 garlic clove, minced
6 tablespoons extra-virgin olive oil
½ teaspoon sugar
Juice of ½ lime
Kosher salt and white pepper

FISH

1 tablespoon unsalted butter
2 (7- to 8-ounce) pieces skinless wild striped bass, pin bones removed
Kosher salt
1 tablespoon packed fresh dill
1 tablespoon packed flat-leaf parsley leaves
4 tablespoons dry vermouth
Flaky sea salt, such as Maldon
1 lemon, halved (optional)

1. Arrange two racks in the oven at a fair distance from one another. The foil-enveloped fish will need some room to expand as they cook. Preheat the oven to 400°F.

2. Bake the potato: Put the potato in the oven and bake until tender throughout, 50 minutes. (Leave the oven on for the fish.)

3. Prepare the fish: Meanwhile, spread a 1-foot length of foil, shiny side down, on a flat surface. Fold the foil in half to create a 6 × 12-inch double-layered rectangle. Repeat so you have 2 foil rectangles. Open the foil and put half of the butter in the middle of each. Season the fish with salt on both sides and sprinkle liberally with the dill and parsley. Put on top of

recipe continues

the butter and add about 2 tablespoons vermouth and a splash of water to each packet; the liquid will create steam to cook the fish and help the foil packet puff as it cooks. Fold the foil back over the fish (so the shiny side of the foil is showing) and roll the edges of the foil down around the fish to make a small package, with all the sides sealed. Leave enough room above the fish to allow for steam to build as the fish cooks, creating an inflated envelope around the fish.

4. Make the sauce: When the potato is completely cooked and hot, split it open lengthwise. Use a tablespoon to scoop out the flesh and put it in the food processor. Add the egg yolk and garlic and puree the mixture until smooth. With the machine running, add the olive oil in a slow, steady stream. Add the sugar and lime juice and season with salt and pepper. If the mixture is too thick, add a little warm water to loosen the texture. It should be loose enough to drizzle. Taste for seasoning.

5. Cook the fish: Place each of the foil envelopes on a separate rimmed baking sheet and add a little water. The water will create additional steam in the oven as the fish cooks. Put the fish on the two oven racks and bake, undisturbed, until the envelopes begin to puff, about 15 minutes. Don't worry if they don't fully puff. It is more about sealing and steaming the fish with aromatics to create clear, deep flavors. Remove from the oven and immediately transfer to 2 dinner plates. Serve the aioli on the side. Break open the foil and drizzle with the aioli. Sprinkle with Maldon salt and lemon juice, if needed.

Striped Bass

This is one of my favorite fish because it's so clean and steaky. There are many farmed striped bass fillets, usually ranging from 6 to 8 to 10 ounces. Try to avoid those and buy the wild striped bass in portions cut from larger fish. Whole, larger striped bass fillets range from 10 to 16 pounds. Buy a couple of portions cut from a fillet this size. That's what is ideal for this recipe.

MY GREAT FRIEND AND FISH CONNOISSEUR, LOUIS ROZZO

more fish tales

I can still remember how hungry I was that morning. It was a day when all the deliveries were late. I was waiting on 30 monkfish tails from the fish company and a crate of artichokes from the produce company. To top it off, my beurre blanc looked more like a beurre broken, the meat cook had stolen the only heavy-bottomed pot in the kitchen, and the dishwasher wouldn't wash the special baking sheets I needed to cook salmon.

11:26 a.m. A random taste test reveals that the parsley I had so meticulously washed, dried, and chopped for lunch service was gritty.

11:28 a.m. A hush falls over the kitchen and I can hear Chef Daniel Boulud yelling for people to move out of the way. I watch as a hand truck snakes its way through the kitchen carrying some strange cargo. It's a giant (about 20-pound) Alaskan king crab, still alive and moving its legs. The head is fairly large and the eyes relatively small, but I swear this crab makes eye contact with me as it is wheeled, kicking and flinching, over to my station. Toto, the restaurant's steward, stops the hand truck right in front of me and gives me a sadistic grin. "I know you're really busy and it's almost lunchtime but . . ." and then Daniel steps in with, "Cook this crab, Alexandra, and we will shell it and serve it to the president of the French Republic who is coming for lunch in forty-five minutes!"

11:32 a.m. Using all my strength, I gingerly drop the crab into the simmering water and watch it turn bright red. I lift it up out of the water and onto a tray and stash it, to cool off, in the walk-in refrigerator.

11:56 a.m. T-minus 34 minutes until the French president arrives for his chilled crab. I look over at the stove and wonder how many things could be burning. Did I have something in the oven? I can't think straight. With newfound resolve, I go into the walk-in refrigerator and stand in front of the crab. In one deft motion, I twist off one of its long legs and cover it with my apron.

11:57 a.m. I snake my way down the back staircase and scoot down the hallway to the employee bathroom. Yes. The bathroom. The only place that is really safe in the whole restaurant if you want a moment to yourself. I test the doorknob, praying there isn't someone in there already. Imagine trying to look natural standing in a hallway holding a king crab leg: "Hey, how's it going? How are the wife and kids doing?" I imagine myself saying. Luckily, the door is unlocked.

11:59 a.m. I lock the bathroom door and look down at the crab leg, glistening, fresh, still slightly warm from being cooked, and realize I can't remember the last time I ate anything. I tear at the shell and pry a huge chunk of the meat from inside. I take a bite. It tastes like the ocean but so sweet. The meat is the perfect temperature and the flesh so tender. I tear at the rest of the crabmeat like a wild animal.

(To this day, this is the best thing I ever ate. And, just to provide perspective, I ate that crab fourteen years ago.)

12:04 p.m. I realize that I am standing in the middle of a bathroom holding a crab shell. I wrap the shell in towels and wash my face and hands of the crime. On my way back to my station, I grab a few legs and stash them in the fridge below my cutting board to shell them for the French president. I smile at the thought that, in some very small way, he and I were sharing lunch.

blackened salmon

The classic way to blacken fish is to take the fillets, dip them in melted butter, and then coat them with a spice or blackening mixture and fry them up. The butter adds richness and gives the spices an opportunity to stick to the fish. One might argue my method is less than authentic because I cook the fish in hot oil. I just find browning fish so much easier in oil, which has a higher smoke point. The key here is to be fearless. This method of cooking creates a fair amount of smoke in the kitchen. Tools for success? A good cast-iron skillet to cook the fish in and fresh spices that provide maximum flavor. In the photo, the salmon was deboned without separating the two fillets, then put back together, cut into steaks, and tied with string. **SERVES 4**

Spices

This is an investment I believe in making. For every jar of spice you buy, your cooking will be enhanced many times over. But keep in mind that spices lose their zing over time, so always buy the smallest amounts possible and replenish as you need them. I grew up on Spice Islands and really love that brand to this day. I also love Penzey's and the Spice House (see Sources). I could invest in five types of cinnamon alone from them! Another thing, buy what you love. My dad's favorite salad dressing when I was a kid was built on a mound of garlic powder. If you like it, buy it and use it!

SPICE MIX

1 tablespoon hot paprika
2 teaspoons cayenne pepper
2 teaspoons garlic powder
2 teaspoons kosher salt
1 teaspoon ground black pepper
1 teaspoon dried oregano

FISH

8 tablespoons (1 stick) unsalted butter, 4 tablespoons (½ stick) melted, plus 4 tablespoons cut into small cubes
4 (7- to 8-ounce) pieces skin-on wild salmon, preferably center cut, pin bones removed, each 1¼ to 1¾ inches thick
2 tablespoons canola oil
1 lemon, halved

1. Over low heat, start to heat a cast-iron skillet large enough to hold the fish in a single layer.

2. Make the spice mix: In a small bowl, combine the paprika, cayenne, garlic powder, salt, pepper, and oregano. Mix to blend.

3. Prepare the fish: Spread the spice mixture on a plate. Pour the melted butter onto a plate with low edges. Working with one piece at a time, dip both sides of the salmon in the melted butter and then in the spice mix. Arrange the fish carefully on a baking sheet.

4. Cook the fish: When the skillet is hot, shut off the heat and add the oil. When the oil begins to smoke quite heavily, add the salmon, one by one, flesh side down, in a single layer in the oil. Turn the heat back on under the pan to high heat and cook for 2 to 3 minutes. Use a spatula to flip the pieces of fish over. Cook the salmon over medium heat until the skin becomes crisp, 5 to 8 minutes. The inside should be between medium-rare and medium. During the last 2 minutes of cooking, add the cubes of fresh butter to different areas of the pan and baste the fish with the butter. Squirt some lemon juice over the fish. Arrange on a platter and serve immediately.

roasted whole mackerel

I comb cookbooks all the time for ideas about what to cook. I am a firm believer in constantly feeding the imagination with ideas, old and new. When I come across this type of recipe, it's actually a pet peeve: Take fish, season it with salt and pepper, and douse it with lemon. Why is this recipe cookbook-worthy when I can bumble my way through that simply enough as a home cook? The answer is that sometimes the way you cook a fish can change your perspective on something you've cooked many times before.

So, here I am plugging an undercelebrated fish—mackerel, either Boston or Spanish (bluefish is just as delicious)—and cooking it whole. Like meat, fish is wonderful roasted on the bone. Use this recipe as a jumping off point to roasting other types of whole fish. I am also advocating a different method of getting the fish into the oven, one my dad used while I was growing up. I loved watching him run over to the oven, fish cradled under one arm (as if it were a football), tossing the fish onto the hot pan, and quickly closing the oven door. Fun. Athletic. Simple. **SERVES 2**

---

1 whole mackerel, 2 to 3 pounds, gutted, gills removed (or 2 smaller fish)
Extra-virgin olive oil, for drizzling
Flaky sea salt, such as Maldon
3 lemons, 2 cut into ¼-inch slices, plus 1 lemon, cut into wedges
1 small bunch fresh thyme

1. Preheat the oven to 450°F.

2. Put a baking sheet on the rack in the center of the hot oven and close the door. Let it heat for at least 10 minutes.

3. Cook the fish: Drizzle both sides of the fish with olive oil and season inside and out with salt. Stuff the head and cavity with the lemon slices and thyme sprigs. The cavity is shallow so some may fall out. You can tie the fish closed in a few places using kitchen string if you'd like, but it's not strictly necessary.

recipe continues

4. Open the oven door and carry the fish over squarely in both of your hands. Squirt a little olive oil on the baking sheet, put the fish in the center of the hot baking sheet, and quickly close the door so minimal heat escapes. You should hear the fish sizzle slightly as it hits the hot pan. Cook for 10 to 15 minutes for smaller fish and 20 to 22 minutes for larger ones. Open the door to look at the fish. The eyes will turn white when it's cooked. Pierce the flesh near the head with the tip of a knife. It should be flaky, if cooked. Remove the baking sheet from the oven and allow the fish to rest for a few minutes on the pan.

5. Serve the fish: Use two metal (or at least fairly rigid) spatulas, one under the head and the other under the midsection of the fish, to transfer the fish to a serving platter. Use a paring knife to gently cut around the head and tail. Then cut down the length of the back until you can insert one of your spatulas down the length of the top fillet and lift it off the bone. Then, lift the head and the full backbone off the fish, unveiling the second fillet. Season the fish with salt to taste. Serve with lemon wedges.

Vegetable Garnishes

1. Tomate Confite – for preparation, see "saveurs d'agneau."

2. Cherry Tomato Confite – In a casserole of oil "pepins de raisin" add thyme, bay leaf, rosemary and confit the cherry tomatoes until they are cooked but not too cooked. Remove and drain.

3. Strips of zucchini – for basic preparation, see "saveurs d'agneau" coated well w/ a bit of tomato concassée (and a drop of red wine - I think)

To make the sauce: Take the tuna bones and cook them in the oven, like for a beef stock. Deglaze afterward with sherry vinegar and cover with chicken stock. Let reduce, then add salt and pepper.

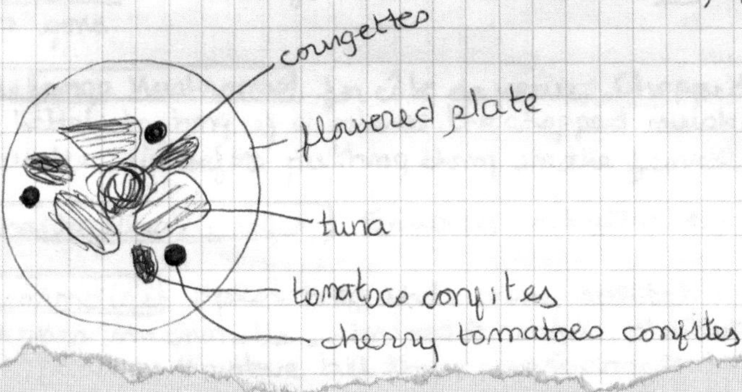

broiled bluefish with corn and bacon

I had sticker shock when I last hit the retail fish counter. How does anyone pay their rent or mortgage and buy and cook fish at the same time? Bluefish remains relatively cheap and very flavorful, provided you like your fish to taste like something. Here, the sugar in the corn is meant to heighten the natural sweetness of the fish's flesh, and the smokiness of the bacon brings out the bacony flavor the bluefish skin has once seared and crisp. This is a dish that makes me feel truly American, with great American ingredients grouped together to taste even better. **SERVES 8**

Cleaning Corn

Sometimes I feel like old school defines itself with a rustic touch and with food that isn't perfect or manicured. I love corn on the cob and getting it stuck in my teeth and using it as an excuse to eat a stick of butter. But for this recipe, you want the corn kernels only. Shuck your corn, remove the silky strands, but don't trim the stalk at all. Wipe the corn with a damp kitchen towel to really clean it. Then, holding onto the stalk at the end, rest the tip of the cob on a cutting board, holding the cob at an angle. Use a fairly large knife and slide it down the length of the cob to cut away the kernels. Don't dig too deep with the knife; take the kernels and leave the chewy cob behind. Rotate the cob after each cut so you go around the whole of it.

8 slices bacon, cut into ½-inch pieces
Kernels from 8 to 10 ears of corn (3½ to 4 cups total)
1 teaspoon packed dark brown sugar
Kosher salt
3 tablespoons canola oil
8 (6- to 7-ounce) skin-on pieces bluefish
1 scallion (green and white part), cut into thin rounds
1 teaspoon red wine vinegar
1 to 2 lemons, to taste, halved

1. Preheat the broiler.

2. Cook the bacon and corn: Heat a medium skillet over medium heat and add the bacon. Cook the bacon, stirring often, until crisp, 5 to 8 minutes. Use a slotted spoon or spatula to remove the bacon and keep it on a kitchen towel someplace warm. Add the corn and brown sugar to

recipe continues

the skillet. Stir to coat with the bacon grease and season with salt. Add ¼ cup water and cook, stirring from time to time, until most but not all of the liquid evaporates, 2 to 3 minutes. The corn should be lightly browned but also juicy.

3. Broil the fish: Meanwhile, put an ovenproof sauté pan on top of the stove over low heat. Add the canola oil. Season the pieces of bluefish on both sides with salt and put them, skin side up, in the sauté pan. Put the pan under the broiler and cook until the fish crisps and the fish flesh is opaque, 5 to 7 minutes, depending on the thickness of the fish. If the skin starts to burn before the fish is cooked, finish cooking the fish in the oven at 350°F.

4. Serve the fish: Stir the scallions and vinegar into the corn mixture. Arrange the bluefish on a platter or individual plates. Squeeze the lemon juice directly on the fish. Top with the corn mixture. Serve immediately.

vegetables
like I remember them

grilled radicchio with honey and hazelnuts

braised savoy cabbage with jalapeños

smoky shallots

roasted garlic

roasted brussels sprouts

beer-braised carrots

corn on the cob with aleppo-garlic butter

mashed potatoes "chantilly"

mashed and oven-dried sweet potatoes

green bean casserole

slow-roasted tomatoes with tarragon dressing

my favorite rice pilaf

My love of vegetables was renewed by an unusual source.

Sometime around midnight, we heard Prince was planning a late-night dinner. No further detail was given. I felt like someone was going to sprinkle purple glitter in front of the restaurant in honor of his arrival.

At 12:30 a.m., the dinner service ends and we clean the kitchen. Three cooks and I each crack a cold beer and sit down to wait. 1 a.m. Second beer. 1:30 a.m. Third and fourth beers. 2 a.m. Making grilled cheese sandwiches and burritos and drinking more beer. We finish with a nap in a couple of the booths downstairs.

2:45 a.m. "Chef." Mike, the dining room manager, taps me gently on the shoulder and I jump up out of my cocoon in the booth that makes up table 52. "He's here," he says with a grin, "with two guests. And he has some rules. . . ."

I am given the following instructions: Go to the table and ask him what he wants to eat but *do not* make eye contact with him or any of his guests and *do not* offer any meat or fish whatsoever.

I go to the table, shaky, sleepy, and somewhat tipsy to greet Prince, Lenny Kravitz, and saxophonist Maceo Parker.

"What can I make for you?" I ask timidly, looking at the floor.

Silence.

I lift one eyelid a little and see that he really is wearing a purple suit.

"Um . . . Do you have some vegetables . . . Maybe some pasta?"

"Sure . . . Maybe some pasta with bacon?" Oops. Did I really just say that?

"No bacon," he answered softly.

"OK. Sure." I spin on my heels and go back to the kitchen.

We pillage the walk-in fridge, gathering all of the vegetables from the market.

"Let's make little plates of different vegetables," I say excitedly.

I make asparagus dressed in a sherry vinaigrette with sesame seeds, batter-dipped zucchini blossoms with paprika, roasted potatoes with pickled onions, grilled eggplant with garlic, farfalle with mushrooms and cream, and marinated beets with scallions.

We bring out the food and then return to the kitchen to pack up and go home.

It is now 4:34 a.m.

"Chef!" Mike comes barreling into the kitchen. "Prince wants to talk to you for a minute."

"Your food was great," Prince says softly. "You have a real command of food and ingredients."

"Thanks," I say to the floor.

"Who are some chefs who inspire you?" he asks.

"I have many," I answer, half thrilled, half wanting to melt into the floorboards.

"Would it help you if I told you some of the musicians that inspire me?" he asks.

"Yes," I respond.

"Me!" he answers simply.

"And for the record," he adds, "I think you are part of the New Power Generation."

I look up and right into the eyes of his Purpleness. Stunning. Everything I imagined he would be and more.

And I have had the honor of cooking for him many times since.

grilled radicchio with honey and hazelnuts

I know. You don't want to buy radicchio because you think that it's bitter. I understand. But that bitter edge is actually delicious and even more so when you cook radicchio simply, with a char from the grill, finish it in the oven, and pair it with raspberries to add sweetness and hazelnuts to add richness. I love when the edges of the radicchio get crisp like parchment. **SERVES 8**

---

3 medium heads radicchio (about 3 pounds total), outer leaves trimmed, quartered through the core
½ cup extra-virgin olive oil, plus more if needed
Kosher salt
½ cup honey
½ cup raspberry vinegar
⅓ cup fresh raspberries
¼ cup hazelnuts, roughly chopped

1. Preheat the grill to high heat. Clean the grates well and lightly oil them. Preheat oven to 350°F.

2. Cook the radicchio: Pour ¼ cup of the olive oil onto a baking sheet and arrange the wedges of radicchio in a single layer. Drizzle with the remaining ¼ cup olive oil and then massage them so the oil has a chance to soak into the layers. Season generously.

3. Arrange the radicchio in a single layer on a moderately hot part of the grill and cook on the first flat side until browned and lightly charred, 5 to 8 minutes. Grill on the second flat side for an additional 5 to 8 minutes. Put them back on the baking sheet and roast in the oven until tender when pierced with the tip of a knife, 10 to 15 minutes. Taste and season with salt.

4. Make the honey sauce: Cook the honey in a medium saucepan over medium heat until light to medium brown, 3 to 5 minutes. If you can't see the color of the honey because of the foam, remove the pan from the heat and gently move the foam aside with a spoon. Add the vinegar (it will bubble up) and raspberries and then return the pan to the heat. Simmer over low heat until it becomes syrupy and can coat the back of a spoon, 2 to 3 minutes.

5. Serve the dish: Arrange the radicchio on a platter and drizzle liberally with the sauce. Top with the hazelnuts and serve immediately.

braised savoy cabbage with jalapeños

I love cabbage, and this is my favorite way to cook it. The flavors of these spices and the addition of tomato and jalapeño make it addictive. I have eaten a bowl of this on its own; I have paired it with chicken; I have even put a mound of it on a turkey sandwich instead of regular coleslaw. While I appreciate the romance of using fresh tomatoes in most cases, I actually welcome the juices from the can in this recipe. It's almost as if the tomatoes sink in and become a part of the cabbage party much faster this way. This is not a dish that needs to cook forever because you develop deep flavors as you go along, especially when you toast the spices in the beginning to wake them from their slumber in your kitchen cabinet. If you like it less spicy, reduce the amount of jalapeño. **SERVES 4**

---

2 tablespoons unsalted butter
2 teaspoons cumin seeds
2 teaspoons caraway seeds
2 teaspoons coriander seeds, lightly crushed
2 small heads Savoy cabbage, cored, ribs removed, leaves thinly sliced into 3/8-inch slices
Kosher salt and white pepper
2 (2-inch) knobs fresh ginger, peeled and finely grated (2 tablespoons)
1 teaspoon ground ginger
1 (28-ounce) can whole peeled tomatoes and their juices
1 small jalapeño chile (seeds, ribs, and all), cut into thin rounds
2 tablespoons fresh cilantro leaves, finely chopped
1 tablespoon cider vinegar

1. Toast the spices: In a large sauté pan, melt the butter over medium heat. Add the cumin, caraway, and coriander seeds and toast them slightly for 30 seconds. Do not let them brown.

2. Cook the cabbage: Immediately add the cabbage. Toss to coat with the butter and spices. Season with salt and pepper and stir to blend. Cook over medium heat, stirring from time to time, until wilted with a slight bite, 10 to 15 minutes. Taste for seasoning. Stir in the fresh ginger, ground ginger, tomatoes (with their juice), and jalapeños. Simmer until the cabbage is tender, 5 to 8 minutes. Taste for seasoning. Add the cilantro and cider vinegar. Enjoy!

chiles new york 1978

Esteemed Indian food authority Julie Sahni was there, in my parents' kitchen, to cook a feast. My mother discovered her by reading a few sentences about her in some obscure section of the *New York Times* and invited her to cook dinner.

Pierre Franey and Paula Wolfert (both famous cooks and food writers) were to be the dinner guests that night.

She came dressed in a beautiful sari, arms loaded with grocery bags. In simple, ten-year-old child terms, she smelled strange to me. Like an odd blend of some potpourri mixed with the aroma of garlic and chiles I sometimes smelled coming out of the Chinese restaurant on my block. She pulled out ingredients, various spices (such beautiful colors!) like turmeric and cumin, fresh cilantro, basmati rice, and an array of different chiles (they looked innocent enough). In fact, many were a beautiful, vibrant green color.

I had never seen any of these things before.

She removed one of the burners on the stove and began heating a wok partially filled with oil. It looked like a volcano ready to blow.

The oil fizzled and sizzled from time to time as she prepared the ingredients and began a steady chatter in my direction as if I were a fully grown person and a chef to boot. I couldn't stop staring at the wok. "We're going to fry some of these beautiful chiles to mellow out their flavor and enhance their texture," she said, grinning. She tossed some poblanos straight into the oil and I shielded my eyes. I had never felt scared in the kitchen before. The chiles hissed and spit like ferocious mountain cats as they hit the oil and suddenly the air was thick with the spice. She immediately shut off the gas underneath the wok. I opened the front door and ran all the way down the hallway of my apartment building gasping for breath. Spicy air? Never thought that could happen.

A few minutes later, I returned to the kitchen as she fished the chiles from the oil.

This is the part where you think I tell you those chiles were the best thing I ever tasted and how I have loved them ever since, right?

Hope not. Because the meal was delicious *except* for the chiles, which burned a hole in my mouth and then my belly. It took me many years to develop a trusting relationship with fresh chiles, in fact. One of the recipes that made me fall in love with them was braised cabbage with jalapeños (opposite).

smoky shallots

These are so delicious next to a steak, roasted chicken, or meaty fish. The technique is simple enough and the kind that leaves you feeling so satisfied when you pull it off at home. I am mostly an applewood chip gal myself, but smell the chips available at the store and go with the type that resonates with you. The aroma of burning wood actually makes my stomach growl! **SERVES 4 TO 6**

---

1 cup wood chips, preferably applewood
18 medium shallots (about 1 pound total), all relatively the same size, peeled
1 tablespoon extra-virgin olive oil
Kosher salt
2 tablespoons unsalted butter
1 teaspoon sugar
1 tablespoon sherry vinegar

1. Preheat the oven to 350°F.

2. Prepare the wood chips: Soak the wood chips in cold water for about 15 minutes.

3. Smoke the shallots: Line a large wok with foil if you like, or use a Dutch oven. Drain the wood chips from the water and put them in the wok. Set a steamer basket over the wood chips and put the shallots in the basket. Cover the entire wok with large sheets of foil, crimping to create a tight seal. Heat the wok over medium heat until smoke starts to emerge from the chips. Lower the heat and allow the shallots to smoke for about 1 hour without disturbing them. Carefully remove the lid and check the shallots. They should smell smoky. Set them aside to rest until cool enough to handle.

4. Finish the shallots: In a large skillet, heat the butter over medium heat. Add the sugar and shallots and cook over medium heat, tossing to coat with the butter, until the shallots are tender, 5 to 8 minutes. Stir in the vinegar and allow it to reduce for a minute. Season with salt to taste.

roasted garlic

I have eaten this by simply scooping the soft garlic cloves from their little homes and sprinkling them with Maldon salt. You can add a few cloves of roasted garlic to a vinaigrette and blend it until smooth to give it body and richness; I have also enriched gravy this way instead of whisking in flour. But I really love pan-frying roasted garlic for a few minutes in some oil until the cloves develop a crispy exterior but are still tender inside. To me, they taste almost like candy. Eat as is or toss on top of some hanger steak (page 106), roasted chicken (page 130), into a sandwich, or even on top of a salad (such as Greenmarket Caesar; page 76) for cool gluten-free croutons. I also love these with some creamy cheese, like Brie, and grilled bread.

SERVES 4 TO 6 AS A SIDE COMPANION

---

4 medium heads garlic (about 12 ounces total), halved crosswise
¼ cup extra-virgin olive oil
Flaky sea salt, such as Maldon
1 tablespoon canola oil
Splash of red wine vinegar

1. Preheat the oven to 350°F.

2. Prepare the garlic: Arrange the 4 bottom halves of the garlic heads in a single layer on a sheet of aluminum foil large enough to fold back over the garlic. Drizzle with the olive oil and sprinkle with salt. Top with the other halves so it looks like 4 heads of garlic that have been split and reassembled. Fold the foil back over the garlic and crimp the edges to seal it.

3. Roast the garlic: Put the foil package into the oven and cook until the garlic is tender when pierced with the tip of a knife, about 1 hour. Remove from the oven, carefully open the foil, and allow the garlic to cool slightly.

4. Pan-fry the garlic: Use a small spoon to scoop out the garlic cloves; discard the papery casing. Heat a large skillet over low heat. Add the canola oil. When the oil begins to make waves when you tilt the pan but isn't yet smoking, remove the pan from the heat and sprinkle the cloves over the oil in a single layer. Return the pan to the heat and cook over low heat, turning the cloves so they don't become overly brown. You want a crisp exterior, light to golden brown; this should take 1 to 2 minutes. Remove cloves as they become light brown. The smaller ones will cook more quickly. Season immediately with salt and a splash of red wine vinegar and serve.

roasted brussels sprouts

I innocently put a side of Brussels sprouts on the menu when I opened The Darby. I thought we would sell a few here and there to the few people who don't go for the crispy potatoes or the baked macaroni. The preparation is simple enough. In fact, when I cooked them for the first time, I worried they needed more. I ate Brussels sprouts in various restaurants around the city and found that they often (and rightfully) get drowned in bacon or maple syrup. Delicious. But not what I wanted. This recipe is all about texture. The crispy leaves on top almost taste like dried seaweed to me, making this a great companion for any fish dish. **SERVES 6 TO 8**

1½ pounds Brussels sprouts, ends trimmed
2 tablespoons extra-virgin olive oil
1 teaspoon sugar
½ teaspoon grated nutmeg
Kosher salt
1 quart canola oil
¼ cup reduced balsamic vinegar (see Tip)

1. Preheat the oven to 350°F.

2. Cook the Brussels sprouts: Trim the end of each Brussels sprout so that the first few layers of leaves come off easily. Peel away a couple layers of leaves. Set those leaves aside in a large bowl. Halve each remaining sprout lengthwise. Put the Brussels sprout halves in a bowl and toss them together with the olive oil and a couple pinches of salt. Put the nutmeg in a fine mesh strainer and dust the Brussels sprouts evenly with it. Arrange in a single layer on a baking sheet. Put a baking dish in the lower part of the oven and fill it with an inch or so of water. This will create some steam as the Brussels sprouts cook. The combination of the steam from the water and the dry heat from the oven will give your Brussels sprouts a more intense flavor and texture. Cook the Brussels sprouts until tender, 20 to 25 minutes. Taste one and season with salt as needed.

3. Fry the Brussels sprout leaves: In a large, deep, heavy-bottomed pot (or deep-fryer), heat the canola oil slowly to 375°F. Line a baking sheet with a kitchen towel to drain the leaves. Drop a small batch of the leaves in the oil (watch out, the oil will spatter and bubble up; wear a long oven mitt and hold the pot cover loosely over the pot to use as a shield). Fry the leaves until crisp, 30 to 60 seconds. Use a slotted spoon to transfer the leaves to the baking sheet to drain. Season immediately with salt so it sticks to the leaves while they're hot. Repeat until all of the leaves are fried. (Go ahead. Taste one. Aren't those leaves good? I have served these on their own as a snack like potato chips.)

4. Finish the dish: Remove the Brussels sprouts from the oven, season to taste with salt, and drizzle with a little bit of the reduced balsamic vinegar to taste. Arrange on a platter and top with the fried leaves. Serve immediately.

Old-school tip

There is nothing like aged balsamic vinegar. When you think about vinegar sitting for that many years before we enjoy it, it's as amazing as a fine wine. The taste is one thing, but you also get that wonderful syrupy texture. But boy is it expensive! So let's go rogue for a minute: Pour 1 cup regular balsamic vinegar into a saucepan and slowly simmer over low heat to reduce it until it is about ¼ cup or until it holds a line when drizzled on a plate. Be careful because it will go from syrup to burned vinegar quickly. So watch it. Immediately transfer it to a bowl to cool so it stops cooking and doesn't reduce too much or burn.

beer-braised carrots

These are simple to make. I have tried this recipe with many different types of more expensive beer and have drawn one conclusion. Pour the fancy beer in a glass and drink it with a steak and some of these delicious carrots. For cooking purposes, Heineken leaves behind a pleasant sweetness and a faint yeasty taste that I love. The brown sugar and the flavor of the carrots are a complete throwback to childhood for me. This recipe, less the beer, is something I requested as the ultimate comfort food—and when comfort food usually leaves you in a sea of macaroni and potatoes, carrots can be a welcome change and a real sleeper hit with your family.

SERVES 4 TO 6

---

4 tablespoons unsalted butter
1 teaspoon coriander seeds
½ teaspoon caraway seeds
12 medium to small carrots (about 1¼ pounds total), thoroughly peeled, stems removed, and halved lengthwise
Kosher salt
3 tablespoons packed light brown sugar
1 (12-ounce) bottle lager, such as Heineken

1. Cook the carrots: Heat a skillet large enough to hold the carrot halves in a single layer over medium-high heat and add the butter. When the butter melts and starts to brown, add the coriander and caraway seeds and toss to coat with the butter. Toast the spices for a minute in the butter. When they become fragrant, add the carrot halves and toss to coat with the butter. Season with salt and add the brown sugar.

2. Finish the dish: Continue to cook the carrots over medium heat until the sugar dissolves and coats the carrots, another minute or two. Add the beer and continue cooking the carrots until they are tender when pierced with the tip of a knife, 25 to 30 minutes. If the beer cooks down completely before the carrots are tender, add a splash of water to finish the cooking process, if needed. Taste for seasoning. Serve immediately.

Old-school tip

Painstaking carrot peeling? I'd love to say "don't sweat it!" but the fewer nicks you make as you peel, the smoother it will be once cooked. Rest the carrot tip at an angle on a flat surface. Hold the other end and peel in long strokes from one end down to the other. That smoother texture changes how you eat it and how your mouth evaluates the carrot (and the taste).

corn on the cob with aleppo-garlic butter

It's hard to beat the taste of corn bought from a roadside stand. I always pick the ears where the outer leaves cling tightly to the cob. They are the most freshly picked. Similarly, I avoid buying corn wrapped in plastic or trimmed on both ends for "easier" eating; these ears tend to be dry and less fresh tasting. For this recipe, remove the outer leaves and inner layer of silk. Then wipe the corn with a damp cloth to remove any stubborn excess strands that may cling directly to the kernels. I have made corn so many different ways, but this is my favorite way to cook it whole. I cook it in water first to make it juicier and then intensify the flavor with roasting and brushing with tasty butter. Why Aleppo pepper? The Turkish pepper has a unique smoky flavor. It also rides the line between sweet and spicy, which makes the corn taste like a better version of itself! **SERVES 6**

Kosher salt
6 ears corn, shucked
2 tablespoons granulated sugar
4 tablespoons (½ stick) unsalted butter
2 tablespoons packed dark brown sugar
6 medium garlic cloves, grated
1 tablespoon Aleppo pepper

1. Preheat the oven to 350°F.

2. Cook the corn: Bring a large pot of water to a boil. Add salt until it tastes like mild seawater. Drop the ears of corn and sugar into the boiling water and allow them to cook for about 5 minutes. With a slotted spoon, transfer them to a kitchen towel to drain.

3. Prepare the butter: In a small saucepan, gently melt the butter. Use a small whisk to incorporate the brown sugar, garlic, and Aleppo pepper. Simmer for a few seconds, stirring until it forms a paste. The butter will want to separate out. Keep whisking to hold it together.

4. Roast the corn: Lightly brush the ears of corn on all sides with the butter mixture and arrange them in a single layer on a baking sheet. Roast until they start to brown, 8 to 10 minutes. Remove from the oven and brush with the remaining butter.

mashed potatoes "chantilly"

My mother made this every year in the same cranberry-colored baking dish. In fact, when I see anything cranberry-colored in a cookware store, I start to think of eating a huge bowl of these mashed potatoes. A "luxe" version of mashed potatoes, these have whipped cream folded in (hence the "Chantilly" part of the name) as well as Parmesan cheese. Alas, this is a recipe that shouldn't be made in advance. The potatoes become like a soufflé. Sublime. **SERVES 8**

4½ to 5 pounds Idaho potatoes (about 10 medium), peeled and cut into 1-inch chunks
Kosher salt and white pepper
¾ cup whole milk
8 tablespoons (1 stick) unsalted butter, cut into slices, plus 1 tablespoon for greasing the baking dish
2 tablespoons plain dried bread crumbs
1 cup heavy cream
¾ cup finely grated Parmesan

1. Preheat the oven to 375°F.

2. Boil the potatoes: In a large pot, add the potatoes and cover amply with cold water. Bring the water up to a boil and reduce the heat so that it simmers. Add a generous pinch of salt to the water and allow the potatoes to cook until tender when pierced with the tip of a knife, 15 to 20 minutes. Drain the potatoes in a colander. Return the empty pot to the heat and add the milk. Bring the milk to a simmer and gingerly add the potatoes back into the pot. Season with salt and pepper and whisk in the sliced butter. Whisk until all of the ingredients meld together. Taste for seasoning. Remove from the heat.

3. Use the remaining tablespoon butter to grease the sides and bottom of a 9 × 13-inch baking dish with 2-inch sides. Add the bread crumbs and roll them around to coat the inside of the dish.

4. Bake the potatoes: Using a whisk (or an electric mixer fitted with the whisk attachment), whip the heavy cream until fairly firm. Season with salt and pepper. With a rubber spatula, gently fold the whipped cream and about ½ cup of the Parmesan into the mashed potatoes. Taste for seasoning. Transfer the potatoes to the baking dish and top with the remaining ¼ cup Parmesan. Bake until the top is light brown and the potatoes are hot, 15 to 20 minutes. Serve immediately.

mashed and oven-dried sweet potatoes

I love roasting whole sweet potatoes. I also love making mashed sweet potatoes without boiling them in water. No fuss. No mess. Once the potatoes are baked, split open, and the flesh recovered, it almost feels as if maximum flavor potential has been decided. Drying out the sweet potatoes after mashing them intensifies their flavor even more. Though I always love milk and cream, I find they actually detract from the true taste of the sweet potatoes. A little orange juice, sherry vinegar, and maybe some butter to brighten them and I call it a day. I won't rule out the tiniest drizzle of honey, if you find this needs a little sweetness. **SERVES 4**

---

2 pounds medium sweet potatoes (about 5), scrubbed
Kosher salt
2 tablespoons orange juice, not freshly squeezed
1½ teaspoons sherry vinegar
4 tablespoons unsalted butter, melted (optional)

1. Preheat the oven to 400°F.

2. Cook the sweet potatoes: Put the potatoes right on the oven rack. No foil. No baking sheet. This will allow the oven heat to circulate more freely around the potatoes as they cook. Put a layer of foil on the floor of the oven to avoid messy cleanup. Roast until the potatoes are completely yielding in the center when pierced with the tip of a knife, 1 hour to 1 hour 30 minutes, depending on their size. Remove from the oven and lower the oven temperature to 300°F.

3. Mash the sweet potatoes: Use a sharp knife to cut lengthwise down the middle of each sweet potato. Scoop out the flesh with a tablespoon, leaving the skin behind. Transfer the flesh to a food processor and pulse to blend until smooth. Do not overblend or it will make the potatoes gummy. Put the potato in a medium ovenproof dish. Spread it out in an even layer.

4. Bake the sweet potatoes: Once the oven registers 300°F, bake the sweet potatoes for 10 minutes and then give the flesh a stir again. Bake for an additional 10 minutes. Remove from the oven. Transfer the sweet potato flesh to a medium bowl and season with salt. Stir in some of the orange juice, the sherry vinegar, and butter, if using. Taste for seasoning. Add more orange juice, if needed.

green bean casserole

This recipe was cleverly conceived by Campbell's Soup in the fifties to encourage the use of their products and the result has been millions of bastardized versions of a perfectly good dish. Here, we will make it from scratch and enjoy the richness with the different textures. I look at this as a form of vegetarian stew. The mushrooms and cream make the green beans so juicy. I am always surprised at how much taste the green beans have in this recipe. **SERVES 8 TO 10**

Kosher salt
1 pound string beans, ends trimmed, halved
4 tablespoons unsalted butter
1 pound white mushrooms, stemmed and sliced into ½-inch slices (about 4 cups)
1½ teaspoons cayenne pepper
1 teaspoon Dijon mustard
4 garlic cloves, minced
¼ cup plus 2 tablespoons all-purpose flour
1 cup low-sodium chicken broth
1 cup heavy cream
1 cup sour cream
4 cups canola oil
2 medium red onions, cut into thin rounds

1. Bring 6 quarts water to a boil in a large pot. Fill a large bowl halfway with ice cubes and add some cold water. Set a colander squarely inside the ice bath. The colander will keep you from having to pick the ice out of the beans.

2. Prepare the green beans: When the water boils, add 2 tablespoons salt and the green beans. Cook until the beans yield slightly when pierced with the tip of a knife, 4 minutes. Using a strainer, remove the green beans from the hot water and transfer them to the colander inside the ice bath. Swirl the beans around in the bath so they cool quickly. Drain and set aside.

3. Make the mushroom base: In a 10-inch cast-iron or other ovenproof skillet over medium heat, melt the butter and add the mushrooms. Season with salt, 1 teaspoon of the cayenne, and the mustard. Stir to blend and cook until the mushrooms give off most of their liquid, 3 to 5 minutes. Using a whisk, add the garlic and 2 tablespoons of the flour. When all of the flour has been incorporated, add the chicken broth. Bring to a boil. Taste for seasoning. Stir in the cream and sour cream and simmer gently. Continue cooking over low heat

recipe continues

until the mixture thickens, 3 to 5 minutes. You should have about 2 cups

4. Preheat the oven to 350°F.

5. Fry the onions: Meanwhile, pour the oil into a medium frying pan. Heat to 350°F. Line a baking sheet with a kitchen towel and have ready a slotted spoon.

6. In a medium bowl, combine the remaining ¼ cup flour and remaining ½ teaspoon cayenne. Toss the onion rounds in the flour and shake off excess by shaking the rounds in a strainer. Test the oil by dropping in one onion slice. It should begin to bubble and fry gradually. Drop a small batch of the onions into the oil and gently swirl them as they fry. When they are light to medium brown, 1 to 2 minutes, remove with the slotted spoon and lay them out on the kitchen towel to cool. Sprinkle with salt. Repeat until all of the onions have been fried.

7. Assemble the casserole: Stir the green beans into the mushrooms. Simmer on the stove, over low heat, until the green beans become tender when pierced with the tip of a knife, 10 to 15 minutes. Stir in half of the onions. Transfer the skillet to the oven for 10 minutes to give the casserole that baked effect. Top the outside of the dish with the remaining onions and serve.

MASHED AND OVEN-DRIED SWEET POTATOES

GREEN BEAN CASSEROLE

Old-school tip

Here's a way to make tomatoes taste more like their true selves: Sprinkle powdered sugar on them. It will not only add sweetness but also enrich the red color. We associate our best tomato memories with a certain sweetness against the tang of the skin and bitterness of the seeds. That bit of sugar will bring you closer to that dream tomato.

slow-roasted tomatoes with tarragon dressing

I am always looking for a new way to serve tomatoes. They are underrated as a side dish because they are too often busy doing salad or sauce duty. I like using standard plum tomatoes for this but whatever looks best is what you should buy; I have also made this with cherry and heirloom tomatoes. The taste of the toast in the dressing acts almost like an herbed bread crumb mix, but the vinaigrette also gives welcome acidity, making the tomatoes pop more. Make the whole thing in advance and enjoy cold or serve hot out of the oven. **SERVES 2 TO 4**

TOMATOES

8 plum tomatoes (about 1¼ pounds), halved lengthwise
1 teaspoon confectioners' sugar
1 teaspoon flaky sea salt, such as Maldon
¼ teaspoon black pepper
2 tablespoons extra-virgin olive oil

DRESSING

2 sprigs fresh tarragon, leaves chopped (2 teaspoons)
¼ cup low-sodium chicken broth, boiled and cooled
½ (4-inch square) slice of bread, preferably white or brioche, toasted
1 tablespoon cider vinegar
1 small shallot, chopped (1 heaping tablespoon)
¼ cup canola oil

1. Preheat the oven to 375°F. Line a baking sheet with foil or parchment paper.

2. Roast the tomatoes: Put the tomato halves cut side up in a single layer on the baking sheet. In a bowl, whisk together the sugar, salt, pepper, and olive oil. Drizzle the mixture evenly over the tomato halves. Put the pan in the oven and roast until the tomatoes are tender, about 1 hour.

3. Make the dressing: In a food processor, blend the tarragon leaves, chicken broth, toast, vinegar, and shallot. With the machine running, slowly drizzle the oil into the mixture so it emulsifies. Taste for seasoning.

4. Drizzle the tomatoes liberally with the dressing and serve.

my favorite rice pilaf

In the case of basmati rice, no matter what my preparation is, I always soak it and use that liquid from the soaking, with precious starches in it, to cook the rice. First I rinse the rice to clean out any small particles and then I cover it with cold water to soak and use as the cooking liquid. I have overcooked and ruined more rice than any human should be allowed to. But this recipe is hypnotic and makes cooking such a simple ingredient easy. I leave the spices in the rice when I serve it. **SERVES 8 TO 10**

---

2 cups basmati rice
2 teaspoons cumin seeds
3 green cardamom pods, lightly crushed, black seeds removed, pods discarded
1 teaspoon fennel seeds
1 (3-inch) cinnamon stick
12 whole black peppercorns
2 tablespoons unsalted butter
2 bay leaves
1 large red onion, finely diced (about 12 ounces)
Kosher salt

1. Preheat the oven to 250°F.

2. Prepare the rice: Put the rice in a strainer and rinse quickly in cold water. Put the rice in a bowl, add 4 cups cold water, and let soak for 30 minutes.

3. Make the spice mix: On a rimmed baking sheet, combine the cumin, cardamom, fennel, cinnamon, and peppercorns. Put in the center of the oven to lightly toast the spices and awaken the flavors, 3 to 5 minutes. Remove the pan and allow the spices to cool.

4. Cook the rice: Heat a medium sauté pan over medium heat and add the butter, bay leaves, and onion. Season with salt and cook until the onion is translucent but not browned, 3 to 5 minutes. Stir in the spices. Drain the rice but reserve the soaking water. Stir in the rice and cook for 2 minutes, until you hear it crackling. Lower the heat if needed. Then add the reserved water. Stir gently. Season with a generous portion of salt and bring the liquid to a simmer over medium heat. Cook the rice over medium-low heat, uncovered and undisturbed, for about 8 minutes. Take a fork (so as not to damage the rice) and flake a few grains off and taste for doneness. It may need another 2 to 4 minutes until cooked. Remove from the heat and allow the rice to rest for 10 minutes before fluffing it gently into a bowl and serving. Remove the bay leaf and cinnamon if desired.

old-school variation

After cooking this, heat some vegetable oil in the bottom of a medium skillet. When the oil begins to smoke lightly, add a thin layer of cooked rice to the pan. Cook over medium heat, stirring from time to time, until the rice starts to crackle and get crisp, 8 to 10 minutes. Season with salt. Serve some of the rice pilaf topped with the crisped rice or put the crisped rice on top of fish or meat and the softer rice underneath it.

dessert

it’s never about hunger

yellow cake with chocolate frosting
and caramel top

orange and dark chocolate tart

enriched chocolate sauce

indian pudding

raspberry doughnuts
with vanilla dipping sauce

sugar-cranberry pie

sour cream pumpkin pie

apple crisp

banana betty

quickie strawberry tartlets

cherry, pasilla chile, and vanilla
custard tart

coffee granita

chewy chocolaty ice cream
cookie sandwiches

butter cookies made for filling

When I am hungry, I imagine myself a wolf in the tundra, my senses sharp, my mind clear: I'm in search of food. But what about dessert? Has anyone ever said, "I'm starving—can't wait to have dessert!"?

The reality is that the recipes in this chapter are good for emotional and culinary well-being but have nothing to do with basic survival. While I believe dessert can take many forms—big or small, simple or complex—it should always be something that you absolutely crave. For me, that is a sweet that does two things: It should take me back to my childhood and bring up all kinds of good taste memories. And it should have an element of surprise, whether from the texture or the temperature of its components.

These recipes try to strike that perfect balance between watching my mother put a Charlotte Russe into the fridge to set up—and the ensuing anticipation of imminent deliciousness—and recreating something I have eaten that I love, like a flourless chocolate tart with a chewy interior from my local bakery.

yellow cake with chocolate frosting and caramel top

The classic name of this dramatic cake is Dobos Torte, which is like a Hungarian little drum cake. At the end, after the towering cake is assembled, you pour warm caramel over the whole thing. It will dry and harden into a crunchy caramel topping, turning this drum-shaped cake into something that crackles when you tap the top. This recipe makes a layer cake into something reminiscent of a crunchy candy bar. Don't be afraid of the caramel. Just cook the sugar over low heat until dark amber and then pour it right over the cake. The cake will melt a little when the hot sugar hits the frosting and that makes the cake slightly imperfect and messy but that adds to the charm. I love it. It's mischievous and unusual. It also happens to be my childhood birthday cake—and, now, Ava's. **SERVES 10 TO 12**

CAKE

2 cups all-purpose flour
2¼ teaspoons baking powder
¾ teaspoon kosher salt
16 tablespoons (2 sticks) lightly salted butter, at room temperature, plus more for greasing the pans
2 cups sugar
6 large eggs
Grated zest and juice of 1 lemon

FROSTING

14 ounces bittersweet chocolate, roughly chopped (about 2¾ cups)
1¼ cups sugar
½ teaspoon kosher salt
2 cups heavy cream
1 teaspoon vanilla extract
12 tablespoons (1½ sticks) lightly salted butter, cut into thin slices

CARAMEL TOP

1 cup sugar
2 teaspoons light corn syrup
Flaky sea salt, such as Maldon (for garnish)

1. Preheat the oven to 350°F. Grease two 8-inch round cake pans with butter.

2. Prepare the cake batter: In a bowl, stir together the flour, baking powder, and salt. In the bowl of a stand mixer fitted with the paddle attachment, beat the butter until smooth, 2 to 3 minutes. Add the sugar and continue beating until the mixture becomes fluffy, 5 to 8 minutes. Add the eggs, one by one, taking care that each one is thoroughly integrated before adding the next. Add the lemon zest and lemon juice and then the flour

recipe continues

mixture and mix until fully blended. Do not overmix.

3. Bake the cake: Divide the batter between the prepared cake pans. Bake until the centers are firm and the tip of a small knife emerges clean when it pierces the center of each cake, 30 to 40 minutes. Remove from the oven, unmold the cakes, and allow to cool thoroughly on a rack.

4. Make the frosting: In a medium bowl, combine the chocolate, sugar, and salt. In a medium saucepan, bring the cream and vanilla to a simmer, about 5 minutes. Pour over the chocolate and stir until all of the chocolate has melted. Gently whisk in the butter slices. Set aside to cool.

5. Frost the cake: When the frosting is cool, whip the frosting in the bowl of a stand mixer fitted with a whisk attachment to lighten it, 1 to 2 minutes. Split each cake in half horizontally so you have 4 equal layers. Put the first cake layer on a rack set over a baking sheet, cut side up. Frost the layer and the remaining ones, stacking them neatly and uniformly on top of each other. Frost the entire outside of the cake as well. Refrigerate for at least 30 minutes so it gets cold.

6. Make the caramel: In a large skillet, heat the sugar and corn syrup over low heat until the sugar melts and turns a caramel color. Swirl the sugar gently in the pan as it cooks so it browns evenly. Take the skillet and pour the caramel over the top of the cake, allowing it to drip down the sides and onto the pan below. It is normal that the hot caramel will melt the frosting slightly. Try to pour it in as even and as thin a layer as you can over the cake. Have fun with it! If the caramel cools before pouring, warm it gently over low heat to loosen it again. Allow the caramel topping to cool and harden on top of the cake, at least 5 to 10 minutes before serving, or up to 1 hour. Do not refrigerate. Sprinkle with a pinch of Maldon salt.

7. Cut the cake: I will not lie. This is not a "neat" cake. When ready to slice,use the heel of a knife to crack the caramel top before cutting slices.The caramel can be a little uneven but I have always found people like it so much, it doesn't matter. This cake is best served at room temperature.

orange and dark chocolate tart

I had my first chocolate-covered orange peel when I was about thirteen years old. I was standing with my parents on a Parisian street corner when my father broke open the fancy little box, parting the tissue paper to reveal these little dark chocolate sticks. I bit into one, anticipating a deep chocolate taste. And I got it. But the chewy orange center was the flavor that really stayed with me. Tangy, pleasantly bitter, and somehow so ideal as a companion for the chocolate. It inspired the flavors of this tart. **SERVES 10 TO 12**

DOUGH

2 cups all-purpose flour, plus more for rolling the dough
¼ cup sugar
½ teaspoon kosher salt
Grated zest of 1 lemon
16 tablespoons (2 sticks) unsalted butter, cut into small cubes, at room temperature
¼ cup ice water

ORANGE TOPPING

½ cup orange marmalade, preferably "chunky"
4 oranges (about 2 pounds), washed

GANACHE

1 cup heavy cream
¼ teaspoon ground cinnamon
9 ounces semisweet chocolate, chopped (1½ cups)

ME WITH MY GOOD FRIEND AND GREAT PASTRY CHEF, COLLEEN GRAPES

1. Preheat the oven to 350°F. Set two racks in the oven.

2. Make the dough: In a food processor, pulse together the flour, sugar, salt, and lemon zest to blend. Transfer the mixture to a bowl and toss (like a salad!) with the cubes of butter. (This mixes the ingredients and reduces the chances of overworking them with the butter. Less mixing means you're less likely to overwork the gluten in the flour and have a tough dough.) Return the mixture to the food processor and pulse 10 to 15 times until crumbly. The butter should be almost thoroughly integrated with the dry ingredients. Pour the ice water through the hole in the top of the machine as you pulse until the ingredients form a loose ball when you pinch them together. Pulse as few times as possible. Transfer the dough to a flat surface and roll into a

recipe continues

ball. Flatten it, wrap in plastic wrap, and refrigerate for at least 1 hour or overnight to let it rest.

3. Bake the oranges: Meanwhile, slice the oranges as thinly as possible into wheels about ⅛ inch thick. Remove any seeds. Lay the orange wheels in a single layer without overlapping them on 2 baking racks each set over a baking sheet. Bake until soft in the center and slightly golden brown around the edges, about 25 minutes. Remove from the oven and let cool.

4. Make the ganache: In a small saucepan, heat the cream and cinnamon over low heat. Put the chocolate in a small heatproof bowl that fits over the saucepan. Use the saucepan of cream as the bottom of a double boiler and melt the chocolate over the cream. When the chocolate is melted and the cream heated, remove both from the heat. Transfer the cream to a separate bowl and allow the chocolate and cream to cool slightly, separately. When they are both somewhat warm, whisk together until smooth. Keep the ganache at room temperature, stirring it from time to time as it cools, while you continue to prepare the tart.

5. Roll the dough: On a lightly floured surface, roll the dough into a circle about ¼ inch thick and about 13 inches across. Transfer to a parchment-lined cookie sheet and refrigerate for 15 minutes.

6. Bake the tart crust: Use a fork to prick the dough all over. Bake until golden brown on the edges, about 35 minutes. Transfer to a rack to cool.

7. Assemble the tart: Spread the ganache evenly over the tart dough and spread the marmalade on top. Cover with the orange slices, overlapping them slightly. Cut into slices and serve.

Old-school tip

Ganache is just a fancy term used to describe melted cream and chocolate. For some of its other uses, see page 225.

enriched chocolate sauce

For years, I whisked boiling hot cream into chopped (and essentially cold) chocolate to make chocolate sauce. It's so satisfying to feel the chocolate melting into the cream. Then, I had a change of heart. By melting the chocolate and simmering the cream, the two parts of the sauce are closer to the same temperature when they're mixed together. Because there is little temperature difference, it's a much less traumatic introduction and the result is a glossy and smoother chocolate sauce. The cinnamon, rum, and orange make the chocolate taste more like chocolate to me.

MAKES ABOUT ¾ CUP

½ cup heavy cream
1 teaspoon ground cinnamon
4 ounces semisweet chocolate, roughly chopped (about ¾ cup)
2 teaspoons dark rum, preferably Myers's
A few light grates of orange zest (⅛ teaspoon packed)
Pinch of kosher salt

In a medium saucepan, whisk together the cream and cinnamon and bring to a gentle simmer over low heat. Put the chocolate in a medium heatproof bowl and set it on top of the pan of cream to make a loose double boiler. Make sure the bowl doesn't touch the cream. The chocolate will melt gently as it covers the simmering cream. When the cream is really hot, shut off the heat and allow the chocolate to finish melting. Stir the chocolate with a heatproof spatula until smooth. Remove from the heat and pour the cream into the melted chocolate. Stir in the rum, orange zest, and salt. Use this sauce warm. I love it, piping hot, poured over ice cream. If using it from the fridge, reheat gradually over low heat in a shallow water bath. If the texture becomes grainy, whisk in a splash of cream or water to loosen as needed.

What to do with this chocolate sauce:

- *I love to pour this over a cake when I'm not in the mood to go crazy making frosting. It will set once cool and make a shiny chocolaty glaze that looks rather inviting.*
- *Let this cool a bit and then use as a filling between cake layers, frosting the outside of the cake with something different to create a contrast of flavors. For example, a yellow cake with marshmallow frosting and a layer of this chocolate meandering innocently through the middle? Yes, please.*
- *Pour it over ice cream.*
- *Keep a container of this in the fridge and the next time you make chocolate cakes or muffins, sink a spoonful into the center and it will melt as the cake(s) cool. The result will be a chocolatier, juicy center.*
- *Stir a spoonful into your morning coffee. You might never be the same.*

Or . . . you can make this:

hot chocolate

This recipe can be made even more old-school (read: richer) by substituting 1 cup cream for 1 cup of the milk.

SERVES 4 TO 6

---

3 cups whole milk
½ cup Enriched Chocolate Sauce (opposite), warm
2 tablespoons unsweetened cocoa powder
½ cup whiskey, such as Bushmills (optional)
1 cup whipped cream (optional)

1. Heat the milk in a saucepan until it simmers.

2. In a medium bowl, whisk together the warm chocolate sauce and cocoa powder until smooth. Whisk in the hot milk. Pour into individual cups and top with the whiskey and whipped cream, if using.

old-school variation

Slightly "al dente" wedges of caramelized apples make a nice textural companion to the pudding. Peel and core 2 Granny Smith apples and cut them each into 6 wedges. Heat a medium skillet over medium heat. Add 2 tablespoons unsalted butter and wait for it to turn golden brown. Add the apples slices in a single layer and sprinkle with 1 tablespoon sugar. Add ¼ to ½ cup cider—enough to coat the bottom of the pan—and cook the apples, stirring them from time to time, until golden brown and slightly tender to the touch, 10 to 15 minutes. Transfer to a plate to cool. Grate the zest from ¼ lemon on top and add a squeeze of lemon juice. Serve in bowls with the pudding.

indian pudding

This is a classic New England dessert, one my mother would make during the fall months. A bowl of comfort. Golden raisins pack astonishing tang, adding acidity the way vinegar is the spark plug in a vinaigrette. For an even deeper flavor, try plumping your raisins in a little bourbon while you gather the other ingredients.

SERVES 8 TO 10

---

3 cups whole milk
4 tablespoons (½ stick) unsalted butter, plus more for greasing the dish
½ cup coarse cornmeal
2 tablespoons all-purpose flour
¾ teaspoon kosher salt
¼ cup blackstrap molasses
2 large eggs
¼ cup sugar
½ teaspoon ground cinnamon
½ teaspoon grated nutmeg
¼ teaspoon ground allspice
½ cup golden raisins
1½ cups unsweetened whipped cream or ice cream, for serving

1. Preheat the oven to 250°F. Grease a shallow 2- to 2½-quart baking dish with butter.

2. Make the batter: In a medium saucepan, combine the milk and butter and warm over low heat until the butter melts.

3. In a medium bowl, whisk together the cornmeal, flour, and salt. In a separate bowl, whisk together a little of the milk mixture and the molasses and then whisk this into the cornmeal. Add the entire cornmeal mixture to the pan and whisk until the ingredients are fully integrated. Cook, stirring constantly, for 2 minutes.

4. Whisk the eggs in a medium bowl. Gradually whisk in some of the cornmeal mix to temper the eggs. Pour everything into the saucepan and gently whisk in the sugar, cinnamon, nutmeg, allspice, and raisins. Remove from the heat.

5. Bake the pudding: Pour into the baking dish and bake until it looks like a slightly moist version of corn bread or a steamed pudding, 2 hours. Allow the pudding to cool for 15 minutes before topping with the whipped cream.

simplicity

Imagine yourself on a little side street in Nice, France.

The restaurant La Merenda has no phone and no chairs, just a few communal tables with not-so-comfy stools. There are no linens or decorations in the place. You are greeted at the door by an older, kindly woman who graciously and quietly seats you at any open place. And then you wait.

The other half of her duo can be seen just a few feet away, bent over the oven basting rabbits or stirring a pot of simmering vegetables on the stove. His movements, like hers, are thoughtful, careful, and without pretension. He turns from the stove to a table facing me and drops piping hot noodles into a clear glass bowl of vibrant herb pesto. He tosses the pasta over and over, watching it get really green. He is clearly enjoying the aroma of the pasta mixing its starchiness with the grassy sweetness of the pesto. When you make something piping hot and you stand directly over it in a hot kitchen, there is such an intimate moment between you and food where those two flavors meet and decide to make sense. It can almost be more satisfying than eating!

He grates some cheese over the bowl and his cohort, as if she senses just the moment, swoops to gather it up and places that bowl in front of us at the table. I take a bite and could instantly discern the mix of sweet and grassy basil, rich and vegetal olive oil, and the pasta, chewy yet cooked just enough, and everything balanced with the perfect amount of salt. If I could convey to you how good this tasted, you would have tears in your eyes, like I did. A bite of food that good is grounds for dropping everything and becoming a chef. Or at least going home and making something, like a batch of cookies.

raspberry doughnuts with vanilla dipping sauce

This recipe is like a best friend you make gradually over time. And it was born out of necessity: When I started working at Butter ten years ago, the most popular dessert was beignets with a dipping sauce. At the time, it seemed criminal to let go of a signature dish. The problem? The pastry chef left, taking the recipe with him. I tried a million recipes. I wound up with a soggy, deflated beignet every time. I would go to doughnut shops and eat the sugar-raised and honey-dipped doughnuts wistfully, wondering how such texture and cakey fluff had been achieved. Finally, after many attempts, I wound up with this recipe, which works every time, no matter how long it's been since I last made it. Just make sure all of your ingredients are at room temperature. I love these filled with seedless raspberry jam and with a vanilla sauce for dunking, though neither one is necessary if you prefer them plain.

MAKES ABOUT 16 (3-INCH) DOUGHNUTS

DOUGHNUTS

1 cup warm water (about 110°F)

1 tablespoon plus 2½ teaspoons active dry yeast

1 cup all-purpose flour, plus more for rolling the dough

10 tablespoons (1¼ sticks) unsalted butter, at room temperature, plus more for the bowl

⅔ cup sugar, plus more for dusting

3 large eggs, cracked and lightly beaten, at room temperature

1 teaspoon vanilla extract

1 teaspoon kosher salt

3½ cups bread flour

1 quart canola oil

¾ cup raspberry jam, preferably seedless

Vanilla Dipping Sauce (recipe follows)

1. Make the dough: Pour the warm water into a medium bowl. The temperature range for the "warm" water is where the dry yeast likes to wake up from its nap in those little envelopes in the back of your cupboard. (When you run the water from the tap, it's about where water starts to feel just hot to the touch; if it is so hot that you have to pull your hand away, you've gone much too far.) Whisk in the yeast and set aside to dissolve in the

recipe continues

water. After 10 minutes, you should see a few small bubbles on the surface. (If there is nothing at all, start again with fresher yeast.) Stir in the all-purpose flour, cover with plastic wrap, and set aside in a warm place.

2. Meanwhile, in the bowl of a stand mixer fitted with the paddle attachment, beat together the butter and sugar on medium speed until fluffy and light, 8 to 10 minutes. Do not skimp on or rush this time. Scrape down the sides of the bowl as you mix. With the mixer on low speed, add the eggs, one by one, taking care that each one is thoroughly integrated before adding the next. When the mix is smooth, add the vanilla and salt. Scrape down the sides of the bowl. Add the bread flour and mix on low speed until fully incorporated. Add the yeast mixture and mix again until thoroughly incorporated. Transfer the dough to a greased bowl, cover with plastic, and allow to rise in a warm place until the dough has doubled in volume, about 1 hour 30 minutes.

3. Roll and cut the doughnuts: Lightly flour a cool surface and sprinkle the dough with an even layer of flour. Use a rolling pin to roll the dough out to about a 1-inch thickness. Cut rounds of dough with a 2-inch round cookie cutter. You cannot reroll scraps (though you can fry them as is and devour them in the kitchen), so cut your doughnut rounds very close together to maximize yield. Put the doughnuts, leaving room between them for them to grow, on a floured baking sheet to rest in a warm place for 20 to 30 minutes. If you wait longer than that to fry them and they become fairly puffed up, cover them with plastic and refrigerate until you are ready. Leaving them in a warm place for too long can result in overproofing and yield an overly yeasty (and somewhat sour) doughnut.

4. Fry the doughnuts: In a medium, deep, heavy-bottomed pot (or deep-fryer), heat the canola oil to 350°F. Monitor the temperature of the oil with a thermometer.

Old-school tip

I know I'm not alone in admitting that I have taken a recipe that has instructed me to have eggs and butter at room temperature and ignored it. But sometimes, you can't. This is one of those recipes. If they're too cold, the mixture tends to break, or separate, and the resulting texture is not as good.

You may ask yourself: Why the two different flours? The all-purpose is great for density, and the bread flour, with increased protein, contributes to a good rise factor. Make sure when you combine the yeast and warm water that you put them in a warm place (like near the stove when the oven is on). They need that heat to get rolling.

recipe continues

5. Drop a doughnut scrap in the oil to make sure it is hot. It should bubble immediately. Cook until golden brown on both sides, 3 to 4 minutes. Remove it from the oil with a slotted spoon and set on a kitchen towel to drain. Fry the remaining doughnuts in batches.

6. Fill the doughnuts: Fill a pastry bag fitted with a small plain tip (or a zipper-top plastic bag with a corner snipped off) with the jam. Poke a hole into the side of each doughnut with the tip (or with a small spoon) and squirt some jam into the center. While still warm, roll in sugar. Serve immediately with the dipping sauce.

vanilla dipping sauce

MAKES 2½ CUPS

1 vanilla bean, split lengthwise
2 cups whole milk
Pinch of salt
6 large egg yolks
⅔ cup sugar

1. Infuse the milk: In a saucepan, combine the vanilla bean and milk with the salt. Bring to a boil over medium heat and then reduce the heat so that the milk simmers. Cook for 2 minutes and then set the pan aside to steep for 10 minutes.

2. Start the sauce: In the bowl of a stand mixer fitted with the whisk attachment, combine the egg yolks and sugar. Whip on medium speed until the eggs are pale yellow, about 5 minutes. Strain the milk, pressing down to extract the maximum from the vanilla bean.

3. Meanwhile, prepare an ice bath: Fill a large bowl halfway with ice cubes and add some cold water. Set another smaller bowl into the ice bath.

4. Cook the sauce: With the machine on low speed, pour half of the warm milk into the egg yolks and blend well. Return the egg yolk mixture to the saucepan along with the remaining milk and cook over medium heat, stirring constantly with a wooden spoon, until the sauce coats the back of the spoon, 5 to 8 minutes. Pour the sauce into the empty bowl set in the ice bath to speed the cooling process.

5. Serve immediately or refrigerate until ready to serve or for up to 3 days.

sugar-cranberry pie

Ever make something over and over again and suddenly realize a little gesture or change can make it so much better? Every year my mother bakes a pecan pie with a syrupy filling reminiscent of this one. We dig into the pie and wrestle, without much success, to get those first slices out of the pie dish intact. This past year, the pie came out beautifully and the pieces whole. My mother gave me a Cheshire cat grin and revealed her discovery. "I always prick my dough with the tines of a fork so it bakes without puffing up. This year I didn't. I realized that the syrupy filling leaks down the holes into the bottom of the pie dish as it bakes. When it cools, the sugar hardens and makes the bottom layer of dough stick to the bottom." Proof that you never stop learning from cooking, no matter how many times you make a dish.

The unique quality this pie has, other than a great, tangy filling, is the additional texture and sweetness from the liberal sprinkling of sugar on top once the pie is baked and cooled. There's something about that snowy, gravelly mouthful of sugar and cranberry filling that makes this one of my absolute favorite pies.

SERVES 8 TO 10

FILLING

1 tablespoon unsalted butter
5 ripe but firm medium Bosc or Anjou pears, peeled and diced (about 2 cups)
1½ (12-ounce) bags fresh cranberries
1½ cups sugar
1 tablespoon cornstarch
1 tablespoon light corn syrup
2 whole cloves
Juice of 1 lemon (3 tablespoons)
Grated zest of 1 orange (2 teaspoons)
1 large egg, lightly beaten, for sealing the pie crusts

CRUST

2½ cups all-purpose flour, plus more for rolling the dough
1 teaspoon sugar
1 teaspoon kosher salt
1 cup shortening, chilled
8 tablespoons (1 stick) unsalted butter, cold, cubed, plus more for the pie pan
⅓ cup plus 1 tablespoon ice water

½ cup sugar, for sprinkling

recipe continues

1. Make the filling: Heat a medium skillet over high heat until it begins to smoke lightly. Remove the pan from the heat, add the butter, and immediately toss in the pears and cranberries. Return to high heat and cook until the fruit is slightly tender, 2 to 3 minutes. Add the sugar, cornstarch, corn syrup, cloves, lemon juice, and orange zest. Mix to blend and cook over high heat for 1 minute so all of the ingredients meld together. Remove from the heat and scoop into a bowl. Refrigerate to cool. Remove the whole cloves from the filling.

2. Generously grease the bottom and sides of a 9-inch pie pan and refrigerate.

3. Make the crust: In a large bowl, whisk together the flour, sugar, and salt. Work the shortening and butter in with your fingers until the mixture resembles small peas. Add almost all of the ice water and continue to mix with your fingers. Add the remaining water if the dough feels too dry or crumbly to come together. Transfer the dough to a flat surface, roll into a ball, and cut in half. Shape each half into a smaller ball. Flatten the balls, wrap each in plastic, and refrigerate for at least 30 minutes before rolling to allow the dough to rest.

4. Transfer the dough to a lightly floured flat surface. Using a rolling pin, roll half until it is at least 4 to 5 inches wider than the pie pan and about 3⁄16 inch thick. Gently fit the dough into the pie pan, pressing it into the bottom and sides. Leave a 1-inch overhang at the top and put the pan in the refrigerator.

5. Roll the second half of the dough to about 3⁄16 inch thickness for the top of the pie. Put it on a baking sheet and refrigerate.

6. Preheat the oven to 425°F.

7. Assemble the pie: Pour the filling into the bottom pie crust. Brush the edges of the crust with the beaten egg. Remove the top crust from the refrigerator and put it over the top of the pie. Pinch around the top edge of the pie crust to seal the top and bottom crusts all around the pie, removing any excess dough with a paring knife. Use a paring knife to cut an "x" opening, 1½ to 2 inches across, in the center of the top. Fold back the dough so it looks like open pages of a book. Put the pie on a rimmed baking sheet.

8. Bake the pie: Bake the pie for 10 minutes. Lower the oven temperature to 375°F. Bake until the crust is light golden brown, an additional 30 minutes. Remove from the oven and allow to cool completely on a rack. Sprinkle the top with sugar.

old-school tip

Put your flour for dusting and rolling your dough into a strainer and sprinkle the rolling surface like you're crop dusting. An even layer of flour means you will likely use less flour for rolling and there won't be any clumps or excess flour rolled into your dough, which can make the texture tough.

MOUNTAIN LAUREL
AZALEA

sour cream pumpkin pie

I am a greenmarket lover. I am especially partial to all of the local varieties of squash and their unique flavors. I have tried them all as the centerpiece for this pie filling and have decided to come clean with my feelings. I like a can of pumpkin puree for this pie more than anything else. It may be because the taste is so familiar and what I grew up eating or because the results are the same each time—but what does it matter why if it's the most delicious? The sour cream is the unique touch to this recipe. The slight tang really illuminates the spices and the inherent sweetness of the pumpkin. I make this pie all season, starting with the first acceptable cool day in fall. **SERVES 8 TO 10**

CRUST

1¼ cups all-purpose flour, plus more for rolling the dough
1½ teaspoons confectioners' sugar
¾ teaspoon kosher salt
½ cup shortening
4 tablespoons (½ stick) unsalted butter, cold, cubed, plus more for the pie pan
3 tablespoons ice water

FILLING

1 (15-ounce) can unsweetened pumpkin puree, preferably Libby's
1 cup sour cream
3 large eggs, separated
1 cup granulated sugar
½ teaspoon kosher salt
1½ teaspoons ground cinnamon
1 teaspoon ground ginger
½ teaspoon grated nutmeg
¼ teaspoon ground cloves
¼ teaspoon cream of tartar

1. Preheat the oven to 350°F. Generously grease a 9-inch pie pan with butter.

2. Make the crust: In a medium bowl, combine the flour, confectioners' sugar, and salt. Work the shortening and butter in with your fingers until the mixture resembles small peas. Add almost all of the ice water and continue to mix with your fingers. Add the remaining water if the dough feels too dry or crumbly to come together. Transfer the dough to a flat surface and roll into a ball. Flatten the ball, wrap in plastic, and refrigerate for at least 30 minutes before rolling to allow the dough to rest.

3. On a lightly floured surface, roll the dough out until it is at least 2 to 3 inches wider than the pie pan, about 3/16 inch thick. Gently fit the dough into the pie pan, pressing it into the bottom and the sides. Trim off any excess at the top and make a decorative edge if desired. Put the pan in the refrigerator to rest.

4. Make the filling: In a large bowl, whisk together the pumpkin puree, sour cream, egg yolks, ¾ cup of the granulated sugar, the salt, cinnamon, ginger, nutmeg, and cloves. Do not overmix.

5. In the bowl of a stand mixer fitted with the whisk attachment, beat the egg whites on medium-high speed until they double in volume, about 1 minute. Add the cream of tartar and continue to beat until soft peaks form, 1 to 2 minutes more. Gradually add the remaining ¼ cup granulated sugar and beat until the whites become stiff and shiny, about 2 minutes more.

6. Assemble and bake the pie: Using a rubber spatula, gently fold the egg whites into the pumpkin filling. Take care not to overmix. Set the pie pan on a baking sheet. Pour the filling into the pie pan. Bake until the top browns lightly, about 45 minutes. Gently shake the edge of the pie pan. The filling will jiggle slightly but should appear set. Allow the pie to cool on a rack before serving.

Old-school tip

The rustic cracks that often happen with pumpkin pies don't bother me, though I'll admit a smooth top is impressive. The easiest ways to avoid the cracks begin when you assemble the filling. Don't overmix the ingredients; stir gently to blend. Don't overwhip the egg whites and fold them in as tenderly and with as few strokes as possible. Lastly, bake the pie at a reasonable temperature and do not overbake it.

apple crisp

I would love to take full credit for this recipe but it is simply another one my mother made year after year when I was growing up. The only thing that changes is the type of apple I use. I pick a few new favorites every year, like Braeburn and Rome varieties, which are tart and hold up well when cooked. However, I usually use pure Granny Smith here—tart, tried, and true. I think crisps are best when the fruit is cooked through. I use a large baking dish so that the layer of apples is thin—because everyone loves the topping most. Let's face it: When no one is looking, we scoop out a portion that has much more topping than it should. **SERVES 8 TO 10**

APPLE FILLING

3 pounds Granny Smith apples (about 8 large)
1 tablespoon blackstrap molasses
Grated zest and juice of 1 lemon, plus additional lemon zest for optional garnish
Grated zest and juice of 1 orange
1 teaspoon ground cinnamon
½ teaspoon grated nutmeg
¼ teaspoon kosher salt

TOPPING

1⅓ cups packed light brown sugar
1 cup all-purpose flour
1 teaspoon kosher salt
½ teaspoon ground cinnamon
⅛ teaspoon grated nutmeg
8 tablespoons (1 stick) unsalted butter, cubed, plus more for the dish
1 pint vanilla ice cream for serving

1. Preheat the oven to 375°F. Generously grease the bottom and sides of a shallow rectangular baking dish (about 9 × 13 inches) with butter.

2. Make the filling: Core and peel the apples. Cut each in half and then into thin slices. Put the slices in a bowl and toss with the molasses, lemon zest, lemon juice, orange zest, orange juice, cinnamon, nutmeg, and salt. Toss to blend.

3. Make the topping: In another bowl, combine the brown sugar, flour, salt, cinnamon, and nutmeg. Add the butter to the bowl and use your fingers to integrate the flour with the butter.

4. Bake the crisp: Layer the apples in the buttered dish and top evenly with the topping. Bake until the apples are tender when pierced with the tip of a knife and the topping is golden brown, 40 to 45 minutes. Set aside to cool for at least a few minutes before serving. Top with additional lemon zest, if desired.

banana betty

Something about the deep sweetness of banana encased in an eggy custard is so simple and tasty. Turns out this is a great place to hide overly ripe bananas. I mean, how many loaves of banana bread can you bake? When I make the custard for this dessert, I struggle not to eat half of it before getting the ramekins into the oven. I still love to crush up cookies and top the Betty with them for added personality. Though gingersnaps are an obvious winner, I also love almond cookies, like amaretti, or crisp dark chocolate ones. **SERVES 6**

1½ cups heavy cream
½ cup whole milk
2 tablespoons dark rum, preferably Myers's
2 teaspoons vanilla extract
Pinch of kosher salt
5 to 6 ripe bananas (about 1¼ pounds), sliced ¼ inch thick
6 large egg yolks
¼ cup sugar
1 cup coarsely cracked gingersnaps (optional)

1. Preheat the oven to 350°F. Fill a large tea kettle with water and bring to a boil.

2. Infuse the cream: In a small saucepan, bring the cream and milt to a gentle simmer. Stir in the rum, vanilla, and salt.

3. Prepare the ramekins: Fill six 6-ounce ramekins a little more than halfway with banana slices. Set the ramekins in a large roasting pan (about 10 × 15 inches).

4. Make the custard: In a medium bowl, whisk the egg yolks and sugar until thoroughly blended and pale yellow in color, about 2 minutes. Pour some of the simmered cream over the eggs and whisk until incorporated. Pour everything back into the saucepan with the cream and cook over low heat, stirring constantly with a wooden spoon, until the custard is thick enough to coat the back of the spoon, 5 to 8 minutes. The bubbles will diminish when it's done. Transfer the custard to a liquid measuring cup.

5. Bake the custard: Pour the custard over the banana slices, filling each ramekin about ½ inch from the rim. Tap each one gently to assure there are no gaps between banana slices. Set in the oven. Carefully pour the hot water from the tea kettle into the dish so that it comes halfway up the sides of the ramekins. Cook until the custard sets, 25 to 30 minutes. Remove from the oven and from the water bath and let cool. Refrigerate for at least 1 hour or up to 2 days. When ready to serve, top with crushed cookies, if desired.

quickie strawberry tartlets

I love a simple fruit tart. During my many years living in France, I enjoyed countless tarts with crisp buttery shells laced with traces of almond flour or extract or lemon zest. When I'm at home, I often find that the prospect of tackling a good tart dough, a filling, and a fruit topping feels like a lot. So I cheat a little and use a very thin cookie, or tuile, batter to make the tartlet shells. The tuile shells are thinner, crisper, and more rustic looking than a classic pie or tart shell shape. Each one has its own unique shape. As far as the fruit goes, strawberries are my first choice because the slightly seedy exterior combined with the meaty inside is impossible to improve upon. The tartlet shells and strawberry mix can be made in advance but do not fill the shells with the sour cream and strawberries until just before serving; the juice from the strawberries makes them soggy quickly. **MAKES 30 TO 35 TARTLETS**

---

1 lemon
¼ cup granulated sugar
1 pound small to medium strawberries, hulled and sliced ¼ inch thick
1 cup confectioners' sugar
½ cup all-purpose flour
2 tablespoons unsalted butter, melted
¼ cup orange juice, *not* fresh squeezed
Cooking spray
½ to ¾ cup sour cream

1. Prepare the fruit: Using a vegetable peeler and a light touch, remove the zest from half of the lemon. Try to remove the zest in small pieces and leave the pith (the white part) behind. Juice the lemon into a medium bowl and mix in the zest, granulated sugar, and strawberries. Cover the bowl and refrigerate until ready to assemble the tarts.

2. Preheat the oven to 375°F.

3. Make the batter: Using a fine-mesh strainer or sifter, sift together the confectioners' sugar and flour into a medium bowl. Use your hands to push the sugar and flour through the strainer to make sifting easier. Whisk in the butter and orange juice.

4. Use a cookie sheet or invert a rimmed, baking sheet onto the counter, making sure the bottom is clean. Coat with a thin layer of cooking spray. Spoon a generous teaspoon of the batter near the corner of the sheet and use a small offset spatula to spread it thinly into a small, imperfect oval, about 3½ by 2½ inches. Take care to leave about an inch between the ovals because they will spread a bit when they

recipe continues

are baked. You should be able to fit about 10 on the sheet at one time.

5. Bake the tart shells: Have ready a mini muffin tin or clean egg carton. Put the tuiles in the oven and bake until light brown, 8 to 11 minutes. Remove the baking sheet from the oven and while the tuiles are still warm, use an offset spatula to transfer a tuile from the baking sheet to the muffin tin. Using your fingers, press down in the center to create a shell that mimics the shape of each muffin cup. The sides will overlap or be higher than the muffin cup. That's fine. Your goal is to make a mini tart shell to fill with the strawberries. Repeat with the remaining tuiles, working with only one at a time. If the tuiles cool too much on the baking sheet before molding and aren't flexible, return the sheet to the warm oven for a minute to loosen them up before continuing. Let the tart shells cool completely.

6. Glaze the berries: Strain the liquid from the strawberries and pour it into a small pan. Simmer over medium heat to reduce until it becomes syrupy and reduced by half, about 4 minutes. Allow to cool slightly, then pour it back over the strawberries, and toss to blend.

7. Serve the tarts: Remove the shells from the muffin tin. Put a small dollop of sour cream in the bottom of each shell and top with some of the strawberries. Assemble and then eat immediately. They become soggy quickly.

Old-school tip

If you do not own flat cookie sheets, baking these tuiles on the back of a rimmed baking sheet means they will brown faster because they are baked on a tray without walls, which can prevent moisture from escaping. Drier tuiles mean crisper tuiles, which is what we want. They are also easier to remove from the back of the baking sheet than when the walls prevent clean sweeps with an offset spatula. If the tuiles become brittle or hard to remove, put the baking sheet into a warm oven for a minute to loosen them and resume.

ME AND MY DAUGHTER, AVA

cherry, pasilla chile, and vanilla custard tart

This is the tart that I made on the finale of *Next Iron Chef.* The task was to create one dish for each Iron Chef, one that represented their essence through ingredients the chairman had chosen—but with a dish that was my style. For Bobby Flay, I skipped the avocado and corn and went for the pasillas and limes. Pasillas (also known as "little raisins") are almost sweet, earthy, with hints of tobacco—and a serious taste of raisin! But how to do this ingredient justice? And limes can be tricky, too, going from sexy to soapy in a heartbeat. I decided on a tart bursting with cherries and chiles balanced by a lime-yogurt sorbet. The combination of the tangy golden raisins with the chiles and fresh cherries is surprising and unusual. **MAKES ONE 9-INCH TART**

TART DOUGH

2 cups all-purpose flour
½ teaspoon kosher salt
Pinch of black pepper
1 tablespoon plus 2 teaspoons sugar
12 tablespoons unsalted butter (1½ sticks), cubed and cold
Grated zest of ½ lemon
½ cup ice water

PASTRY CREAM

6 large egg yolks
¾ cup sugar
3 tablespoons cornstarch
1½ cups whole milk
2 vanilla beans, split lengthwise and scraped
2 tablespoons unsalted butter
1 tablespoon heavy cream
½ teaspoon vanilla extract

TOPPING

4 cups rich red wine, preferably merlot or zinfandel
½ small cinnamon stick
3 pasilla chiles, stemmed and soaked in warm water until softened
4 to 5 tablespoons packed dark brown sugar
2 tablespoons unsalted butter, plus more for greasing the pan
1 pound fresh cherries, split and pitted (2⅓ cups)
½ cup granulated sugar, plus more for sprinkling
⅔ cup golden raisins
2 limes
½ cup almonds with the skin on, toasted and coarsely chopped
1 pint tangy, plain frozen yogurt

1. Make the tart dough: In a food processor, pulse together the flour, salt, pepper, and sugar. Add the butter and lemon zest and pulse to blend until the mixture resembles coarse crumbs. Do not overmix. Overworking the dough will make the texture tough. Pour in the ice water and pulse until the dough forms a loose ball. Remove the dough from the machine and press it between two sheets of wax paper to about ¾ inch thickness. The more you flatten the dough now, the less work you will have later rolling it. Wrap in plastic and chill in the refrigerator for at least 1 hour before rolling.

2. Make the pastry cream: In the bowl of an electric mixer fitted with the whisk attachment, whip the egg yolks with the sugar until it turns pale yellow and you can see the trace of the whisk as it moves through the yolks, 5 to 8 minutes. Add the cornstarch and whip until fully integrated.

3. Pour the milk into a medium saucepan and add the vanilla beans and seeds. Bring to a simmer over medium-high heat. With the mixer on low, pour about half of the milk into the eggs in a slow steady stream; keep the vanilla beans in the saucepan. Pour the entire mixture back into the saucepan and bring to a boil over medium-high heat. Lower the heat to medium-low and cook, whisking constantly, until the mixture becomes thick, 3 to 5 minutes. Remove from the heat and stir in the butter, cream, and vanilla. Pour the pastry cream onto a baking sheet lined with plastic wrap and immediately cover it with a layer of plastic wrap pressed against the surface of the cream so it doesn't form a skin as it cools. Refrigerate until cold.

4. Start the topping: In a medium saucepan, heat 3 cups of the wine and the cinnamon stick. Remove the chiles from the water, opening them up and rinsing out the seeds; discard the soaking liquid and seeds. Tear the chile flesh into small pieces and add it to the saucepan along with 4 tablespoons of the brown sugar. Bring the mixture to a simmer over medium heat. When the wine starts to boil, lower the heat and cook gently until the chiles are tender and falling apart and you have about 2 cups liquid remaining, 15 to 20 minutes. Taste the mixture. It should be earthy with notes from the wine and a little heat from the chiles. If it's a little tart, stir in the remaining tablespoon brown sugar. Strain through a fine-mesh sieve, pressing as much of the solids through as you can to give the sauce body. You should have 1 to 1¼ cups puree.

5. Cook the cherries: Heat a large sauté pan over medium heat. Add the butter, swirling it around until it melts and turns light brown. Quickly add the cherries in a single layer and turn the heat to high. Cook until the cherries sear lightly and release some of their liquid, 1 to 2 minutes. Sprinkle them with the granulated sugar and add the remaining

recipe continues

1 cup wine and the raisins. Cook over high heat until the red wine loses its alcohol taste, 2 to 3 minutes. Squeeze the juice from ½ lime over the cherries. Transfer to a bowl and refrigerate until cool.

6. Preheat the oven to 350°F.

7. Bake the tart shell: Liberally grease the bottom and sides of a 9-inch round tart pan with a removable bottom. Lightly flour a flat surface and roll the dough to a circle a couple of inches larger than the tart pan. Gently roll the tart dough around the rolling pin and unroll it loosely over the tart pan. Ease the dough onto the bottom and against the sides of the pan. Don't stretch the dough or it will shrink when you cook it. Grease the dull side of a sheet of aluminum foil and press it, greased side down, on top of the dough. Fill with dried beans. Bake for 20 minutes. Remove the tart shell from the oven and gently remove the foil and the beans. Return the tart shell to the oven and bake until the dough is light brown and fairly firm to the touch, 10 to 12 minutes more. Remove from the oven and set aside to cool.

8. Assemble the tart: Spoon the pastry cream into the tart and top with a light dusting of grated zest from 1 of the limes. Toss the cherries with the red wine sauce and spoon them and some sauce all around the top of the tart. Arrange the golden raisins on top of the cherries, tucking some of them inside the crevices of the cherries. Drizzle with a little more sauce and top with the toasted almonds. Sprinkle with a touch of sugar for texture. Serve with the frozen yogurt on the side topped with a little grated lime zest from the remaining ½ lime.

coffee granita

I love coffee in the morning and I also love it with dessert. If I had to live without one, I think I could more easily live without dessert than without the coffee! But so as not to have to make that awful choice, I propose this small and refreshing dessert, which is something like a sweetened cup of iced coffee. One of my absolute favorite desserts is a big mound of this, freshly scraped, on top of really creamy vanilla ice cream. It's like an icy version of, in my opinion, the best Italian dessert, *affogato:* a shot of espresso poured over a scoop of ice cream. **SERVES 6 TO 8**

2 tablespoons sugar
1¼ cups brewed strong coffee, cooled
2 tablespoons coffee liqueur, such as Tia Maria or Kahlúa
Grated zest of ½ lemon

1. Make the syrup: In a small saucepan, combine 1 cup water and the sugar. Bring to a simmer, stir until the sugar dissolves, about 5 minutes, and then pour into a bowl to cool. Refrigerate.

2. Whisk the coffee, liqueur, and lemon zest into the cooled syrup. Pour into a shallow baking dish and put in the freezer until the mixture hardens, 3 to 4 hours.

3. Serve the granita: Scrape the surface with the tines of a fork to remove the granita in large flakes. Scoop into bowls.

chewy chocolaty ice cream cookie sandwiches

These cookies have slight brownie qualities and, for that reason, I like to eat them on their own as much as when they are part of an ice cream sandwich. They are thin and chewy and chocolaty. After the cookies are baked and cooled, soften the ice cream and mold it with a spoon so it's ready to be sandwiched between two of the cookies. Pressing the cookies to make the ice cream behave will only break them and make messy sandwiches. These can be made and devoured on the spot (my favorite way to do it) or premade, wrapped in wax paper or foil, and returned to the freezer for an old-fashioned homemade ice cream sandwich. My favorite flavors of ice cream to use? Butter pecan, vanilla, coffee, and strawberry. I love to roll the sides in various toppings as well, from salted, roasted nuts to dried fruits or chopped pieces of chocolate. Do what you like! **MAKES 9 COOKIE SANDWICHES**

2½ ounces semisweet chocolate, roughly chopped (heaping ½ cup)
1½ ounces unsweetened chocolate, roughly chopped (about ⅓ cup) cut into pieces
3 tablespoons lightly salted butter, plus more for the pan
1 large egg
⅓ cup sugar
1 teaspoon vanilla extract
1 tablespoon plus 2 teaspoons all-purpose flour
⅛ teaspoon baking powder
¼ teaspoon kosher salt

1 pint ice cream

1. Preheat the oven to 350°F. Grease 2 baking sheets with butter.

2. Melt the chocolate and butter: In a medium bowl, combine the two kinds of chocolate and the butter. Create a makeshift double boiler by filling a pot that will hold the bowl snugly with 1 inch of water. (The bowl should not touch the water.) Bring the water to a boil. Lower the heat so the water is hot but not boiling. Keep the bowl there, stirring with a heatproof spatula from time to time, until the chocolate and butter melt. Remove from the heat.

3. Make the batter: In the bowl of an electric mixer fitted with the whisk attachment, beat the egg on high speed for 1 minute. Add the sugar and vanilla and beat until the mixture thickens slightly and becomes a pale yellow color, 3 to 5 minutes. Scrape down the sides of the bowl and add the chocolate mixture. Using a rubber spatula, mix gently to blend. Sift together the flour and baking powder and stir into the chocolate. Stir in the salt. Slowly add the flour mixture to the chocolate mixture and stir until all of the ingredients are blended.

4. Bake the cookies: Drop 1-tablespoon lumps of the cookie batter onto the baking sheets, leaving about 1½ inches between the cookies; they will spread as they cook. You should have about 18 cookies total, 9 per baking sheet. Bake for 4 minutes, rotate the pan from front to back, and bake until they spread and crack slightly, an additional 4 minutes. Let the cookies cool for 10 to 15 minutes on the pan before transferring them to a rack to cool completely.

5. Assemble the sandwiches: Molding the ice cream is key. I like to scoop a heaping tablespoonful or two, depending on the size and shape of the cookies, and press it into a fairly round 2-inch-thick shape. Then sandwich it between 2 cookies and press gently. Repeat to fill all of the cookies.

Old-school tip

My mom has one of those old-fashioned flour sifters and I have vivid memories of her delicately sifting dry ingredients into cake batters. Why do it? Aerating and fully integrating dry ingredients before mixing them into cakes or cookies is underrated. It helps the texture. Got a strainer? Mix your dry ingredients together and dust them over the wet ingredients. This is a little step toward a nice fluffy cake or tender cookie. Sift the dry ingredients but simply add the salt; it doesn't sift well.

butter cookies made for filling

You know that jar of jam you bought on a whim when you went on that trip two years ago? Or those fruits you have sitting on your kitchen counter that are getting too ripe? This is the perfect place to use them to make an unusual jam filling. I bake these simple butter cookies almost every Christmas but fill them with something different each year. That way people won't catch on that I'm secretly making the same cookie over and over again! While I love gingersnaps and chocolate chip, this is the OG cookie. It goes with anything and can be dressed up or down, depending on your mood. You can also replace the vanilla extract with almond extract to go with cherry jam filling or chopped almonds and raisins. **MAKES ABOUT 5 DOZEN, OR ENOUGH FOR 2½ DOZEN SANDWICH COOKIES**

1½ cups (3 sticks) unsalted butter, at room temperature
¾ cup confectioners' sugar
2 cups all-purpose flour
1 cup cornstarch
1 teaspoon kosher salt
½ teaspoon vanilla extract
1 cup finely ground almonds, toasted

1. Preheat the oven to 325°F.

2. Make the dough: In the bowl of a mixer fitted with the paddle attachment, beat the butter and sugar on medium speed until smooth, 3 to 5 minutes. Using a fine mesh strainer or sifter, sift the flour and cornstarch over the butter mixture. Add the salt and mix until blended. Stir in the vanilla and almonds. Use a heaping teaspoon measure to divide the dough into little balls. You should have about 5 dozen. Refrigerate on a baking sheet until the dough becomes cold, at least 30 minutes.

3. Bake the cookies: Use your hands to roll the dough pieces into even balls and then put them on a baking sheet, leaving about an inch of room between each ball of dough. Press each ball down gently, making in indentation in the middle with your index finger. Put the baking sheet in the oven and bake until golden brown, 10 to 12 minutes. Allow to cool at least slightly before filling.

Old-school tip

A simple cookie recipe doesn't have to end there. I have used this single dough to make a really varied platter of cookies. Gussy these butter cookies up if you like, cutting them into different shapes and, once baked, decorating them in different ways: Dust some with sugar, make some of them into sandwiches with jam in the middle, whisk together some sour cream with chocolate chips for another sandwich filling, and drizzle some with honey or melted chocolate. A drizzle of caramel and a sprinkling of lemon zest is another great combination. Use what you already have on hand to create variations from the mother recipe.

"Cacao"

½ l de crème
½ l de crème Chantilly
500 g de chocolat
1 café sucre
3 banane
200 l Rhum
25 g de beurre

Meringue Cookies

2 kg sucre semoule
1 l egg whites

break whites with whip (Hobart Mixer) on a low speed. 30 seconds. Put in all of the sugar and

sunday brunch dishes

from my mom's pantry to yours

chilled cantaloupe soup

quickie corn bread

tasty dill bread

evil cheese biscuits

deluxe coffee cake

your own pork sausage patties
with eggs

spice-rubbed bacon

omelet with fried sage
and gruyère

cinnamon sourdough pancakes

There is nothing like waking up in the morning, feeling your stomach growl with hunger, a battle cry, and then smelling coffee cake wafting from the oven. Or corn bread. My corn bread recipe is a version of the very first recipe I ever made by myself from scratch on page 495 of the *Fannie Farmer Cookbook*. A simple little recipe on a page with a few others, but in my mom's copy, that page is stuck to the page before it with batter and errant grains of sugar from the hundreds of times I would crack the book open. Even when I knew the recipe by heart, I liked that part of the ritual—opening the book; I knew this to be the first step to making something good.

When savory seems the way to go on a weekend, I like there to be a special, homemade touch. I spice my bacon; I make my own pork sausage. I also enjoy baking something sweet to go with the first cup of coffee and then moving onto eggs or something spicy or really savory. Going between hints of brown sugar, cinnamon, or fresh fruit flavors and then graduating to spicy pork, peppery bacon, or a simple omelet with sage gives my brunch table the kind of variety that transforms my favorite meal of the week into a breakfasty amusement park.

chilled cantaloupe soup

A chilled soup for brunch? While I love to sit around and drink too much coffee and eat that third slice of coffee cake, sometimes something cool and clean like this can be a welcome addition to the brunch table.

I suppose you expect me to say I went to the Hamptons, dressed in a perfectly starched chef's jacket, and gathered an apronful of melons to unearth the true essence of this voluptuous fruit. Not exactly. I learned to love this melon at various diner counters with my dad. I grew up on a steady diet of the finest cantaloupes . . . from midtown Manhattan coffee shops; my father insists that they have a monopoly on the best melons. Try this with other kinds of melons: Galias, which taste tart and tangy like passionfruit spiked with 1% pineapple, are a worthy substitute. Buy what looks good! **SERVES 6 TO 8**

---

2 medium cantaloupes, cold, flesh cut into small pieces (3 packed cups)
Pinch of kosher salt
1 cup apple cider
Juice of 1 to 2 lemons
½ to 1 cup ice water, if needed
1 to 2 teaspoons honey

1. Working in two batches, purée the cantaloupes with the salt, cider, and lemon juice to taste in a blender on medium speed. While you want the mixture to be smooth, keep the blender running on medium speed to avoid whipping unnecessary air into the melon and lightening the flavor along with the color. Add some ice water if the blender has trouble blending the melon and, if you feel the melons lack sweetness, a little honey to taste.

2. Transfer all of the soup to a bowl and put the bowl over ice. Taste for seasoning. Add a squeeze of lemon juice if the flavor needs brightening. Serve very cold.

old-school variation

The last time I made this soup, it was so cold I got an ice cream headache after my first spoonful. The obvious conclusion was to pour this into a glass and add sparkling wine. Delicious. I measured about 1 part melon soup and 2 parts sparkling wine. Or try my dad's Old-School Melon Cocktail (recipe follows).

A couple of brunchy cocktails . . .

the old-school melon cocktail

I do have another childhood memory involving melon and my dad. He used to make (every once in a blue moon) some Midori sours with melon liqueur. Go old school, take a jump back into the '70s, and garnish the drink with some melon balls (you just need that melon baller, which you probably have in a back drawer somewhere; now is the time to dust it off and put it to work). With this recipe, the colder the ingredients and the glasses, the better the result.

SERVES 2

3 ounces (6 tablespoons) gin, such as Bombay Sapphire, chilled
4 ounces (½ cup) Chilled Cantaloupe Soup (opposite)
½ ounce (1 tablespoon) fresh lemon juice, or more to taste
1 lemon wedge
Melon balls, for garnish

Put the gin, soup, and lemon juice in a shaker (or any container with a fitted lid) with a few ice cubes and shake until blended and cold. Strain into 2 chilled glasses. Rub the rim of the glass with the lemon wedge for a little added acidity when sipping and garnish with melon balls.

muddled screwdrivers

My other favorite brunch cocktail is a classic. I love what the muddled orange peel does to this drink. I have also sliced the oranges and let them sit overnight in the fudge with a pinch of sugar and a touch of ground clove for deeper flavor.

SERVES 4 TO 6

2 oranges, washed and cut into ¼-inch-thick wheels
Juice of ½ lemon
Pinch of kosher salt
8 ounces (1 cup) vodka, preferably Stolichnaya, chilled
2½ cups freshly squeezed orange juice, chilled
1½ to 2 cups crushed ice, as needed

Place the orange slices in a sturdy bowl and add the lemon juice and salt. Use a wooden spoon to bruise the orange slices so that the oil in the peels emerges and the pulp from the orange mixes with the lemon juice. Add the vodka and continue to muddle. Pour into a pitcher and stir in the orange juice. Divide the ice among 4 to 6 glasses and pour the mixture into each. Serve immediately.

quickie corn bread

My parents were seriously late sleepers and I actually credit that as another one of the reasons I became a chef. I would wait and watch cartoons and eventually end up foraging in the cupboards for something to eat. Early *Chopped* format breakfasts: four ingredients, thirty minutes, hungry child. I always gravitated to the *Fannie Farmer Cookbook* because the recipes seemed short and simple enough. It was the first time I remember making something and feeling the essence of timing in cooking: the buttered dish, the preheated oven—these were steps I could follow. And those baking recipes really delivered. SO satisfying—as was the amazed look on my mom's face when she would stumble into the kitchen and see me eating a wedge of this slathered with jam. The coarse cornmeal gives this corn bread texture and crunchy edges—perfect for lots of jam. **SERVES 8 TO 10**

1¼ cups coarsely ground cornmeal
¾ cup all-purpose flour
¼ cup sugar, plus more for sprinkling
1¼ teaspoons kosher salt
2 teaspoons baking powder
½ teaspoon baking soda
⅓ cup whole milk
1 cup buttermilk
2 large eggs, lightly beaten
8 tablespoons (1 stick) unsalted butter, melted, plus 1 tablespoon for the pan
Jam or Gussied-Up Jam (recipe follows), for serving (optional)

1. Preheat the oven to 400°F and put a 9-inch cast-iron skillet inside. Getting the skillet hot makes a better crust on the bottom of the corn bread.

2. Make the batter: In a large bowl, whisk together the cornmeal, flour, sugar, salt, baking powder, and baking soda. Whisk in the milk, buttermilk, and eggs. Whisk in the melted butter.

3. Bake the corn bread: Carefully remove the hot skillet from the oven and coat the bottom and sides with the remaining 1 tablespoon butter. Pour the batter into the skillet and bake until the center is firm and a cake tester or wooden pick inserted into the center comes out clean, 20 to 25 minutes. Allow to cool for 10 to 15 minutes and then sprinkle with a light layer of sugar for texture. Cut into slices and serve topped with jam, if desired.

gussied-up jam

I love jam. I use corn bread as an excuse to eat a ton of it. While I love blueberry corn muffins, I actually prefer the blueberries over corn bread instead of baked inside. I particularly like Bonne Maman Wild Blueberry Preserves for this recipe. **MAKES 2½ CUPS**

1 cup blueberry jam
1 pint fresh blueberries
Pinch of kosher salt
Grated zest of ½ lemon
1 tablespoon lemon juice

In a small saucepan, warm the jam over low heat until it starts to become slightly liquid. Stir in the blueberries, salt, lemon zest, and lemon juice. Simmer for 1 minute and then transfer to a bowl to cool slightly before eating.

tasty dill bread

Dill has always been an herb I struggle with. It has a deep, anise flavor and an herbaceous, almost metallic quality as well. As far as I'm concerned, it is hard to pair with other foods. Dill in chicken soup? When there is too much, I find it overpowers the chicken flavor. Dill with tomatoes? Even the bright, acidic quality of tomatoes can be obscured by dill. But I felt it wasn't very cheflike of me to abandon such a pretty herb, and I knew there was something about the flavor I do like. I just didn't know how to harness it properly, until now. This bread recipe is a classic and is delicious when slathered with salty butter. I especially love it with egg dishes, which is how it found its way to my brunch table. For something more unusual, make the Cranberry Sauce (page 146) and serve it alongside this bread. That combo is a winner. Keep in mind that the dough requires some time to rise and some time to bake. **MAKES ONE 8-INCH LOAF**

2¼ teaspoons active dry yeast
½ cup warm water (about 110°F)
3 cups bread flour
2 medium shallots, very thinly sliced
2 tablespoons chopped fresh dill
2 teaspoons dill seeds
1 teaspoon caraway seeds
1 teaspoon fennel seeds
1 teaspoon sesame seeds
3 tablespoons honey
1 tablespoon blackstrap molasses
1 tablespoon wheat germ
2 teaspoons kosher salt
½ teaspoon black pepper
1 cup 4% cottage cheese
1 large egg
Butter, for greasing the bowl and pan

1. Make the dough: In a medium bowl, sprinkle the yeast over the warm water and gently shake the bowl to help the yeast mix with the water. Set aside until dissolved, about 10 minutes.

2. In the bowl of a stand mixer fitted with the paddle attachment, combine the bread flour with the shallots, dill, dill seeds, caraway seeds, fennel seeds, sesame seeds, honey, the molasses, wheat germ, salt, and pepper. Mix on medium-low speed to blend. Mix in the cottage cheese and egg.

3. Add the yeast mixture and mix to incorporate. Transfer the dough to a greased bowl. Cover with a towel and put it in a warm place to rise slightly, 1 hour 30 minutes to 2 hours.

4. Grease an 8-inch loaf pan with butter. Gently push the air out of the dough. Put the dough squarely in the pan and cover it with the towel again. Leave in a warm place to rise for 1 hour.

5. Meanwhile, preheat the oven to 400°F.

6. Bake the bread: Lower the oven temperature to 350°F. Put the loaf in the oven and bake until a wooden toothpick inserted in the center comes out clean or the internal temperature of the bread reaches 200°F, 30 to 35 minutes. Remove from the oven and unmold the bread. Allow the bread to rest on a rack for at least 30 minutes before cutting. (Or, if you're like me, tear off the end and nibble on it immediately as you wait for the rest of the loaf to cool!) The crust is addictive.

Pâte Sablée
4,500 g de farine
700 g de sucre glace
380 g de poudre d'amandes
200 g d'eau

Pâte à Choux
1/4 l d'eau
6 g de sel
100 g de beurre
150 g de farine
4 oeufs (entier)

Bread Dough
9,600 g de farine
2,400 g de farine de seigle
7 l d'eau
220 g de sel
270 g de beurre

evil cheese biscuits

When I worked at Larry Forgione's famed An American Place Restaurant, these dastardly biscuits would come out of the convection oven in the back of the kitchen a few minutes before dinner service. All the way over in the pantry area where I was preparing salads, it was like I could sense they were ready. I would cook up some excuse about needing to go to the walk-in fridge for a head of lettuce and then swipe a biscuit on my way through. Fresh out of the oven, the inside was still slightly gummy and volcanically hot. I would let it sit on my station for a couple of minutes to rest and then it would be perfect: moist in the center, with the taste and texture of the cheese front and center. A perfect premeal snack and great with a bowl of soup or a salad. So why are they evil? Because I can never stop eating them!

MAKES 25 BISCUITS

---

3 cups unbleached all-purpose flour, plus more for shaping the dough
1 tablespoon plus ¾ teaspoon baking powder
2 teaspoons sugar
2¼ teaspoons kosher salt
1¾ to 2 cups heavy cream
1½ cups finely grated sharp cheddar
¼ cup finely grated aged provolone

1. Preheat the oven to 400°F. Line a baking sheet with parchment paper or use a nonstick baking sheet.

2. Make the biscuits: Into a large bowl, sift together the flour, baking powder, and sugar. Sifting not only ensures that the dry ingredients will be free of lumps but also mixes them together. Add the salt, 1¾ cups of the cream, and the cheeses and stir to combine. Here's where it gets messy: use your hands to finish mixing the ingredients so they are thoroughly blended. Take care that there is no flour remaining at the bottom of the bowl, but do not overwork the dough. If all of the flour isn't integrating and the dough seems dry and unyielding, add the remaining ¼ cup cream and mix.

3. Turn the biscuit dough onto a lightly floured counter and, with floured hands, pat it down until it is a square about 7½ inches wide and about 1 inch thick, patting the edges so they are mostly straight. As you work, if the outside edges start to show cracks, cup the outer edge with your hands and push the dough in, toward the center. Lightly flour a knife (to avoid sticking as you cut) and cut the biscuit dough into 1½-inch squares. This way, you will use all of the dough and won't make any scraps. Arrange the biscuits (with some distance between each) on the baking sheet and refrigerate them for about 15 minutes before baking.

4. Bake the biscuits: Bake until they start to brown lightly, 15 to 20 minutes. Remember that the biscuits will continue to cook even after they are removed from the oven, so if their centers seem a bit moist, that's good! Remove from the oven and let cool for at least 5 to 10 minutes before serving.

Old-school tip

Don't load up a baking sheet with these biscuits; placing them too close together can result in steaming instead of browning. Also, like a steak, the biscuits will continue to cook once they are removed from the oven. So take these out when they are still slightly undercooked in their centers and let them finish cooking on the counter for a little while before digging in. They are also great cooled, split, and toasted.

deluxe coffee cake

This coffeecake was, for me, a real confidence builder. It was one of the first things I made on my own. And considering I grew up next door to a doughnut shop, making this from scratch became a source of pride. I call this my alarm-clock cake because the smell of it baking as a fresh pot of coffee slowly drips its way to completion is a surefire way to get everyone out of bed. **SERVES 10 TO 12**

TOPPING

½ cup walnut halves, coarsely chopped
½ cup pecan halves, coarsely chopped
⅔ cup all-purpose flour
⅓ cup granulated sugar
⅓ cup packed light brown sugar
2 teaspoons ground cinnamon
1 teaspoon kosher salt
5 tablespoons unsalted butter, melted

CAKE

4 tablespoons (½ stick) unsalted butter, plus more for the pan
1 cup granulated sugar
2 large eggs, at room temperature
2 cups all-purpose flour
1 teaspoon baking powder
1 teaspoon baking soda
1 teaspoon kosher salt
1 cup sour cream
½ cup whole-milk yogurt

1. Make the topping: Line a baking sheet with parchment paper. In a medium bowl, stir together the walnuts, pecans, flour, granulated and brown sugars, cinnamon, and salt. Stir in the butter. The topping should form sandy clumps. Sprinkle the topping onto the baking sheet to break it up into smaller clumps. Refrigerate.

2. Preheat the oven to 350°F. Use butter to thoroughly grease the bottom and sides of a 9-inch round baking pan.

3. Make the cake batter: In the bowl of a stand mixer fitted with the whisk attachment, beat the butter and sugar together, on medium-high, scraping down the sides from time to time, for 8 minutes. Lower the speed and add the eggs, one by one, taking care that the first egg is thoroughly integrated before adding the second.

4. Sift together the flour, baking powder, and baking soda. In a separate bowl, whisk together the salt, sour cream, and

recipe continues

yogurt until smooth. Turn the mixer on low and alternate adding some of the flour mixture with some of the sour cream mixture. When all has been mixed in, give the sides and the bottom of the bowl a good scrape and blend to make sure the batter is thoroughly combined. Transfer the batter to the greased baking pan and tap it lightly on the sides so it falls evenly in the pan and to remove any air bubbles. Liberally sprinkle the cake with all of the topping.

5. Bake the cake: Bake until a cake tester or small knife inserted in the center comes out clean, 55 to 60 minutes. Allow the cake to cool for at least 15 minutes before slicing and serving. Once cool, the cake will keep, covered, for up to 3 days.

Streusel

1 kg beurre fondu
1 kg sucre glace
1 kg poudre amande
1 kg farine
20g sel

mix ingredients together and keep in the freezer like a crumble topping. Cook in a ~200°C oven tile lightly colored.

your own pork sausage patties with eggs

I always wish for a pinch more spice or a little more sweetness in most breakfast sausages. This recipe is my way of controlling that balance of pork and pepper flavor at home. Don't be afraid to tinker with the spice levels if you want, going for more or less heat from red pepper flakes and cayenne or more texture from the fennel seeds. Something spicy and one-of-a-kind on your brunch table makes the tang of a good Mimosa come to life. Brunch is about serious flavor. **SERVES 6**

---

1 pound ground pork, preferably from the shoulder
2 teaspoons kosher salt
½ teaspoon red pepper flakes
½ teaspoon fennel seeds
½ teaspoon cayenne pepper
¼ cup plain dried bread crumbs
¼ cup grated Parmesan
1 tablespoon canola oil
4 tablespoons (½ stick) unsalted butter, as needed
6 large eggs

1. Make the sausage: Put the meat in a large bowl and mix together with your hands. Add the salt, red pepper flakes, fennel seeds, and cayenne and mix to blend. Stir in the bread crumbs and Parmesan.

2. Cook the sausage: In a large skillet, heat the canola oil over high heat. Use a ¼ cup measure to form the meat into 6 patties 2¾ inches in diameter and about ⅓ inch thick. When the oil begins to smoke lightly, shut off the heat (to avoid splattering) and arrange the patties in a single layer in the pan. Take care they are spread somewhat apart so they have a chance to brown instead of steaming. Put the heat back on high and brown the sausages on both sides, 1½ to 2 minutes per side. Touch them to make sure they are still somewhat tender and moist in the center. In fact, I always eat one as a snack and taste test. Use a slotted spoon or spatula to remove them from the pan. Transfer the patties to a platter or individual plates.

3. Fry the eggs: Wipe the skillet clean. Put the pan over medium heat and add half of the butter. When it begins to brown, crack 3 eggs, a distance apart, into the pan. Lower the heat, season them lightly with salt, and cook until the whites set, 2 to 3 minutes. Repeat with the remaining butter and eggs.

4. To serve, put the eggs on the sausage patties and serve immediately.

spice-rubbed bacon

This bacon is great with eggs, pancakes, or on toast with some thick slices of tomato. But you knew that already. What makes *this* bacon special is the combination of spices, which complements the salty and smoky aspects of the bacon. It's also the texture: Cooking bacon between two baking sheets flattens it and renders it super crisp, making the bite into a strip more substantial. **SERVES 6**

---

2 teaspoons mild curry powder
½ teaspoon red pepper flakes
2 teaspoons coriander seeds, lightly crushed
2 teaspoons coarsely ground black pepper
⅓ cup packed light brown sugar
12 thin slices bacon

1. Preheat the oven to 350°F. Line a baking sheet with parchment paper or foil.

2. Coat the bacon: In a medium bowl, mix together the curry, red pepper flakes, coriander, pepper, and brown sugar. Add the bacon slices and coat them on both sides with the sugar mix. Arrange the bacon strips in a single layer, gently stretching them so they form a thin layer, on the baking sheet. Sprinkle any sugar left in the bowl over the bacon. Top the bacon with a layer of parchment or foil and lay another baking sheet squarely on top.

3. Cook the bacon: Bake until golden brown and fairly crisp. Check the bacon after 20 minutes by lifting the top baking sheet and parchment. It will go from ready to burned fairly quickly because of the brown sugar. If it's not ready, resist the temptation to turn up the oven temperature; instead, simply bake for 10 to 15 minutes longer before checking again. Keep in mind that when you remove the bacon from the oven and transfer it to a rack to cool, it will crisp up a little more. So be patient! Serve warm or at room temperature.

Old-school tip

Sometimes I want the texture of a seed—whether fennel, cumin, or coriander—rather than using the spice ground. Biting down and having the little burst of flavor in your mouth can be unexpected. To wake up the flavor of coriander seeds, in particular, I toast them in a warm oven (300° to 350°F) until I start to smell the aroma of the coriander, 2 to 3 minutes. I pour the seeds onto a cutting board to cool for a minute and then flatten them by running the bottom of a sauté pan over them a few times to crush them lightly. Then I find the coriander can best work its magic.

omelet with fried sage and gruyère

There is a wonderful place in Los Angeles called Joan's on Third where they make exceptional omelets. Joan's secret (passed down from Dione Lucas) is to add a splash of water to the eggs (instead of milk or cream) to make the omelet light and fluffy. The crispy sage and cheese inside make my favorite combination in an omelet. Gruyère has the perfect amount of barnyard taste, great tang, and good melt factor. Don't give yourself a hard time trying to make a perfectly shaped omelet: If the eggs don't seem to be cooperating, turn them into scrambled eggs with a simple quick stir. It'll be our eggy secret. **SERVES 1**

---

1 tablespoon canola oil
8 to 10 fresh sage leaves, to taste
Kosher salt
3 large eggs
1 tablespoon unsalted butter
½ cup grated Gruyère

1. Fry the sage leaves: Heat a 6-inch nonstick skillet over high heat and add the oil. Have a tray lined with paper towels and a slotted spoon ready. When the oil begins to look thinner and spreads to the sides of the pan, shut off the heat and add the sage leaves. Stir them to coat with the oil and cook, stirring constantly, until the sage pales slightly in color and gets slightly crisp, 45 seconds to 1½ minutes. Use a slotted spoon to transfer the leaves to the paper towels. Season them immediately with salt and allow them to cool. Reserve the skillet.

2. Blend the eggs: In a medium bowl, whisk together the eggs, 1 teaspoon water, and ½ teaspoon salt. Whisk only enough to integrate the eggs; you don't want to whip too much air into them or make them frothy.

3. Cook the omelet: Remove excess oil from the skillet and return it to medium heat. Add the butter. Swirl the butter around as it melts so it coats the whole surface of the pan. When the butter is melted (but not browned), lower the heat and pour in the egg mixture. Use a fork to stir the eggs slightly, as if you were scrambling them. Then, allow the eggs to cook, undisturbed, until the egg starts to set in the middle and the very edges start to brown slightly, 15 to 30 seconds. Sprinkle the cheese and sage leaves over them. Cook until all the eggs look almost fully cooked and only slightly loose, 1 to

2 minutes. I personally like an omelet that is slightly loose in the center and not so browned on the exterior.

4. Serve the omelet: Lift the handle of the pan up, tilting the pan away from you and toward the heat. This tilting should cause the omelet to slide down in the pan a little. Using a heatproof spatula, fold the edge closest to you toward the center. Fold the other edge in toward the center and invert the pan over the center of a plate so that the omelet lands seam side down. Serve immediately.

Old-school tip

I love fresh herbs (and almost always prefer them to their dried counterparts, dried oregano being my one exception to this rule). Lots of fresh herbs—like thyme, tarragon, and basil—play nicely in the sandbox with other ingredients. But some of their herb friends need a little mellowing before being let out for recess. Lightly frying sage leaves or rosemary in a little neutral-flavored oil (like canola) tames their piney, somewhat medicinal flavor and instead brings their rich, almost grassy, mintiness to the forefront.

cinnamon sourdough pancakes

These are my favorite homemade pancakes. Now, don't get me wrong; I will admit freely that I also love pancake mix. Just blend, cook, and eat. But there are times when I crave a deeper flavor and tang. I think it's so cool to add the sourdough flavor of a loaf of great bread to pancake batter. It's not overly acidic but it makes pairing your pancakes with the sweetness of syrup and any fresh fruit all the more special. I have also gone more savory and served these with roasted cubes of squash. Plan ahead, letting this batter rest in the fridge overnight before making the pancakes the next morning. **MAKES 8 TO 10 LARGE PANCAKES; SERVES 4 TO 6**

2½ teaspoons active dry yeast
½ cup warm water (about 110°F)
2 cups all-purpose flour, plus more if needed
3 tablespoons sugar
1½ cups whole milk, plus more if needed
6 to 8 tablespoons (¾ to 1 stick) unsalted butter, as needed
2 large eggs, lightly beaten
½ teaspoon vanilla extract
¾ teaspoon ground cinnamon, plus more for sprinkling
¼ teaspoon ground allspice
Pinch of kosher salt
Maple syrup (optional)

1. Make the batter: In a medium bowl, mix together the yeast and warm water. Allow the mixture to sit in a warm area of your kitchen until the yeast dissolves and the mix is foamy.

2. In a separate bowl, combine the flour and sugar.

3. In a saucepan, warm the milk. Do not let it simmer or boil. Remove the milk from the heat, stir in 3 tablespoons of the butter, and pour into a bowl to cool slightly before mixing with the other ingredients.

4. Stir the yeast mixture and gently whisk in the flour mixture. Finish by blending in the milk mixture. Cover the bowl with a layer of plastic wrap and set aside in a warm place to proof until the batter increases in volume and is somewhat bubbly in appearance, about 1 hour. Refrigerate until the next morning.

5. In the morning, preheat the oven to 300°F. Remove the batter from the fridge, whisk it to wake it up a little, and allow it to come to room temperature, about 15 minutes.

6. Meanwhile, whisk together the eggs, honey, vanilla, cinnamon, allspice, and salt. Stir the egg mixture into the flour batter.

7. Cook the pancakes: Heat a large nonstick skillet (or, if preferred, a griddle). Melt 1 tablespoon of the butter in the pan. Spoon in a little of the batter to make a small test pancake. This batter tends to be a little runny. If it spreads too much in the pan, whisk in some additional flour. Batter too thick? Add a little milk and blend. Once the batter is good to go, cook the pancakes, adding about ½ cup for each one and leaving room between them as they'll spread in the pan, until you see a bubble here and there on the surface, a couple of minutes. Flip, cook for another minute, and then put them on a plate and keep them loosely covered with foil in the oven until you build up enough of a batch to serve. Add additional butter to the pan as needed.

8. Serve stacks of pancakes topped with maple syrup, if desired, and dusted with some additional cinnamon.

Old-school tip

You can enrich your syrup by simmering 1 cup over low heat until you have about ⅔ cup. Add 1 tablespoon sherry vinegar, a splash of molasses, and a pinch of kosher salt and cook for a few additional minutes until the flavors infuse. The acidity of the vinegar picks up on the tang of the sourdough pancakes; dynamite!

make it from scratch
for the fridge door

W&S BUTCHER

homemade ricotta

your own butter

easy pickles

quick marinades or bastes for meats and fish

balsamic-raspberry vinaigrette

purple mustard

harissa

my mom's barbecue sauce

homemade hot sauce

tapenade

infused vinegars

I love Hellmann's mayonnaise and Heinz ketchup. I also love Lea & Perrins Worcestershire sauce. To me, they are iconic American flavors. There was always a jar or bottle of each in the fridge at all times when I was a kid. My mother used to open the fridge door and stare inside as if the solution to all of the world's problems lay within. Was it to spark her imagination for the next meal? My father used to laugh and say, "Close the door and stop gazing into the horizon."

For me, as a professional chef and a mother who likes to make things "on the fly" for my daughter, I find myself gazing into the refrigerator in the same way. I think the heart of the refrigerator is actually the door. Those shelves should house your favorite sauces, condiments, flavor picker-uppers that you can go to at a moment's notice. Let's face it: There are 350 ways to cook chicken but often a small splash of something can transform in a flash a plain-Jane chicken breast into one that tastes like it is wearing the equivalent of a Ferragamo evening gown. Going to your fridge door for a flavor fix can make you feel like a magician in your own kitchen. And who, on a weeknight, after a long day's work, doesn't want that?

I like to make these recipes when I have some free time and use them when I don't!

homemade ricotta

I didn't really think making ricotta could be this simple—or taste so good. Of course, the flavor of the ricotta depends largely on the dairy you use. Minimally pasteurized and nonhomogenized local cream, milk, and buttermilk taste best. I find turning them into ricotta actually makes the distinctness of good dairy come to the forefront. That said, I have also made great ricotta from supermarket milk. The resulting cheese is still fresher than anything you can buy in the store. Be patient. This takes time and it may feel like you didn't do it right. Hang in there.

This ricotta is great on toasted wedges of bread with roasted vegetables and a sprinkle of vinegar or lemon juice. On the other hand, when you're making something more substantial like ravioli filling, where you need a firm ricotta, better to drain a batch of this for a day or two in the fridge or use store-bought. In fact, I have been known to eat some of this ricotta on toast with some raspberry jam or sugar sprinkled on top while using store-bought ricotta to make ravioli.

MAKES ABOUT ⅔ CUP

---

1 cup heavy cream
½ cup whole milk
½ cup buttermilk

1. Make the ricotta: In a medium saucepan, bring the cream, milk, and buttermilk to a gentle simmer over medium heat. Simmer gently until the milk solids rise to the surface and form what looks like a raft, 30 to 35 minutes. Shut off the heat and allow the milk to cool gently on the stove, 10 to 15 minutes.

2. Drain the ricotta: Line a strainer with a few layers of cheesecloth and set it over a large bowl. Use a large spoon to scoop the solids from the surface of the milk mixture into the strainer. Then pour the liquid gently over the solids in the strainer, allowing the liquid to flow through into the bowl beneath.

3. Refrigerate the solids in the strainer for at least a few hours (and preferably overnight) to allow all of the liquid to drain out and for the ricotta to firm up slightly. The ricotta will keep, covered in the fridge, for up to 1 week but is best a day or two after it is made.

Old-school tip

The liquid that results from making this ricotta—the whey—is actually quite useful and delicious. I often make this ricotta and then make a simple tomato soup. I use the whey to enrich the soup in place of the water I might otherwise add. It thickens the texture and adds more flavor. Then I serve the ricotta on toast on the side to dunk into the tomato soup. It makes me feel as if I have come full circle with my cooking. It's so satisfying to make something and use the by-product in something else that then gets served at the same time. The whey can also be used in place of water in homemade bread or pasta dough.

your own butter

I love making my own butter and jams for toast. This butter is also great for spooning over cooked meats or fish to add a finishing touch of richness. I don't use it for cooking, though; it's too delicate for that. I have found it's very important to use a natural sour cream that doesn't have any thickeners (like guar gum) when making this recipe; otherwise, the butter doesn't come together. It's amazing to me that just whipping cream creates something that looks like it took hours and a degree in food science to make. This butter will keep, covered in the refrigerator, for up to a month but is best within a few days. (Dairy acts like a sponge in your fridge, absorbing the aromas of the foods around it.) If you want to make less, cut the recipe in half. Use some of the buttermilk that results from this recipe (about 1¾ cups) to enrich or add tang to tomato soup. **MAKES ABOUT 10 OUNCES BUTTER**

2½ cups heavy cream
1 cup sour cream (without any thickeners or additives, such as guargum)
1 teaspoon kosher salt

1. Whip the creams: Prepare an ice bath: Fill a medium bowl halfway with ice cubes and add some cold water. In the bowl of a stand mixer fitted with the whisk attachment, whip the cream and sour cream together on low speed for about 2 minutes. Cover the space between the mixer and the bowl with plastic wrap. Increase the speed of the mixer and sprinkle in the salt. Whip until the cream separates and the mixture thickens.

2. Finish the butter: Use a rubber spatula to gather up the butter and remove it from the bowl. There will be some liquid, which is actually buttermilk, at the bottom of the bowl. Gather the ball of butter together into a double layer of cheesecloth or a thin kitchen towel. Squeeze it to remove excess buttermilk and plunge it into the ice bath to rinse any buttermilk off the surface. Pack the butter into a bowl or roll it into a log shape using plastic wrap.

old-school variation

For other butter flavors, stir in smoked salt and/or cracked black pepper. If you want added texture, use a coarse sea salt in place of the kosher salt. Bear in mind, though, that flavors intensify over time. So if you refrigerate the butter for a while, the flavors might get stronger than you like.

easy pickles

Submerging vegetables in a salt and water solution (brine) or an acidic ingredient like vinegar makes for the simplest of pickles. Pickling helps preserve vegetables, but, more important, the process adds flavor, brightness, and acidity. Add some slices of fresh chile, like a serrano or jalapeño or a pinch of red pepper flakes, if spice is your game. At the restaurant, after making these pickles, we cut them into spears, batter them, and deep-fry to serve them with spicy mayonnaise. Indulgent and delicious! **MAKES ABOUT 12 PICKLE SPEARS**

⅓ cup flaky sea salt, such as Maldon
2 tablespoons cider vinegar
4½ cups bottled water
¾ pound Kirby cucumbers (about 3 medium or 4 small), all about the same size and thickness, thoroughly washed and dried
2 teaspoons fennel seeds
A few sprigs fresh dill

1. Make the brine: In a medium saucepan, mix the salt, vinegar, and water and bring to a boil. Simmer for 5 minutes. Remove the brine from the heat and allow it to cool slightly.

2. Pickle the cucumbers: Arrange the cucumbers upright in a jar large enough to hold 3 cups of liquid (I like a traditional glass mason jar, but any container you like with a fitted lid will do.) The cucumbers should be tightly packed and should come within ½ inch of the top of the container. Add the fennel seeds and dill sprigs to the container. Fill the container with the brine to the top and tap on a flat surface to remove any possible air bubbles. Top off with additional liquid as needed. Cover and refrigerate (and see if you can wait longer than a few hours before eating one). The pickles will last for up to a few weeks.

quick marinades or bastes for meats and fish

I have a distinct memory of my mother, only occasionally (mom, forgive me), adding powdered salad dressing (was it called "Good Seasons"?) to a jar with some oil and shaking her way to a dressing. Something stuck with me about the jar and this idea that you could shake up some flavor on a night when you're not feeling that creative. Here are a couple of jars I keep in my fridge for up to a couple of weeks.

---

chili garlic paste

I am partial to this on shrimp, fish, or pork dishes, and also like to stir a dollop into sautéed greens.

MAKES ABOUT 1 CUP

½ cup plus 1 tablespoon extra-virgin olive oil
1 medium red onion, cut into ¼-inch rounds
6 garlic cloves, minced
1 tablespoon grated lemon zest
1½ teaspoons flaky sea salt, such as Maldon
1½ teaspoons cracked black peppercorns
1 teaspoon chili powder
¼ cup thinly sliced jalapeños, seeds and all

1. Preheat the grill to medium-high.

2. Spread 1 tablespoon of the oil over the onion slices and grill until charred and tender on both sides, 10 to 15 minutes. Roughly chop the onion. In a jar combine the onion, garlic, lemon zest, salt, pepper, chili powder, jalapeño and the remaining ½ cup oil. Allow the jar to cool before closing the lid, giving the jar a vigorous shake, and refrigerating.

dry vermouth marinade

Love this splashed on broiled fish, braised fennel, or into a pan of cooked chicken. **MAKES ABOUT 1 CUP**

½ cup dry vermouth
½ teaspoon kosher salt
½ cup canola oil
½ cup hazelnut oil (see Sources) or extra-virgin olive oil blended with ¼ cup toasted hazelnuts and strained

Combine all of the ingredients in a jar. Shake before using.

balsamic-raspberry vinaigrette

I love a thick emulsified vinaigrette. Whisking this one together by hand and putting a little elbow grease into getting that nice emulsion is worth it. Can you just toss it all in the blender? Sure. *But* the blender whips more air into it and the air makes the flavors less intense. It's a shortcut I don't find worth it. But I do like to make a salad with this vinaigrette by simply arranging some greens in a casual single layer and then drizzling the dressing over them. Done. Biting into a piece of crisp lettuce and getting a bite that tastes of pure undressed green and then immediately getting a burst of the vinaigrette on another part of the green makes the flavors more intense.

MAKES 3 CUPS

¾ cup balsamic vinegar
⅓ cup raspberry vinegar
¼ cup Dijon mustard
1 tablespoon superfine sugar
1 tablespoon kosher salt
1 teaspoon ground black pepper
1 cup extra-virgin olive oil
1 cup canola oil

In a large bowl, whisk together the balsamic vinegar, raspberry vinegar, mustard, sugar, salt, and pepper. Whisk until well blended and then slowly drizzle in the olive and canola oils, whisking constantly, to make an emulsified vinaigrette. This will keep, covered in the fridge, for up to 3 weeks. Just shake vigorously before using. If it separates, blend it for a minute with a splash of cold water.

purple mustard

Yes, it takes mustard to make this mustard, but the flavor that comes from fortifying it with these additional ingredients is unique: somewhat sweet from the reduced wine (which also gives it its distinctive color), and just a touch spicy from the garlic and horseradish. If you can't find fresh horseradish, use some jarred horseradish as a substitute. I put this on bacon and pork chops, but I also use it as my mustard for salad dressings and on any sandwich that just calls out for mustard. It needs to rest and have time to develop flavor. Be patient with it. **MAKES ABOUT 2 CUPS**

1½ cups dry red wine
1 heaping tablespoon dark raisins
¾ cup yellow mustard seeds
3 tablespoons dry mustard, preferably Colman's
⅓ cup cider vinegar
½ teaspoon Worcestershire sauce
¼ cup Dijon mustard

1. Reduce the red wine: In a medium saucepan, simmer the red wine and raisins over medium heat until reduced to ½ cup. Transfer to the food processor and puree until smooth. Remove from the heat and stir in the mustard seeds. Set aside to cool and to allow the mustard seeds to plump.

2. Make the mustard: In a blender, combine the dry mustard, vinegar, ¾ cup water, and Worcestershire sauce and blend until smooth. This will taste very strong on its own. Transfer this mixture to a bowl and stir in the Dijon mustard and cooled red wine reduction. Cover and refrigerate for at least 2 to 3 days for this mixture to mellow. The mustard will keep for several months in the refrigerator.

harissa

I have many jars of hot sauce that I dip into from time to time in my fridge at home. I think a lot of us have those jars with flames running down the sides or a giant chile looming on the label. I am not a fan of the burn-your-mouth-off sauces. I could almost be accused of not liking spice, in fact. But there are hot flavors—especially those layered with spices like in this harissa, which has the added dimension of texture—that I really love. I like when heat unfolds slowly, with every bite. My kitchen staff makes fun of me, actually, for not being able to eat their spicy concoctions. There are at least three variations of hot sauce floating around in the fridges of the restaurant at all times. This is my favorite. **MAKES ABOUT ¼ CUP**

---

2 teaspoons coriander seeds
1 teaspoon cumin seeds
1 teaspoon caraway seeds
2 tablespoons paprika
1 teaspoon red pepper flakes
3 medium garlic cloves
Flaky sea salt, such as Maldon
2 tablespoons extra-virgin olive oil, plus more as needed

1. Preheat the oven to 300°F.

2. Roast the spices: On a small baking sheet, combine the coriander seeds, cumin seeds, and caraway seeds. Toast in the oven until you detect the faint scent of the spices, 1 to 2 minutes. Set aside to cool. Add the paprika and red pepper flakes.

3. Mash the garlic: Using a mortar and pestle (or, alternatively, a mini food processor), grind the garlic until it turns into a paste. Season with salt.

4. Finish the harissa: Add the spices to the garlic and blend. Work in the olive oil. Transfer to a container and top with a film of additional olive oil. Refrigerate for up to several months.

old-school tip

I always wondered why some things come covered in a layer of fat or oil. For example, sometimes a pot of chicken liver will come topped with a solid layer of fat. That layer of fat actually prevents oxygen from reaching the liver and therefore the liver keeps (and keeps its color) much longer. I like to do the same here with harissa. I think the layer of oil gives the harissa more time to mellow and meld together in the fridge.

my mom's barbecue sauce

When it comes to anything barbecue, you probably shouldn't trust a native New Yorker who grew up in midtown Manhattan. However, this is the best dump-and-stir recipe I have ever encountered. When you first mix it together and get it simmering on the stove, your kitchen will be overpowered by the aroma of vinegar. I always have a moment of doubt when I catch the first scent, like it's not going to come together and be the wonderful sauce I remember. But it has never failed me. The amount of chili powder is not a typo; it adds a little pleasantly sandy texture to the sauce and becomes part of what sticks to your fingers when you eat that fourth drumstick. I have kept a jar of this sauce in the back of my fridge (and in the freezer) for an alarmingly long amount of time. Let's just say it's a sauce that keeps well and is incredible on chicken, pork, or shrimp on a weeknight when you just want to brush this sauce on something and devour. **MAKES ABOUT 3 CUPS**

1½ cups ketchup, preferably Heinz
1 cup cider vinegar
¼ cup Worcestershire sauce, preferably Lea and Perrins
¼ cup reduced-sodium soy sauce
½ cup packed light brown sugar
½ cup packed dark brown sugar
1 tablespoon dry mustard, preferably Colman's
1 tablespoon Dijon mustard
½ cup chili powder
2 garlic cloves, grated
1 (2-inch) knob fresh ginger, peeled and cut into ½-inch rounds
1 lemon, cut into ½-inch-thick slices

In a large saucepan, combine the ketchup, vinegar, Worcestershire sauce, soy sauce, light brown sugar, dark brown sugar, dry mustard, Dijon mustard, and chili powder. Whisk to blend. Bring to a simmer over medium heat. Add the garlic, ginger, and lemon slices. Simmer until the vinegar mellows slightly and the flavors start to meld together, 20 to 25 minutes. Cool before using. Covered and refrigerated, this keeps for a long time. Remove and discard the lemon slices. Over time, they can make the sauce bitter.

VARIOUS POULTRY LABELS COLLECTED WHILE WORKING IN FRANCE

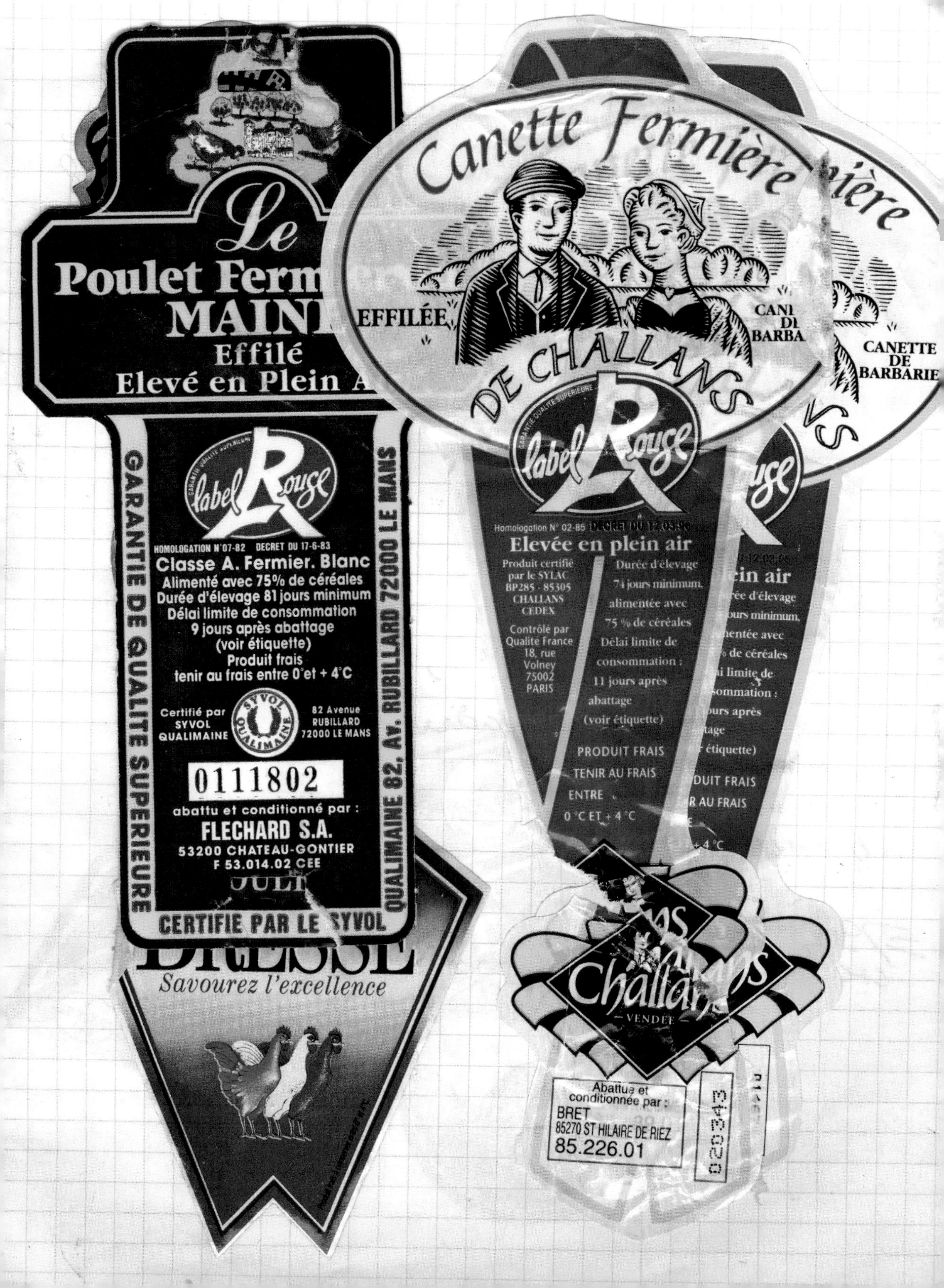
Le
Poulet Fermier
MAINE
Effilé
Elevé en Plein Air
label Rouge
HOMOLOGATION N°07-82 DECRET DU 17-6-83
Classe A. Fermier. Blanc
Alimenté avec 75% de céréales
Durée d'élevage 81 jours minimum
Délai limite de consommation
9 jours après abattage
(voir étiquette)
Produit frais
tenir au frais entre 0°et + 4°C
Certifié par SYVOL QUALIMAINE
SYVOL QUALIMAINE
82 Avenue RUBILLARD 72000 LE MANS
0111802
abattu et conditionné par :
FLECHARD S.A.
53200 CHATEAU-GONTIER
F 53.014.02 CEE
GARANTIE DE QUALITE SUPERIEURE
QUALIMAINE 82, Av. RUBILLARD 72000 LE MANS
CERTIFIE PAR LE SYVOL
Savourez l'excellence
Canette Fermière
EFFILÉE
DE CHALLANS
CANETTE DE BARBARIE
label Rouge
Homologation N° 02-85 DECRET DU 12.03.96
Elevée en plein air
Produit certifié par le SYLAC BP285 - 85305 CHALLANS CEDEX
Contrôlé par Qualité France 18, rue Volney 75002 PARIS
Durée d'élevage 74 jours minimum, alimentée avec 75 % de céréales
Délai limite de consommation : 11 jours après abattage (voir étiquette)
PRODUIT FRAIS
TENIR AU FRAIS
ENTRE 0 °C ET + 4 °C
Challans
VENDÉE
Abattue et conditionnée par :
BRET
85270 ST HILAIRE DE RIEZ
85.226.01
020343

homemade hot sauce

Much like dry yeast or spices, dried chiles need to be plumped and woken up by liquid to reach their full flavor potential. In this case, warming and softening them in vinegar forms an acidic, deep (but not obliterating), and somewhat smoky spice that I haven't found in any bottled sauce. I find chipotles (smoked dried jalapeños) overly smoky in a lot of cases. That's how I arrived at this particular combination. This will keep for a month (if not more) in the fridge. **MAKES ABOUT 1 CUP**

---

1 cup Champagne vinegar
1 dried guajillo chile, stemmed
1 dried ancho chile, stemmed
1 jalapeño chile, thinly sliced (seeds and all)
3 garlic cloves, grated
1½ teaspoons sugar
1 tablespoon kosher salt

1. Hydrate the dried chiles: In a small saucepan, combine the vinegar, guajillo chile, and ancho chile and bring to a simmer over medium heat. Simmer over low heat until the dried chiles are soft, 5 to 10 minutes.

2. Blend the hot sauce: Pour the chile-vinegar mixture into a blender and puree, starting on low speed and moving slowly to high, taking care to cover the top of the blender tightly. Add the jalapeño, garlic, sugar, and salt and blend until smooth. Transfer to a jar with a fitted lid and refrigerate.

oysters

I always thought an oyster was completely submerged in water all of the time. On a recent boat ride through a little inlet outside Charleston, South Carolina, I learned that isn't always true. As the boat ripped through the water (something that would stimulate anyone's appetite), I noticed some unusual-looking plants adorning the shoreline. When the boat slowed, I got a closer look at these "plants"; they were actually oysters, one growing virtually on top of the other, like a fifty-car pileup on the freeway! They were rooted in the sand but, because the tide was low, some were submerged and others not.

The skipper of our boat, Joe, a South Carolina native, saw me staring and pulled the boat over to the edge of a small beach area. "Put those boots on," he instructed with a knowing grin. He handed me a pair of boots and I pulled them on slowly as he passed me an oyster knife. We jumped off the edge of the boat into about 6 inches of water and immediately sank about 4 inches into the muddy sand. We crouched over the oysters and gently pulled a few loose. They were covered in grit but still beautiful. I struggled with the thick gloves he lent me and felt like I might topple over at any moment. I pried the top shell open and tasted the oyster (and the fresh liquor inside the shell) as if it were my first. It was so cold! "Pretty good, eh?" Joe grinned.

Sometimes things are best when enjoyed in their purest form.

Old-school tip

If there's one thing that adds time to prepping recipes, it's mincing garlic or any form of onion, from shallots to leeks. I like to peel garlic and shallots and then simply grate them on a Microplane grater (or box grater). It's much faster and it creates a really fine mince that means the garlic and shallot can infuse quickly with other ingredients.

tapenade

Tapenade is just a fancy term for an olive spread commonly found in the south of France, some of the most delicious olives in the world are grown. I don't add any of the other salty elements (like capers or anchovies) that you commonly see in tapenade recipes. For me, this recipe is about a beautiful power struggle between the olive and the olive oil. I personally favor meaty green olives because they seem mellower and less salty than black olives. But then I miss that salty and slightly vinegary taste black olives so often bring to the table. The result? I add them both to get the best from each. The rough chop of the olive drives the bus and the grated garlic and shallots round out the texture. I not only use this as a spread but also toss it onto cooked pasta and dollop it into a salad dressing that needs a salty kick. It can really perk up fresh vegetables without being heavy. **MAKES ABOUT 1 CUP**

---

2 tablespoons extra-virgin olive oil, or more if needed
1 small shallot, grated
1 garlic clove, grated
½ cup meaty green olives, such as Cerignola or Picholine, pitted
½ cup black olives, such as Nyons or Kalamata, pitted
Black pepper
Grated zest of ½ lemon
1 teaspoon sherry vinegar
1 teaspoon whiskey

1. In a small saucepan, heat 1 tablespoon of the olive oil over medium heat. When it begins to make waves and get hot, remove from the heat and stir in the shallot and garlic. Return the pan to the heat and cook until they soften slightly and become translucent, 2 to 3 minutes. Transfer to a plate to cool slightly.

2. Strain any liquid, reserving it, from both kinds of olives and put them in a food processor. Season with a few twists of pepper. Pulse 5 to 6 times until the olives look roughly chopped. Transfer to a bowl and whisk in the lemon zest and vinegar.

3. Mix in the remaining tablespoon olive oil. For me, the perfect tapenade hits the palate with olive oil richness and finishes with the light (but not overpowering) saltiness of the olive itself. If the olives are very intense, add more oil. If not salty enough, add a touch of the reserved olive brine. Stir in the whiskey and the shallot mixture. For best results, cover the tapenade and let it sit at least overnight in the fridge so the flavors have a chance to meld together. It will keep for up to several weeks in the refrigerator. Top with a layer of olive oil to seal it.

infused vinegars

I remember when I first read Jean-Georges Vongerichten's section on infused oils in his book *Simple Cuisine.* It was a long time ago but the concept stuck with me. I made every oil possible. Some yielded the purest, most distilled flavors, like mustard oil and parsley oil. They revolutionized flavors for me. Some were not so successful; an orange peel oil was less than stellar. The process taught me that trial and error and a little fearlessness in the kitchen always lead to new flavors. Some of these flavors are easy to produce at home. At the time, I only thought about the flavor I was adding in, like parsley, and not so much about the oil I used with the parsley.

And then I met my lifelong friend and companion, vinegar, and a whole new world of possibilities opened up.

Vinegars, like oils, are aromatic, sometimes floral, and sometimes muted. But they also have the capacity to give tremendous acidity to food, my personal favorite.

Here are some infused vinegars that you can keep in the fridge to splash on your food when you want more of a certain taste. As these will last in the fridge for quite some time, each recipe here makes anywhere from 2 cups to 1 quart vinegar.

---

spicy

Ghost peppers are alarmingly hot chiles, but when blended with cider vinegar, the result is tasty. The vinegar interacts some with the chile as it plumps and spices the situation. A splash of this vinegar can impart both a spicy edge and a round, yeasty form of acidity. This is great in salad dressings, on cabbage slaw, or over some inherently sweet vegetables, like carrots. You don't have to use ghost peppers. Any super spicy dried chile will do. **MAKES 1 QUART**

12 dried ghost peppers (see Sources)
1 quart cider vinegar

Put the peppers in a jar with a fitted lid and pour the vinegar over them. Seal and refrigerate. Wait a few weeks (or longer) and then use with wild abandon but at your own risk.

sour

I am such a sucker for verjus, which is simply filtered grape juice made from grapes picked a few weeks before harvest for wine. It can really pack an acidic, cutting punch. While this is not verjus, the flavor this recipe creates replicates it nicely. I also like using the grapes after the mixture sits in the fridge for some time. I have been known to puree a few of the grapes into a salad dressing to add body. I also love soaking onion slices in this vinegar for a little while before using or adding a little to a creamy sauce. I even put some on a sweet fruit salad to temper the sweetness. **MAKES 1 QUART VINEGAR AND 2 CUPS PICKLED GRAPES**

2 cups seedless red grapes, stemmed and washed
1 quart malt vinegar

Put the grapes in a jar with a fitted lid and pour the vinegar over them. Seal and refrigerate. Wait a couple of weeks. The added bonus here is getting to use both the vinegar and the grapes.

sweet

I don't often need to add sweetness to food. It finds its way in there in so many different ways. What I like about this vinegar is that it adds some acidity that has had time to meld with the sugar. It fits in seamlessly—more so, in a lot of cases, than adding straight sugar! I like a little of this on my strawberries, peas, green beans, or corn. **MAKES ABOUT 1 QUART**

1 quart balsamic vinegar
½ cup honey
1 tablespoon blackstrap molasses

In a jar with a fitted lid, combine the vinegar, honey, and molasses. Seal and refrigerate. Wait a couple of weeks.

recipes continue

salty

This is salty more than anything else. But there is a slight and pleasant pungency that comes with it. I love this drizzled on cheese (like goat cheese), in salads, and also on cheeses that can use a little boost (like mozzarella) to present a stronger cheese flavor.

MAKES 2 CUPS

2 cups Champagne vinegar
2 pieces Parmesan cheese rind, each about 2 inches long, with the very outer layer (that may have ink marking) cut off

In a small, nonreactive saucepan, heat the vinegar and Parmesan rinds. Simmer over medium heat for 5 minutes and then shut off the heat and allow the mixture to cool gradually. Pour into a jar with a fitted lid (rinds and all), seal, and refrigerate. Wait a few days. Discard the rinds.

bitter

Use a vegetable peeler to remove the zest in long strips from the orange and lemon. It's OK if a little white pith comes along for the ride but not too much. This will end up becoming more of a condensed bitter flavor and less about the orange and lemon as time goes by. I like a splash of this in sweet cocktails like one would add olive brine to martinis. It's also delicious stirred into anything overly sweet that needs a lift, such as jam. It's almost like bitters!

MAKES 2 CUPS

2 cups sherry vinegar
Zest strips from 1 orange
Zest strips from 1 lemon
1 tablespoon kosher salt
2 whole cloves

In a jar with a fitted lid, combine the vinegar, citrus zests, salt, and cloves. Seal and refrigerate. Wait a few days to a few weeks.

acknowledgments

Thanks most of all to my parents who made me into a cook by way of their cooking.

Everything I do is for my daughter, Ava: great lover of squab, gooseberries, quinoa, and chicken fingers.

Thanks to my great-aunt Agnes Pearson for waking up my palate and love of simple things with a tomato sandwich.

Thanks to Annie Washburn, Emily Giske, and Bruce Seidel for many things.

Annie: thanks for packing my glassware when I really needed it.

Thanks to Colleen Grapes and Patti Jackson for just about everything else but especially for always making great pretzels and ice cream.

The person who made me respect food and believe in myself as a cook: Mr. Guy Savoy.

Thanks to Bobby "The Pope" Flay for keeping the train on the tracks and always saying "let me ask you a question."

Thanks to Alton Brown for being so generous with advice.

Thanks to one of my other great mentors, Daniel Boulud, for making me believe I cried on all those potato-crusted bass because I am "passionate."

To the original group of incredible kitchen staff who made a little joint on Lafayette Street so special: Alvaro Buchelly, Jamaal Dunlap, Wirt Cook, Ashley Merriman, Antonio Morales, Eligio Morales, Miguel Angel Cruz, Bernardino Vega, Flaviano Sosa, Michael Jenkins, Miguel Mendoza, Kevin O'Brien, Tony Ramirez, Eddie Ramirez, Sergio Ramirez, Santos Duarte, Manuel Duarte, Aragon Tapia, Lauren Basco, Tracy Hill, and Aaron Dickens.

Special thanks to Ian Halbwachs, who has tested recipes and created and masterminded many things with me. A true talent.

Special thanks to Simon Akiva, a one-of-a-kind individual, for all his support. And thanks to Madi Clark, another one-of-a-kind person and a great cook.

Thanks Jacqueline Akiva, Richard Akiva, and Scott Sartiano.

To amazing purveyors and great friends: Pat LaFrieda, who has been an incredible support and friend always, Mark Pastore, Louis Rozzo, Benjy Kirschner, Amy Scherber, Alex Paffenroth, Rick Bishop, and the people at Windfall, Stokes, Cherry Lane, and Keith's Farms.

Thanks to my editor, Rica Allannic, at Clarkson Potter, for painstakingly and passionately editing the cookbook of a cookbook editor's daughter. Thanks to creative director Marysarah Quinn for breathing life into this book through brilliant design. Thanks also to Ashley Phillips, Kim Tyner, Ada Yonenaka, Erica Gelbard, Kate Tyler, Donna Passannante, Allison Malec, Doris Cooper, and Pam Krauss.

Thanks to Irika Slavin for giving me both a supportive smile and your famous evil eye. Thanks to Amanda Melnick, Lauren Sklar, Laura Bernard, Jessica Merenich, Norina Li, Allison Page, Brian Lando, Lauren Meuller, Brooke Johnson, Bob Tuschman, Susie Fogelson, and everyone at Food Network for their amazing support.

Thanks to Jennifer Baum and Pamela Spiegel at Bullfrog and Baum for always being there.

Thanks to Josh Bider, Jeff Googel, Bethany Dick, Mark Mullet, Jon Rosen, Andy McNicol, and Ross Raphael at William Morris Endeavor.

Thanks to Michael Pederson for the brilliant and careful (and delicious!) food styling. Thanks to Jill Santopietro for dedicated and passionate recipe testing.

Thanks to Barbara Fritz for prop styling that made the book feel like home.

Thanks to Squire Fox for the edible photography.

Thanks to Anne Burrell, Marco Canora, Dan Kluger, Bill Telepan, Daniel Boulud, Larry Forgione, Ted Allen, Aaron Sanchez, Geoffrey Zakarian, Scott Conant, Chris Santos, Marc Murphy, Marcus Samuelsson, Amanda Freitag, Mark Meyer, Peter Hoffman, Harold Moore, David Meyers, Jehengar Mehta, Elizabeth Falkner, Robert Irvine, Michael Chiarello, Gabrielle Hamilton, Sara Jenkins, Dave Mechlowicz, Dean Rasi, and fellow chefs everywhere. Thanks to Horace Mann for an amazing education and making me realize I can never sit at a desk.

Sources

Here are a few of my favorite old-school places to explore new ingredients or taste a bit of nostalgia:

Here are a few of many wonderful farmers I frequently buy from at the **Union Square Greenmarket:**

Alex and Linda Paffenroth, Paffenroth Gardens, paffenrothgardens@mac.com
Rick Bishop, Mountain Sweet Berry Farm, mountainsweetberryfarm.blogspot.com
Ron Binaghi Jr., Stokes Farms, stokesfarm.com
Ronnybrook Farm Dairy, ronnybrook.com
For more information about the wonderful farmers, check out: grownyc.org

For great information on fish, check out the Save the Oceans/Seafood Watch program at montereybayaquarium.org. For more info, check out frozzoandsons.com.

For meat, check out LaFrieda Meats/Pat LaFrieda at lafrieda.com.

For spices (like Aleppo pepper, dill seeds, and ghost peppers) and special salts (like Maldon salt) and an ingredient haven and food-toy store for grownups, visit Kalustyan's (123 Lexington Avenue, New York, NY; Kalustyans.com). I also love Asia Market (71 Mulberry Street, New York, NY).For mail order, the Spice House (thespicehouse.com).

For an old-school Little Italy experience, go to Ferrara Bakery (195 Grand Street, New York, NY; ferrarabakery.com), have an espresso and a warm sfogliatelle. Then walk across the street to Alleva Dairy (188 Grand Street, NYC; allevadairy.com) for some mozzarella and ricotta and down the street to Di Palo's (200 Grand Street, New York, NY; dipaloselects.com) for some sliced prosciutto and olives.

Check out Faicco's Pork Store (260 Bleeker Street, New York, NY) for an old-world Italian food store with amazing prepared foods and Italian ingredients.

For cheese, check out Lucy's Whey in the Chelsea Market (425 West 15th Street, New York, NY; lucyswhey.com) to discover some of the great cheeses being made in our very own United States of America!

For salt from all over the world, chocolate, and bitters, I like the Meadow (523 Hudson Street, New York, NY; atthemeadow.com) and Halen Mon (halenmon.com).

For chocolate (pricey but delicious), I like Mast Brothers (111 Third Street, Brooklyn, NY; mastbrothers.com).

For an old-school doughnut experience, hit up the Donut Pub (203 West 14th Street, New York, NY). True, there are better and fancier doughnuts, but this place is as much about the experience of sitting at the counter as it is the cinnamon bun or red velvet doughnut.

For an old-school sandwich experience, have a lime rickey and a pastrami sandwich at Eisenberg's Sandwich Shop (174 Fifth Avenue, New York, NY).

For cookbooks, I love Kitchen Arts and Letters (1435 Lexington Avenue, New York, NY; kitchen artsandletters.com) and Bonnie Slotnick (163 West 10th Street, New York, NY; bonnies lotnickcookbooks.com) for old cookbooks. Cookbooks make the world go round. Buy them!

index

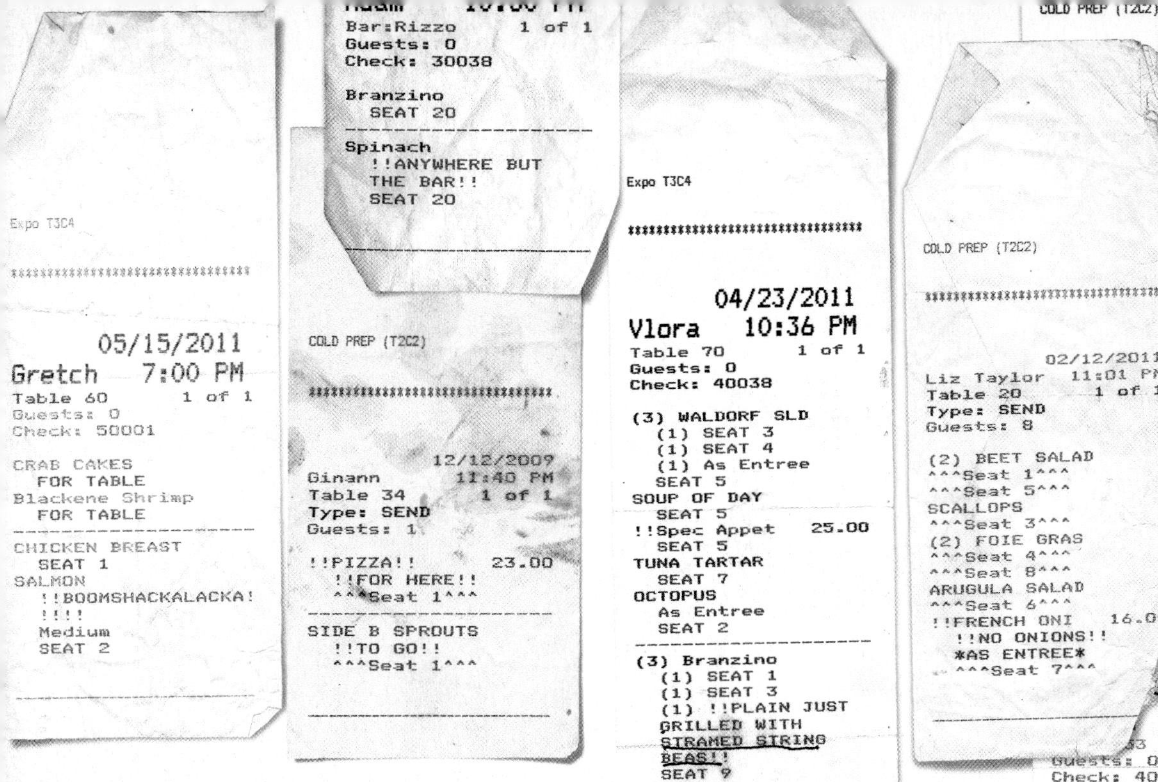

about the author

ALEX GUARNASCHELLI is the executive chef of the New York City restaurants Butter and The Darby. A graduate of Barnard College and La Varenne cooking school, she trained with acclaimed chefs Guy Savoy in Paris and Daniel Boulud in New York. An Iron Chef on *Iron Chef America* and a judge on *Chopped*, she has hosted and appeared on numerous Food Network shows, including *Alex's Day Off* and *The Cooking Loft*, and writes a blog on foodnetwork.com. She makes her home in New York City with her daughter.